I was s[illegible] ore demandi[illegible] I've turned mean. But I think it's helped keep me alive . . .

THE WRECKS

When I went around the bus I discovered it had landed on top of a car. Under the front wheel was a nine-year-old boy. He said, "Mister, would you get this bus off me? I can't breathe. . . ."

THE CRAZIES

I walked up and shined the flashlight, saw a well-endowed girl trying to get her clothes on, and the driver pulling up his pants. She turns out to be his wife. The car was full of Valiums, Quaaludes, marijuana and other controlled substances . . .

THE WIVES

It's a perilous thing to love a man on the highway patrol. Because every time he walks out the door to check on duty, it's like a piece of yourself goes with him . . .

FROM *TROOPER DOWN!*

"Powerful, riveting, moving, frustrating, funny, horrifying, unforgettable— *TROOPER DOWN!* takes the reader for one hair-raising ride on an emotional roller coaster. Congratulations to author Marie Bartlett on a first-rate book!"

—Christopher Andersen, author of *The Serpent's Tooth*

"*TROOPER DOWN!* merits being read by all who care deeply about the protection afforded our basic civil liberties by one of the nation's most elite law enforcement agencies."

—United States Senator Terry Sanford

TROOPER DOWN!

LIFE AND DEATH ON THE HIGHWAY PATROL

MARIE BARTLETT

WITH A FOREWORD BY JAMES J. KILPATRICK

POCKET BOOKS
New York London Toronto Sydney Tokyo Singapore

POCKET BOOKS, a division of Simon & Schuster Inc.
1230 Avenue of the Americas, New York, NY 10020

Published by arrangement with Algonquin Books of Chapel Hill
Library of Congress Catalog Card Number: 88-5896

ISBN: 0-671-67610-5

First Pocket Books printing June 1990

10 9 8 7 6 5 4 3 2 1

Printed in the U.S.A.

To Gary, for his enduring support, and to Aunt Phyllis, who always said I could do it

Contents

Foreword

If we drive long enough, and if we are sufficiently unlucky, most of us eventually will make the acquaintance of a state trooper, and most of us will remember the experience with dismay. We are bowling along, not paying much attention to the speedometer, listening to the radio, hurrying a little to reach an appointment, and then we sense an ominous flicker in the rearview mirror. It is a flashing blue light, and if we have been really inattentive, it is accompanied by the snarl of a siren.

"May I see your operator's license, sir?"

The trooper is in his thirties. He is a big guy, solid as a concrete block, and he is all business. He has no discernible sense of humor. We have been frozen in his radar at seventy miles per hour in a fifty-five-mile zone, and he has heard every excuse ever given. ("I've got the diarrhea, officer, and I really have to go. . . . My kid is sick, and I was just so damned worried about her. . . . I've got to get home before my wife finds out where I've been. . . .") There follows the citation, the instructions on standing trial or sending a check to the clerk of court, and then the impassive dismissal.

"Drive safely, sir, and obey the law."

The only thing that remains is for one's spouse, who has been sitting stone-silent through the whole affair, to say, "I told you to slow down." To which one responds, "I wonder where the sumbitch was hiding." It has not been a day to remember with joy.

This is about the only image most of us have of the state trooper at work: the trim uniform, the Smokey Bear hat, the coolly watchful eyes. We see his patrol car concealed in a byway, and we slide uncomfortably past his presence; we look in the mirror in guilty apprehension: Has he moved? It is the feeling of the field mouse toward the circling hawk. For most of us, troopers are faceless and nameless. Until I read Marie Bartlett's book, it never had occurred to me that troopers shed tears, make love, sire children, get in debt, go to church, and know fear as others do. Now I know.

This is reporting of the old school, nothing fancy, nothing embroidered for effect. In one of the Sherlock Holmes stories—I believe it is *A Scandal in Bohemia*—Holmes is admonishing the long-suffering Dr. Watson. Had Watson seen a flight of stairs? Of course he had seen the stairs. How many steps were there? Dr. Watson had no idea. "That is the trouble," said Holmes, "you see, but you do not observe." By the same token, many of us hear, but we do not listen. It is part of Marie Bartlett's gift to count the stairs—to observe with a camera's silent eye—to observe, and to listen. Her troopers come alive. They speak in their own voices. She writes of the North Carolina patrol *con amore*, but her book is much more than a tribute to a fraternity of men (and a few women also) who serve as officers of the law.

Marie Bartlett covers the training program for cadets and listens to a superior officer talking to the young recruits: "I tell them if they're just looking for a job, they won't make it in the highway patrol because there's something special they've got to have. I explain they'll be gone from home half their lives and their wives will be doing all the grocery shopping and raising the kids. I tell them they can't go to beer joints and nightclubs because people will watch and judge them by their actions. I tell them they'll have to move whenever and wherever the patrol commander wants them to go, and they'll be lucky if they get stationed within a hundred miles of home."

Bartlett's troopers are North Carolina troopers, but they could be troopers anywhere. Typically the entering cadet is about twenty-two years old, a high school graduate, physically fit, with something in his personality that hungers for excitement and action. Those who have the right stuff stay in a state patrol for life—for life, or as the case may be, for death. Few resign; only a tiny handful are booted out for misconduct; the turnover is less than 5 percent a year. The pay compares with pay in the armed services. Considering the hardships, it isn't much.

These patrolling knights of the highway know periods of tedium. They serve routine warrants, change an occasional tire, direct traffic for some official function, fill in forms at the end of a shift. They spend hours just watching the cars roll by. What keeps them in the fraternity, and sometimes leads to burnout, is the knowledge that violence, danger, and bloodshed may be only seconds away.

They work wrecks: "What bothers me most about working wrecks is to see a little kid hurt. If there's anything left in the world that's innocent, it's a child. I've stood at the scene of an automobile accident involving kids and cried. Then I went home and couldn't sleep. Seeing a dead or injured child is something I'll never get used to, though I know it's part of the job."

Often the wrecks are fatal wrecks. Marie Bartlett listens to a trooper who worked a bad one. The car was utterly demolished: It could have been a Plymouth, a Chrysler, a Dodge. The wreckage had burst into flame. The driver obviously was dead. For a time the vehicle was too hot to approach. A local firefighter spoke to the trooper. His twenty-year-old son wasn't home, and "those wheels sort of look like the ones he had on his car.'' The youth was wearing his high school class ring and a belt buckle with his initials on it. The trooper remembered that night:

> ''By the time we arrived at the scene, the wrecked car had cooled down. Not knowing any other way to get the information I needed, I crawled into the front seat. There was nothing left of the boy except bones, scraps of cloth—and a class ring that I found on the floor. The belt buckle, with the boy's initials on it, had fallen off, but I found it on the floorboard and wrapped it in a handkerchief. Then I went back to the patrol car.
>
> ''The fireman was waiting for an answer. I knew I had to tell him the truth. There's no way to sugarcoat that kind of thing, so I just handed him the belt buckle and said, 'It's him.' ''

Troopers grow to despise drunk drivers. With reason: ''I once investigated a wreck where two cheerleaders—daughters of a doctor and a lawyer—turned their car over and were thrown fifteen feet from the vehicle. One of the girls had been hanging out the window and was decapitated. I found her head in the middle of the road. It reminded me of a mannequin wearing a wig, with every hair in place. There was a question about both girls drinking because they had just come from a party—a party given by one of their parents. Here was a young girl with a promising future whose life ended tragically because of drinking and driving. It was also the twenty-third of December, and I thought of all the unwrapped gifts she'd never see and what her family must be going through. That upset me. They buried her the day after Christmas.''

Marie Bartlett's gripping account has its moments of hilarity. There was the trooper who had to grapple with a naked woman, all four hundred pounds of her, who gave him a difficult time. There was another trooper who had his wits badly scared by a chimpanzee riding in the back seat of a car he had stopped. But most of her book deals with danger. For the trooper, danger is always there. In any given year about a hundred law enforcement officers in this country will die in the line of duty. They will be murdered by escaping convicts, or die in accidents while in pursuit of a suspect. They will drown trying to save others. They will know heartache when they must ring a telephone late at night: "It's your daughter, sir. We've taken her to the hospital. No, sir, I can't tell you the extent of her injuries. . . ." The trooper knows the girl is dying.

The constant stress takes its toll of men; it takes a toll of wives as well. To be married to a trooper is like being married to a sailor. The wife who has a full-time job is going to work just as her husband returns from a midnight shift. A trooper's assignment may take him across a state line in hot pursuit. The search for an escaped convict continues without regard to overtime hours. And when a trooper is late getting home, apprehension mounts. Has he been hurt? Is he in danger? Is he working off his tensions with another woman? Is he—dead? Hard lines, as they say, hard lines.

A. E. Housman, the English classicist, had a certain test for poetry. If a line of poetry were perfect, he would sense hairs rising on the back of his neck. I have my own test for excellence in prose. If a paragraph produces a lump in the throat and a sudden watering of the eyes, that paragraph works. It packs a wallop. Marie Bartlett's unadorned narrative works. I don't expect to love the next cop who gives me a ticket, but having read *Trooper Down!*, I'll be happy hereafter that these men in gray are out there on the road.

JAMES J. KILPATRICK

Preface

You know the feeling. You're driving sixty-eight miles per hour in a fifty-five-mile-per-hour zone and suddenly you look up, see a blue light flashing, and realize that at any moment you'll be pulled over and asked to submit your driver's license. At best, you'll be reprimanded for exceeding the speed limit. At worst, your driving history will be thoroughly scrutinized, and you'll be ticketed, fined, and told when to appear in court.

You are apprehensive, and perhaps annoyed, as the trooper approaches your car. The ultimate figure of authority on the highway, he has momentarily detained you from reaching your destination and has the power to curtail your freedom even further.

Calmly, professionally, he requests the information he needs, hands you back your driver's license, and—if you're lucky—tells you to slow it down because next time he'll give you a ticket.

His last name is imprinted on a silver pin over his right shirt pocket. But unless you're arrested, treated improperly, or have special reason to find out who he is, you probably won't notice his nameplate. Moments after he's gone, you may not even remember what he looks like. For he's just another cop.

In North Carolina, which has more patrolled roads than any other state in the union, slightly more than one thousand troopers monitor up to four million drivers each year, on a state highway system that supplies major transportation arteries between north and south, east and west.

That's one of the reasons I chose North Carolina to represent state troopers around the country. They are also considered one of the most thoroughly trained, well-equipped, and respected state law enforcement agencies in the nation. In years past, when highway patrols were officially ranked in terms of which had the highest arrest records and the most favorable public image, North Carolina was consistently listed among the top three, along with Texas and California.

Steve Wollack, a California psychologist who designs attitude tests for a number of state patrols, says North Carolina troopers reflect what is best about the elitist structure of a specialized police agency.

"I've seen cases of such conflict in law enforcement that police were actually shooting at each other," he said. "But there's an *esprit de corps* that exists within the North Carolina highway patrol which is very impressive, and has helped make it a top-notch organization."

While the primary role of the North Carolina state trooper is to police the roads and enforce motor vehicle laws, he performs duties that range from assisting stranded motorists to securing major disaster areas. His job can be as mundane as fixing a flat tire or as perilous as chasing an escaped felon.

In that respect, he shares many of the experiences found among police officers in all types of law enforcement. FBI agents, state investigators, city police officers, and county deputies—whose work often overlaps—can identify with the incidents and attitudes related in this book.

Since the North Carolina Highway Patrol was established by the state's General Assembly in 1929, forty-four patrol officers have lost their lives while on duty. Twenty-three were killed in traffic accidents, seventeen by gunfire, and four in plane crashes. In 1985, a particularly violent year for North Carolina troopers, three officers were shot and killed after stopping vehicles on routine traffic checks. The year prior to that, another patrolman was seriously wounded trying to apprehend two escaped convicts. Every year, in fact, a surprising number of highway patrol officers are injured by persons they attempt to arrest.

According to FBI studies, more law enforcement officers, including troopers, are killed and assaulted annually in the South than in all other regions of the country combined. From 1976 to 1985, for instance, 441 officers were killed in Southern states compared to 154 in the western half of the United States, 160 in the Midwest, and 122 in the Northeast.

While no definite conclusions were drawn as to why this occurs, FBI officials theorize that Southern law enforcement officers may be more susceptible to violent assaults because of several contributing factors: many police officers in the South tend to work in isolated regions, with a scarcity of backup support. There is easy accessibility to handguns and a general intolerance for gun control in the South, and policemen—particularly troopers—convey a "nice-guy, Southern-gentleman" image instilled during training that can work against them on the road, especially when they're faced with dangerous individuals. In fact, some troopers believe that until recently, the North Carolina Highway Patrol was more concerned about maintaining a good public image than it was about promoting safety and self-defense on the job.

Starting salary for a rookie highway patrolman in North Carolina was $17,000 a year in 1987. After seven years, state troopers earn up to $30,000, with top pay for a master trooper at about $32,000. That's a far cry from the early days, when patrolmen typically worked fifteen to twenty hours a day, six days a week, for wages that seldom exceeded $150 per month. Today, officers work forty hours a week, with split shifts, weekend, and holiday duty the norm. When emergencies arise, they are called from across the state, whether they are on duty or off, and are required to respond twenty-four hours a day.

They are told how to conduct themselves and what's expected from their personal behavior, even when they are not in uniform. A few troopers argue the highway patrol virtually controls their lives.

Yet they are among the most dedicated, committed employees found in any profession. Men and women who join the highway patrol don't see it as a job. It's more a calling, a way of life.

Few people really know what a highway patrol officer encounters on the road, how he feels about his job, why his work consumes him, and the ways in which it ultimately affects his life. This book attempts to explore all of those issues.

"Trooper down" is a term used when an officer is out of commission due to an assault or injury received on the job. This book is the story of North Carolina's Highway Patrol, but the attitudes, problems, and day-to-day experiences told by the men and women in these pages represent those of patrol officers throughout the nation.

As much as possible, I have used the troopers' own words to relate their stories because I felt it would give the reader an inside look at how troopers see themselves and others. In a few cases, certain characteristics or facts have been altered to protect the identity of the people involved.

I was surprised and fascinated by what these officers had to say, and grateful for their willingness to say it. Without exception, every trooper I interviewed was not only candid, but courteous and cooperative. Many of them took time from their off-duty hours to sit and talk with me at length. Others went out of their way to see that I obtained all the information I needed.

Some of the material I wanted to include had to be omitted for editing purposes. For example, an entire chapter on the highway patrol's communications system, which serves as a "lifeline" to troopers on patrol, was deleted to save space. I hope telecommunicators across the state, who generously gave of their time and their stories, will accept my apology. Without them, the highway patrol would come to a virtual halt.

At the heart of the book are the accounts of three North Carolina troopers who were killed in 1985. I found these passages difficult to write. In each case, the violence was senseless, and the victims—all of whom were fine people—had their lives prematurely ended. I'm deeply indebted to the families of the troopers involved—Frank and Bonnie Harmon, James and Frances Coggins, and Mrs Jackie Worley—for their faith in this project and for their courage in recounting the painful details surrounding the incidents.

I also wish to thank Colonel Jack F. Cardwell and the North Carolina Highway Patrol for giving me almost unlimited access to the information I needed to complete the book. Without such cooperation *Trooper Down!* would not have been possible.

While nearly everyone I met provided some type of assistance, certain people were particularly kind. My special thanks to the following: Captain William T. Harris, Troop G Commander, who patiently honored all my requests, including rides on patrol "just one more time" so I could experience first-hand the role of a trooper; Major Robert A. Barefoot, Sergeant Braxton B. Oliver, and the instructors at the Highway Patrol Training Center in Garner, North Carolina, who allowed me to roam their campus freely and answered dozens of questions about cadet life, and Communications Center directors Glenn Griffin, Thurmond Perry, R. C. Savage, and Frank Huggins, who explained how the patrol's statewide radio network operates.

Several people were responsible for helping me see this project through. My heartfelt thanks to: Rick Boyer, fellow author, who led me to Catherine Mahar, a wonderful agent in Boston; *Asheville Citizen-Times* western bureau chief Bob Scott, who gave so much and asked so little in return;

Dr. Louis Rubin, publisher, and Susan Ketchin, editor, at Algonquin Books of Chapel Hill, whose excellent ideas enhanced the manuscript greatly; finally, Trooper Joey Reece, who kept me out of trouble by making sure I got the details right.

Through my research—which began as a newspaper feature and grew into a book—I came to see the men and women behind the gray-and-black uniform as individuals, I gained a new understanding and sense of respect for what they do, day in and day out. I met with them on their jobs, in their homes, in restaurants, jails, courthouses, headquarters, patrol cars, and on the side of the road. I took coffee breaks with them, had dinner with their families, spent hours on patrol with them, watched them laugh at their mistakes, cry about their losses. As a result, I came to view them as people, rather than simply figures of authority. Some of these officers I now consider good friends.

I was impressed with their honesty, intelligence, and sensitivity. While a few of the troopers I met were less than sterling characters, the majority were decent, hardworking people attracted not just to the elite image of the highway patrol, but by a sincere willingness to help others.

None of which means that next time I'm caught speeding, I won't be stopped, questioned, or fined. For that's one of the first things I learned about the North Carolina Highway Patrol. It's an organization composed of professionals, people who by and large believe in what they do and take their work seriously, yet who are often misunderstood.

"There are things the public will never comprehend about the highway patrol," said one officer. "They see this guy riding around in a shiny car, or drinking coffee at a restaurant, flirting with women, or writing a few tickets.

"But that just happens on the best damn days. They don't see the times when we're holding a kid whose mother just got killed, or telling somebody's parents their son won't be home, or seeing a teenager so strung out on drugs he'll never be worth anything to society.

"They don't see us at two in the morning on one of these back roads with a car full of drunks—none of them wanting to go to jail. Or see us facing the possibility of getting shot.

"The hours are hard and demanding. We're working nights, holidays, weekends, while our family spends time without us.

"There's just a lot more to it than anyone realizes."

This book is for troopers everywhere, on every highway in every state, and for the public they willingly serve.

MARIE BARTLETT
February 1988
Candler, North Carolina

TROOPER DOWN!

Prologue

"We're state employees with a job to do, but we're a fraternity too. You don't say, 'I work for the highway patrol.' You say, 'I'm a member of the highway patrol.' It's like joining a club, with a very elite membership."

—Anonymous trooper

It is 11:05 on a Friday night and North Carolina highway patrolman Joel K. Reece is parked in a silver, unmarked LTD, calibrating a VASCAR unit. The device earmarks speeding drivers by measuring and computing the distance between two points of reference. Troopers like it because it allows them to spot potential violators without being detected.

There's nothing to do now but wait in the dark. Reece leans back against the seat and taps his hand against the steering wheel, forefinger and thumb pressed together—a sure sign he's getting restless.

At five feet eight and 160 pounds, the thirty-two-year-old officer is small but powerfully built, with dark good looks and an impish grin. The son of a former policeman, he is proud of the patrol's sharp image and works hard to keep himself in shape.

Once called a "golden boy"—a term used for troopers who present a neat appearance, perform their duties well, and don't create problems for the patrol—he is devoted to his job and the organization.

"I guess I'm a company man," he has said during his nine years on the patrol. "I love what I do."

The radio crackles and Reece picks it up. It is another trooper, patrolling another stretch of highway.

"Ten-twenty?" Reece asks the caller (what's your location?).

"Downtown Swannanoa."

"What'd you do? Give up around here?"

"Negative," the patrolman replies. "I'll be back in just a minute. We're looking for a 10-55 (drunk driver)."

A second officer's voice comes over the line.

"This is the pits!" he exclaims. "There's *nothing* going on tonight. When we do find a drunk driver, we'll probably wreck, what with all of us trying to get to him at the same time."

"It's early," says Reece. "It'll pick up."

The men sign off and Reece decides to cruise Interstate 40. In the traffic ahead is a green, dilapidated Buick periodically crossing the midline.

Reece clocks him at a suspiciously slow 28 mph before he flicks on the blue light.

Moments later, the Buick comes to a weaving halt.

In the dark there is no way to tell if the driver is alone, male, female, harmless, or armed to the teeth. Flashlight in hand, Reece approaches the car with a caution born of experience. Ever since his close friend, Giles Harmon, was shot and killed during a routine traffic check, he applies all of his law enforcement training to every stop.

Reaching the left rear of the car, he swipes his hand lightly across its side, making sure his fingerprints are left behind. Such prints could serve as evidence against a driver who fires at an officer, then takes off, claiming he was never stopped.

Then he does a quick but professional scan of the car's interior. How many occupants? Any weapons in sight? Signs of drugs? What's the driver up to? Has he turned around or is he sitting face forward? Is he reaching for anything and what is it? Are his hands in plain view?

Reece stops just short of the driver's window, his body close to the car for protection.

A bearlike man with stringy hair and a scruffy yellow beard looks up.

"Evenin', officer," he says, slurring his words.

"Let me see your driver's license," Reece says calmly. The man hands him a small plastic card and Reece holds it under the light to check its validity.

"Okay," says Reece, opening the car door. "You'll have to come with me."

His name is Devlin Farmer (the person is real, the name is not). Twenty-six years old, he is wearing a dark purple T-shirt, mud-splattered jeans, and a pair of black canvas shoes that curl at the toes.

And he is huge. So big that he dwarfs his arresting officer, who has just told him he's being taken into custody for drunk driving. Reece has already handcuffed him and placed him in the front seat of the patrol car.

"Sir, uncuff me, sir," Farmer pleads. "These things are killin' me!"

Reece, struggling to get a seat belt around the man's enormous midriff, ignores him.

"Hell," he mutters, jerking the seat belt forward, "I don't know if I can get this thing around you or not!"

"My arms is cut in two, sir."

"No, they're not."

"Yeah, they are, sir."

The belt finally snaps into place and Reece returns to the driver's seat, where he radios in his position. He will ask the telecommunicator to verify Farmer's license and check the vehicle registration. Then he'll inform them he has a 10-55 (intoxicated driver) in custody.

"Turn around and face me now," he instructs Farmer. "I'm gonna give you a little test. See the black tip of this pen?"

Farmer nods, his head bobbing unsteadily.

"Follow it with your eyes."

The man tries, but can't seem to focus.

A slight edge creeps into Reece's voice.

"Can you not do it?" he says.

"Sir, I'm nervous."

"Well this isn't too hard to do—to look at a pen. Don't move your head. Keep your head still."

Farmer squirms and the cuffs bite deeper into his wrists.

"Sit still," Reece says, "and it won't hurt so bad. Now tell me how many beers you've had today."

"One or two," says Farmer.

Reece eyes him warily.

"One or two beers won't make a man your size stagger around."

"I ain't lying."

"Had any liquor or drugs?"

"Nope," says Farmer. "I ain't that kind of guy."

Reece shakes his head and puts the cruiser in gear. He has yet to meet a drunk driver who's had more than "one or two beers."

"Where are you taking me?" Farmer wants to know.

"To the breathalyzer room at the courthouse."

"Well, can't you please uncuff me first?"

"No, I can't," says the trooper. "You might reach over and grab the steering wheel."

"I won't do nothin'. I promise."

Reece tells him to sit back and relax. They'll be at the courthouse in five minutes. At the entrance to the booking room, the officer unbuckles his holster and steps into a cubicle to deposit his gun. Twelve years earlier, in this same building, North Carolina troopers Dean Arledge and Lawrence Canipe were killed in the breathalyzer room when a drunk driver grabbed Canipe's pistol and shot both men in the back. As a result, law enforcement officers are now required to put their weapons aside while administering breathalyzer tests.

Inside the booking room, Reece starts the paperwork while a sheriff's deputy frisks Farmer. Behind them is the "drunk tank," a grimy concrete enclosure designed to hold up to twenty or thirty inebriated adults. Three men, all in various stages of intoxication, are sitting on a wooden bench against the wall. One has been protesting his innocence all night; he wasn't driving the car in which he was found, he says, he was walking alongside it.

"Yeah, and doing about eighty miles an hour at the time," says the trooper who arrested him. "You must have a great set of legs."

Farmer is spread-eagled against the counter, ready for the routine search that is part of every arrest. With the cuffs removed, he seems faintly bored, as though he's done this several times before.

"Take your shoes off," the deputy tells him. "Now your socks. Turn them inside out. That's right. Now put 'em back on." His brown leather wallet, a set of keys, and seventy dollars in small bills are on the counter.

A few minutes later, Reece, who's been busy with paperwork since he and Farmer arrived, escorts him down the hall. In the breathalyzer room, no larger than a bedroom, are three desks, five folding chairs, and—at the moment—eight people. Half are waiting their turn at the breathalyzer machines. The other half are troopers. Two of the officers are sergeants who routinely administer drunk driving tests.

Inside the small, windowless room it is hot and stuffy. Reece pulls up a chair and loosens his tie before turning to Farmer.

"Welcome to the circus," he says. "Grab a seat 'cause it looks like we're gonna be here awhile."

On weeknights, it takes up to an hour to process one drunk driver. Fridays and Saturdays are worse.

In a corner of the room is a heavyset woman wearing

tight black pants and a low-cut top, exposing parts of her considerable breasts.

"So what are the charges?" she asks the trooper seated before her.

"Lots of stuff," he says, smiling. "But first we've gotta get the basics. How old are you?"

"Twenty-five."

"Color eyes?"

"I don't know," she says, leaning forward. "Look for yourself."

Every trooper in the room grins.

"Occupation?"

"None right now," she says.

"Ever been arrested before?"

"Yeah, for all kinds of things."

"What?"

"I said all kinds of stuff."

The officer looks up sharply, his good humor gone.

"What?" he says impatiently. "You might as well tell us because we can find out anyway."

"Then go ahead and find out."

"Anything bad? Ever had any felonies?"

"No."

"Any drug charges?"

"No."

She sits back while the officer prepares the breathalyzer test. After blowing into the machine and waiting for the results, she registers .11, one point over the legal limit. A few minutes later, she is on her way to the magistrate's office to post bail.

"Don't we know her from somewhere?" Reece asks when she leaves the room.

"Yeah," says a sergeant, "she's that hooker who got busted for cutting up a customer. Hurt him pretty bad too."

"You mean guys actually *pay* for that?" says another officer.

Reece laughs and looks at his watch. It's nearly 2:00 A.M. and he's brought in only one drunk driver tonight. Still, he expects to hit triple figures soon, when he arrests his one hundredth drunk driver for the year. That makes him feel good.

It is Farmer's turn at the breathalyzer and Reece completes the paperwork while the sergeant explains to Farmer that he has the right to refuse the test, the right to call an attorney or to have another witness on hand. Most people waive these rights when they realize the delays will wind up costing them more time and money. Farmer agrees to take the test.

At an adjoining table is a short, slender man, early twenties, wearing glasses, jeans, and a sleeveless black T-shirt. He was at a bar when a friend convinced him to go to a restaurant and bring back some food. On the way, he was stopped by a sharp-eyed trooper and arrested for drunk driving. The breathalyzer shows a .14 score, four points above the North Carolina legal limit. He will automatically lose his driver's license for the next ten days and, if convicted, could have his license suspended for up to a year.

He is shaking his head over the news.

"My wife is gonna hate me for the rest of my life," he moans. "She's gonna kick my ass. I can't believe I did this."

No one appears to be listening.

Reece is intent on watching the sergeant complete the first half of Farmer's test.

"I say at least .14," he predicts.

"Umm, maybe," the sergeant responds. "With this guy's size, he'd have to drink a case of beer and a pint of liquor before it would even tell on him."

Farmer looks dejected.

"I've got to quit this drinkin'," he says. "It's killin' me."

"I'd like to stop," he adds softly.

He scores .13 on the breathalyzer.

"Can you come to court on the twenty-second?" Reece asks him. Farmer nods.

"Then let's talk to the magistrate and get your bail set. As long as you can post bail and get someone to pick you up *who isn't drunk*, you're free to go."

"How much is it gonna cost me?" Farmer says.

"That's up to the magistrate," Reece replies.

Half an hour later, the legalities complete, Farmer is on his way to find a phone.

For Reece, hours away from the end of his shift, the night is still young. So far, everything's been normal . . . even quiet. Yet that is subject to change, and quickly, as every state trooper well knows.

Just ask Louis B. Rector.

1

"Am I Gonna Die?"

> "It's always in the back of your mind. You use all the precautions you can, but when you're out on the road alone, you're vulnerable. And there's not much you can do about it."
>
> —*Patrol sergeant*

Trooper Louis Bryan Rector almost didn't make it into the highway patrol.

Born in the small coastal town of Elizabeth City, North Carolina, he tried to join the N.C. State Highway Patrol after high school, but failed to pass the entrance exam. For a while he forgot about his yen to be a trooper, went on to complete college with a degree in drafting and design, and took a job in Suffolk, Virginia, at the Highway Department, drawing road plans.

One day he got a call from a highway patrol sergeant who said that Louis could take the entrance exam again. This time he passed and was accepted at the patrol academy in Chapel Hill.

But it was 1970 and the Vietnam War, like a bad case of flu, was hanging on, spreading its virulence. Several days after Louis found out he could join the patrol, he received notice that he had been drafted into the army. Again, he put his plans for becoming a trooper on hold, and enlisted in the Air Force. He spent the next three and a half years stationed in Las Vegas, Nevada, all the while thinking of the North Carolina Highway Patrol.

"I'm not sure what it was that fascinated me about the highway patrol," he said later. "I had an uncle who was a trooper in the 1930s and I can remember being very impressed with him as I was growing up. I guess part of it was the uniform, the shiny car, and the prestige."

It is the prestige that draws most troopers into the North Carolina Highway Patrol.

"In this state, the patrol is like being in the major league of law enforcement," said one officer. "In the town where I grew up, even people who didn't like cops respected the patrol."

Louis now believes that, for him, finally being able to join the highway patrol was an act of God, a predetermined fate that would challenge and change him in ways he would never have imagined.

By 1974, he was out of the Air Force, married, and living in Mount Airy, North Carolina. Uncertain about his future, he returned to college for technical courses and says he would have become a professional student had it not been for his wife.

"You can't stay in school for the rest of your life," she told him. "Get a job."

Still drawn to law enforcement, Louis became a sheriff's deputy in Greensboro, North Carolina, where he stayed for two years. Then the highway patrol beckoned again. On November 15, 1976, he was officially accepted into the organization and began basic training as a cadet. It was his third try at becoming a trooper.

The course was hard for Louis. At twenty-eight, he was older than most cadets, and he did not fit the mold of the classic hard-nosed, aggressive trooper who "kicks ass and takes names."

Six feet tall, 175 pounds, he is dark-haired and fair skinned, with warm brown eyes, and a shy smile that masks a strong sense of purpose. A sensitive, soft-spoken man, he gives the mistaken impression that he is more at home with a good book than a .357 Magnum. Yet underneath that mild manner is a steely, stubborn determination to succeed at whatever he sets out to do. And in 1976 he was determined to become a state trooper—with some prodding that is.

"I was the type who had to be pushed," he recalled. "The physical training was especially rough. We had to be out of bed at 5:00 A.M. and were expected to run up to seven miles a day. There were many mornings when my physical training instructor literally moved me along with his foot."

Even after Louis graduated from the patrol academy (third from the top in his class) he found his first few weeks as a trooper relentlessly difficult.

"The first night on the job my training officer took me into the patrol office and dumped a huge stack of paperwork on the desk. Then, with no instruction, he said, 'Here, do it.' I thought, this isn't for me. I wanted to go back to the security of the sheriff's department, where I knew what to do and everybody knew me."

Throughout this time Louis wanted to quit, and proceeded to tell his sergeant so.

"If you're gonna quit," replied the officer, "at least wait until you get out of training. That way, I won't look so bad."

Louis, however, decided to stay, and by the end of the six-week training period he was feeling better. A trooper at last, he was ready, willing, and able to work alone.

March 6, 1984: Louis, thirty-six, was now in his eighth year with the North Carolina Highway Patrol. After completing on-the-job training he was stationed first in Hoke County, a rural community eighteen miles west of Fayetteville, then sent to Burke County in 1979. Once known for its backwoods violence, the region, situated in the foothills of the Appalachian Mountains, had grown and matured into a respectable, pleasant place to live. By 1984, the county, named for Revolutionary War governor Thomas Burke, was 506 square miles of farmland and furniture factories, with a population of 75,000 and an average per capita income of just over $10,000.

Cutting through the center of Burke County is Interstate 40, a major transportation artery that channels the flow of traffic heading east from Tennessee and states beyond.

During his eight years as a trooper, Louis had distinguished himself as an active, competent officer, having encountered his share of drunk drivers, speeders, violators, accident victims, and other motorists in distress. And, not surprisingly, he'd gotten into a fight or two, once with a 240-pound drunk who had wrapped his arms around Louis, nearly squeezing him to death, and once with an irate driver who, in a fit of temper, pulled a gun.

Though aware that the potential for danger lurked daily in a trooper's job, Louis truly believed nothing serious would ever happen to him on the road. It would always be the other guy, another trooper whose name and face would appear on the six o'clock news. As a result, he was more enforcement-conscious than safety-conscious, a lopsided attitude inadvertently encouraged by highway patrol policy. Since an officer's abilities as a trooper were measured by the number of tickets he wrote weekly and the types of arrests he made, it was imperative that he present himself as an active, aggressive trooper who did his job well (i.e., wrote a lot of tickets). Conscientious patrolmen like Louis were particularly susceptible to such internal pressures.

That March night, Louis's shift began as a routine patrol.

Louis left the house around midnight in his unmarked cruiser, checking on duty through the Newton Communications Center.

"F-138, Newton," he said, identifying his call number. "I'm now 10-41 (beginning tour of duty)."

"Ten-four," the telecommunicator replied.

Since the patrol was short-handed in both Burke and adjoining Catawba County, troopers shared the responsibility of patrolling long stretches of Interstate 40. So for the next hour, Louis headed west before turning around at the McDowell County line (which also adjoined Burke) to backtrack east.

About midway on his assigned route, he clocked several tractor-trailer rigs exceeding the fifty-five speed limit. One trucker was barreling along at seventy, so Louis pulled him over and, after arresting him, took him to the Morganton County Jail, where he was fined forty-seven dollars for speeding and then released.

Heading back toward the interstate, Louis should have patrolled the stretch of of highway he had not yet covered. Instead, without knowing why, he turned and drove to the same location he had just patrolled. When he reached the McDowell County line he crossed over as he had done earlier, cruising toward Morganton.

Moments later he spotted a light gray 1978 Cadillac in the westbound lane going much too fast. Using his radar, Louis clocked the driver at seventy-four miles per hour and crossed the grassy interstate median to pursue him. Nearing the McDowell County line, he caught up with the car, activated the blue patrol light, and turned on the siren. But the driver sped forward.

The chase continued across the county line until the Cadillac finally slowed, then eased onto the right emergency lane to stop. Louis pulled up behind. With the engine still running, he stepped out of the patrol car. The air surrounding him was gray and foggy, heavy with the threat of a bone-chilling rain.

In his left hand he carried a patrol-issued flashlight. Inside the car lay his bulletproof vest, slung carelessly across the front seat. Hot and bulky, it was an optional piece of equipment that Louis and other North Carolina state troopers seldom bothered to wear.

As soon as his feet hit the pavement, instinct took over. Something told him not to move too quickly, for this would be a traffic stop like none he had ever encountered. Yet he still had to act.

Slowly and methodically, Louis moved to the left rear door of the Cadillac. The back window was halfway down, and he could see a portion of the driver's head. At first he thought the man was wearing an orange hat, then realized that what he had seen was a thick, curly mop of reddish hair.

Neither the man nor his passenger spoke, moved, or turned around. The trooper felt a sudden stab of fear.

"Driver! Put your hands up on the steering wheel!" Louis demanded.

Without warning, the man turned and fired a single shot from a .22-caliber revolver. The bullet passed through the half-open back window and struck Louis in the left side of the chest, glanced off a stainless steel pen in his shirt pocket, and entered his lung.

Staggering backwards, he fell to the ground, then got up and ran between the patrol car and the Cadillac. Grabbing his .357 Magnum, he intended to fire at the driver, but as he reached up to aim, he saw the passenger get out of the car and aim a .22 revolver at him. The man fired six times, hitting Louis in the upper left leg, right knee, and right side of the stomach. Seconds later, he jumped into the Cadillac and the car sped away.

Bleeding heavily but still conscious, Louis managed to fire all six rounds from his gun. Two bullets shattered the Cadillac's back window, but missed both occupants.

Alone now and seriously hurt, Louis struggled to return to the patrol car that would link him to help. On the pavement behind him lay his hat and the flashlight, along with the scattered remains of numerous .22 shells.

Crawling towards the safety of the patrol car, he was engulfed with a sense of shock and anger. This wasn't supposed to happen to him. As he climbed into the driver's seat, he looked down. There was little pain from the wounds but he could see thick red stains seeping across the front of his shirt and trousers. Afraid to examine himself further, he concentrated on getting his gun back into its holster.

Despite his condition, his first thought was, "I have to get my gun back where it belongs." Over and over he tried replacing the weapon, but each time, the empty holster on his hip swung round and round.

Finally, still holding the gun, he picked up the radio.

"Signal 25, Newton," he gasped into the mike (I need immediate assistance). "This is F-138. I've been shot."

"Ten-four," the telecommunicator responded. "Can you give us a description of the vehicle and the direction it was traveling?"

Louis provided what details he could and in turn was reassured that help was on the way.

Convinced he could help himself, Louis turned the wheel of the patrol car and started east on the interstate, unaware in his state of shock that he was driving in the westbound lane. The last thing he remembers was slamming on the brakes as the guardrail rushed towards him. It was 1:36 A.M.

Less than a mile away, John Angley and his wife were sound asleep when the police scanner next to their bed relayed a message that a highway patrol officer needed assistance on Interstate 40 near Dysartsville Road. An emergency medical technician and paramedic for the McDowell County rescue squad, Angley was on call as a "first responder" to any crisis that arose within his district during the night.

Without a word, he got up, dressed, and was out the door. Randall Brackett, McDowell County fire chief, and Bruce Gwyn, another local fire fighter, had also responded to the call. All were en route to Louis at about the same time.

Angley and Gwyn arrived at the scene simultaneously. As they ran towards the patrol car, both men noted it was stopped in the wrong lane, with all four headlights burning. The blue light, sitting atop the dashboard, was still spinning, and a blood-splattered bulletproof vest was draped across the passenger seat.

Angley saw Louis slumped forward in the driver's seat, his gun still in his hand. Turning to Gwyn, he cautioned him not to open the door until they had clearly identified their purpose.

"Sir," said Angley, leaning towards the patrol car. "We're here to help you, sir. Can we open the door?"

Louis's head moved slightly and he mumbled.

Reaching into the car, Angley gently pulled the officer back against the seat to check his vital signs. He could tell by the trooper's ashen color and weak pulse that he was in deep trouble. Louis was also having difficulty breathing. As he gasped for breath, he looked up at John and asked imploringly, "Am I gonna die? Am I gonna die?"

"Not if we can help it," said Angley.

The Burke County rescue squad was the first ambulance to arrive. Emergency medical technicians Tommy Waters and Phillip Reece began preparing IVs while Angley and Gwyn administered oxygen to Louis. As the medics were lifting the trooper out of the patrol car and onto the stretcher, he suddenly vomited and stopped breathing. Angley quickly repositioned him and Louis took one breath, then another.

A short, stocky man in his late thirties, Angley took his work seriously, sometimes getting emotionally caught up in the traumas he witnessed as an EMT. He hoped fervently that the trooper would make it and the night would end on a happier note.

At Grace Hospital in Morganton, nineteen miles from where Louis had been shot, doctors, nurses, and other emergency medical personnel were waiting for the ambulance to arrive. They had already been notified that a highway patrol officer was badly wounded and would probably require immediate surgery. Among the operating room nurses off duty that night was Scottie Rector, Louis's thirty-two-year-old wife.

The call came shortly before 2:00 A.M. Scottie, a medium-built woman with brown hair and a soft, lilting voice, picked up the phone. A registered nurse, Scottie couldn't understand why the hospital was calling her when she wasn't scheduled to work.

"It's Louis," said Scottie's nursing supervisor. "He's been shot and you need to come to the emergency room."

"Are you kidding?" she said. "How bad is it? How bad is he hurt?" She sat up in bed, now wide awake.

"I don't know," answered the woman.

He's dead, Scottie thought. Louis is dead and they don't want to tell me.

"I'll be right there," she responded. Dressed in a pair of faded jeans and a sweatshirt, she drove through the rain to Grace Hospital, certain that all of her fears over Louis's job had finally come to pass. At home, their daughter, Chanda, twelve, and son, Bryan, eight, slept on.

In the hospital emergency room, John Angley and the ambulance crew had completed their job and were waiting for word on how Louis was doing. Almost immediately, he'd been whisked into a trauma room and surrounded by physicians and a well-trained medical staff who knew exactly what to do. The E.R. was teeming with law enforcement officers, reporters, hospital personnel, and patients.

Almost immediately after the telecommunicator at Newton received word that Louis had been shot, highway patrol officers from Burke and surrounding counties were alerted to stand by for emergency duty. Many off-duty troopers donned their uniforms and checked on voluntarily so they'd be ready when the first official orders came through.

One of those troopers was Don Peterson. He heard the news through a telecommunicator who called him at home.

"I went straight to the McDowell County line, where other troopers were already securing the area," Patterson recalled. "We set up roadblocks, stopping to check all traffic going through. Detectives from the State Bureau of Investigation were there too, taking photographs and looking for evidence. Louis's patrol car was still running, the radar unit still flashing 74 mph where he had clocked the Cadillac. Even the commercial radio was on. Then I saw

Louis's revolver lying in the front seat. At that point, all we could think of was, 'What happened here? Who did this? And when are we going to find them?' "

Nearby, at Grace Hospital, Louis was undergoing emergency surgery. Though he had lost a substantial amount of blood, all four bullets had passed through his body and he was expected to recover. Days later, he would learn that the ballpoint pen had saved his life. Had the first bullet not deflected off the pen, the surgeon told Louis, it would have entered his heart instead of his lung.

While Louis lay in the intensive care unit following surgery, McDowell County deputies, asked to assist in the manhunt, located the ditched Cadillac behind an elementary school in Nebo, a tiny community a few miles from where the shooting took place. There was no sign of the driver and his passenger. Several troopers were dispatched to Nebo, where they joined the deputies in sealing off the area. Not yet sure who they were looking for, the patrolmen stopped everyone coming through Nebo and checked their licenses.

Meanwhile, with help from the FBI and other law enforcement agencies, the highway patrol office in Morganton began gathering the first important bits of information about the Cadillac's occupants. What eventually emerged was a chilling portrait of two deadly criminals on the run.

The driver was Ronald Sotka, forty-one, better known as Ronald Freeman, a Tennessee prison escapee who was serving consecutive life sentences for the 1970 murder of his pregnant wife and stepdaughter. A former church deacon from Knoxville, Freeman had maintained his innocence even after he had been found guilty and sentenced to 198 years in prison.

His passenger was James E. Clegg, thirty, a habitual criminal who had escaped with Freeman and three other inmates from Fort Pillow State Prison in Tennessee on February 18. Two of the five convicts had been captured within days. Clegg, Freeman, and a third man were still at large.

Authorities considered Clegg and Freeman "extremely

dangerous." Three days after their escape from prison, the pair had walked out of the woods near Brownsville, Tennessee, and shot and killed a fifty-nine-year-old businessman who was grilling steaks in his backyard. Afterwards, they kidnapped his wife and drove her 400 miles across the state to a rest stop near Knoxville, where she was released unharmed. The fugitives were then picked up by an unidentified woman who apparently harbored them in her home.

From there, Clegg and Freeman drove to Ashville, North Carolina, where they rented a car and traveled to Cleveland, Ohio, to see Freeman's brother, who gave them $1,200. Returning to Asheville, Clegg and Freeman purchased a two-tone older-model Buick for $850. On their way east, seventy miles past Morganton, the engine gave out. The men ditched the Buick and stole a 1978 Cadillac from a Mocksville garage. In an apparent effort to mislead police, they got back on Interstate 40, heading west again, when they were stopped for speeding by Louis Rector.

Trooper Don Patterson remembers the first few frustrating hours of the search.

"In the beginning, we had about thirty or forty troopers working on the scene, in addition to other law enforcement officers. Tracking dogs were brought in, but they didn't find anything. Around 7:00 A.M. we realized we were hunting for two Tennessee escapees. We got a highway patrol helicopter from Raleigh but it was too foggy to go up. Later, when the weather cleared, I accompanied the helicopter crew since I knew the area, but that didn't help either. All we could see from the air were patrol cars and roadblocks."

Troopers at ground level weren't doing much better. Excitement mellowed to boredom as the hours dragged on and the search through rain-soaked woods led to one dead end after another. Bloodhounds picked up a scent near the abandoned Cadillac, which led to a cemetery half a mile away. Then the trail stopped. At one point, troopers thought they had someone cornered in a house, only to discover that their "fugitive" was an old man who had failed to open the door because he was hard of hearing.

By mid-evening, bleary-eyed troopers—some of whom had been on duty eighteen hours or more—were beginning to feel the strain. Yet no one complained or asked to be relieved. A trooper was "down," and they were determined to locate the men responsible.

"It didn't matter if we ate or slept or went home," said Don Patterson. "We wanted to find those guys."

That night, Patterson went to the intensive care unit at Grace Hospital to check on Louis. During the visit, he recapped the manhunt and asked Louis if he could describe either of his assailants. But all Louis could remember was that both men were white.

"He was alert and could talk," Patterson said. "So I felt good about him when I left."

Just before dawn on Wednesday morning the McDowell County sheriff's department got word that a man had broken into a house in Marion, five miles west of Nebo, wanting food.

A town of 3,680, Marion was known as a tough mountain community where locals were raised to eye most strangers with suspicion. During the night, Freeman and Clegg had hidden in the fields along the railroad tracks in Nebo, working their way west toward Marion. When they reached town they had decided to split up and take their chances separately.

Freeman made attempts to break into two east Marion homes but was shot at by gun-toting residents. He then ran into the woods before authorities could catch him. On his third try, he kicked in the back door of a house belonging to Rass and Molly Harvey in south Marion, and demanded something to eat. The Harveys were asleep, but a daughter-in-law living in the house fixed Freeman's breakfast and pleaded with him to give himself up. He said no, he'd already vowed he'd never be taken alive. Then he told her he was taking her with him as a hostage. Frightened at this turn of events, she got up, went to check on the Harveys, and found them both wide awake, listening to every word Freeman said.

Molly Harvey, sixty-three, was legally blind and diabetic. She knew about the manhunt in Nebo and Marion, but could not believe one of the fugitives was actually sitting at her kitchen table eating breakfast. The shock was more than she could bear, and she began having chest pains. In a strange show of compassion—or perhaps because he didn't know what else to do—Freeman allowed the daughter-in-law to call an ambulance and admit relatives and a minister into the house. At the same time, he warned the family he would kill anyone who tried to notify the police.

Emergency Medical Technician John Angley, the first person to reach Louis Rector after the shooting, was called to the scene.

"Me and my partner, Joe, pulled up in the front yard about five in the morning," said John. "The porch light was on and everybody was up. When we went in, there were eight or ten people, including kids, just sitting around the living room. I saw this guy standing against the door with his hands behind his back, but I didn't know who he was. He was wearing an old army jacket and never said a word or offered to help. All I remember is the look on his face—a cold expression, like he knew where he was headed but he didn't care."

The daughter-in-law took the medics into the bathroom, where Molly, prostrate on the floor, was now in cardiac arrest.

Angley radioed for more assistance while his partner tried to revive the stricken woman. He remembers the telecommunicator—who had heard about Freeman's whereabouts—asking them if they were both all right, and feeling puzzled by her concern.

Freeman, intent on watching the medics attempt to revive Molly, didn't notice that a family member had slipped out the back door. Moments later, the Harveys' son-in-law notified the sheriff's department that Freeman was in the house.

A few minutes later, as Angley was bending over Molly to help get her onto a stretcher, a deputy sheriff tapped him on the shoulder and whispered, "Where is he, John?"

"What are you talking about?" John whispered back.

"That convict," said the officer. "We were told he's here in the house somewhere."

Somewhat shaken, John replied, "I think he went into the bedroom behind us."

"You boys go ahead and get her out of here," instructed the deputy, pointing to Molly. "There may be some shooting."

Freeman, hunched over a bed with a pistol in his hand, was waiting when officers entered the house. Following a brief exchange of gunfire, Freeman escaped through a bedroom window, ran down an embankment, and into a neighboring yard.

Desperate, Freeman ran almost a mile before he came upon a green, two-room, tar-paper shack. Close behind him was a group of determined state and local police, including Trooper Larry Carver. Within seconds, the shack was surrounded by officers and Freeman was told to surrender. In response, he fired several times from behind an unhinged door he was using for cover, hitting Carver in the shoulder. Suddenly, there was a barrage of gunfire and Freeman was struck repeatedly. He died almost instantly.

At Grace Hospital, when Louis Rector heard that Freeman was dead, his only reaction was one of relief.

Throughout the tense hours leading up to Freeman's death, Clegg was never more than half a mile away.

About four-fifteen on Wednesday afternoon, state trooper "Junior" Arrant and a small group of other officers were conducting a house-to-house search when they noticed a pants leg protruding from under a pile of plywood. Arrant motioned for a deputy to come over so he could show him what he'd seen. As the deputy flipped back the plywood, Clegg looked up and placed one hand on his chest, the other palm up, letting the men know right away that he was unarmed.

Cold, tired, and hungry, he was ready to surrender.

"He knew his life was hanging by a thread," said Arrant.

Shortly after James Clegg was captured, Molly Harvey died at Grace Hospital in Morganton.

Louis continued his recovery, keeping tabs from his hospital bed on all aspects of the manhunt. Clegg was taken to the McDowell County jail, where he was charged with assault with a deadly weapon with intent to kill, inflicting serious injury, and assault with a firearm on a law enforcement officer. He was also served with a fugitive warrant for escaping from prison. Extradition proceedings began almost immediately. Clegg was sent back to Tennessee, where he faced charges of murder and kidnapping in connection with the slaying of the Brownsville businessman and the abduction of the man's wife. Pleading guilty to the first set of charges involving Louis Rector, Clegg was sentenced to twenty years in a North Carolina prison, with the term to begin after he had served his time in Tennessee. In a statement issued by his attorney, Clegg asked that the $10,000 reward for the capture of him and Freeman be given to Molly Harvey's family.

Louis spent the next three months at home recovering from his gunshot wounds. Physically, he did fine. But Scottie Rector recalls that after the shooting, her husband underwent a distinct personality change.

"He was very quiet and withdrawn, almost passive," she said. "I worried about what would happen when he returned to work. If I could have, I would have kept him from going back."

Every night for weeks, Louis tossed and turned, wondering how he could have prevented the shooting, or how he might have killed the two men who had assaulted him. Then, turning the episode over and over in his mind, he'd seethe with rage.

"It didn't take me long to realize that my animosity toward Freeman and Clegg was consuming me," he said.

"I knew that before I could get on the road to recovery, I'd have to resolve my anger."

For help and comfort he turned to friends, and for spiritual guidance, to his Baptist faith.

On June 1, 1984, Louis went back to work. The first night proved traumatic for both him and his family. Not only was he confronted with his own fears, but Scottie and the children all burst into tears, pleading with him not to go on patrol.

"It was a real scene," he said later. "My wife said she wasn't going to be subjected to this again—having someone call her and tell her I'd been shot. The whole thing was emotionally draining for us all. Finally, I hit rock bottom. So I did the only thing I knew how to do. I went into my bedroom and got down on my knees. I told God I was afraid, and so was my family, and I asked Him to give us more strength and courage than any of us had at the moment."

A short time later, Scottie walked with her husband to his patrol car, waiting while he radioed to a telecommunicator that he was now on duty. As the clock struck 6:00 P.M., Trooper Louis Rector was officially back on patrol.

Yet problems stemming from the shooting continued to plague him. Trooper Don Patterson and other colleagues weren't sure what to expect out of Louis from one day to the next.

"None of us knew his feelings or could identify with what he'd gone through," said Don. "He'd be short-tempered, flying off the handle at the least little thing. Then he'd withdraw. We discussed his behavior among ourselves, but we didn't know how to help him. It was a hard thing to cope with, but we tried to understand."

From Louis's perspective, he felt he was constantly being tested to see if he still had what it takes to be a trooper.

"I thought everyone was watching me, waiting to see when I was gonna break under the pressure, when I was gonna mess up."

On patrol, Louis worked hard at hiding his fears. Then

one night something happened to shatter the fragile wall he had built around himself.

"Not long after I came back to work, I clocked a car speeding in the eastern part of the county," Louis recalled. "I chased him for about seven miles until he turned down a dirt road and stopped. The guy jumped out of the car and I followed him. We ran across a concrete barrier but I tripped and fell. I looked up as he was entering a wood thicket and saw him pointing a gun. He fired on me twice and I drew my weapon and fired back. Then he disappeared into the woods. At that point, I lost control."

The shooting made Louis so physically ill that he crawled to a nearby ditch and threw up.

Several months later, Louis's anger finally came to a head.

A trooper had been shot and killed in western North Carolina and Louis was scheduled to join other officers in the manhunt. At the last minute his name was taken off the list.

"I wanted to go up there bad, to be accepted again as part of the group. I felt that after my recovery I'd earned the right to help my fellow officers. When I found out I wasn't allowed to go, I went crazy. It was like they still had reservations about me. I couldn't handle it."

That night, Louis, upset and angry, stomped into the first sergeant's office at Morganton headquarters.

"Why in the hell can't I join the manhunt?" he ranted. "It's not fair that you're leaving me behind!"

The sergeant tried to calm him down.

"I won't tolerate that kind of behavior," he said. "All we're doing is looking out for your best interests. This is more a scheduling problem than anything else. We put you where we need you the most."

But for Louis, the emotional turmoil persisted. In fact, he says now he was headed toward a downward spiral.

"I had a lot of family problems, and still a lot of anger. My wife almost left me and my job became a daily struggle. Worst of all, despite my faith, I was trying to handle it alone. I kept telling myself I was doing fine. But I really wasn't."

The turning point came when a new supervising officer, First Sergeant Cliff Walker, arrived in Morganton. Walker, who had suffered through a serious auto accident while on patrol, recognized the trauma that Louis was going through. He strongly suggested—even demanded—that the trooper seek professional counseling.

Louis's wife, Scottie, was urging him to do the same.

"At first I refused," he said. "When I finally gave in and went, I was able to admit to myself that I needed some help. I also realized the importance of getting it out into the open so I could learn how to deal with it."

Before the shooting, he said, the highway patrol was his first and most important love.

"I *still* love the patrol. But I've rearranged my priorities so that my family and my faith are now the most important part of my life."

He also has a zealous desire to promote safety, and often appears by request at the highway patrol's school to share his experience with troopers who attend the patrol's Officer Survival Training courses.

"Sometimes, especially at night," he tells them, "I have to literally force myself to get out of the patrol car and walk up to the driver. When I do, I can see that hand coming around, the gun pointed toward me. But you know, I still feel like I'm rendering a valuable service out there. When I investigate a wreck, or assist a stranded motorist, for instance, I'm doing something to help people. And I find that very satisfying. I just wish the public realized we're not out there to 'get' anyone. Sure, there are a few bad apples in our organization—what company doesn't have them? But the majority of us are people who have an inward desire to serve the public, and that's all we're trying to do. Yeah, I still like being a trooper. In fact, I can't think of anything else I'd rather be."

2
Cadets

"We're gonna eat with you, sleep with you, and sweat with you, twenty-four hours a day. But you're gonna have to do the work when I tell you to do it. This is *not* the YMCA. And if you don't like it here, I don't give a shit."

—Instructor to new cadets
North Carolina Highway Patrol Training School

Most troopers share Louis Rector's feeling that, no matter how dangerous or frustrating the job can be, there is no career they would rather pursue. Such collective dedication to the highway patrol bonds them to each other and contributes to the sense of brotherhood that runs like a thread throughout the organization.

"If I need help in a dangerous situation, I can call any fellow officer in that black-and-silver patrol car, whether I know him by name or not," said one trooper. "And he knows he can count on me for the same."

The bonding process begins in cadet school, when fifty or more carefully selected individuals come together and gradually merge into one strong, cohesive unit.

Enlistment procedures operate basically the same for state police agencies around the country, but North Carolina's standards are considered somewhat more stringent than most. The highway patrol in North Carolina accepts between one and two thousand applications each year from men and women who want to become state troopers. Out of those applicants, about two hundred are chosen for a ten-hour screening, led by a high-ranking officer on the patrol's administrative staff.

"First, I answer questions about the highway patrol, from what it's like chasing cars to basic requirements and benefits," said Lieutenant Billy Day, director of administrative services. "Then I tell them if they're just looking for a job, they won't make it in the highway patrol because there's something special they've got to have.

"I explain they'll be gone from home half their lives and their wives will be doing all the grocery shopping and raising the kids. I tell them they can't go to beer joints and nightclubs because people will watch and judge them by their actions. I tell them they'll have to move whenever and wherever the patrol commander wants them to go and they'll be lucky if they get stationed within a hundred miles of home.

"I tell them that law enforcement is one of the worst jobs in the world as far as the pay and the hours are concerned. Then I tell them if they don't want to meet all of our requirements, or no longer think they want to be a highway patrolman, they're free to go. We want each person to make the decision about what he really wants to do."

Those who stick around for the second phase of the screening fill out a series of forms and write a narrative explaining their reasons for joining the highway patrol. Applicants are then given a psychological test that measures their attitudes about use of force, the role of authority, race relations, and police work in general.

Steve Wollack, a California psychologist who designs attitude tests for a number of highway patrols around the nation, says he's found that, contrary to public opinion, there's no single personality "type" who goes into law enforcement as a career.

But according to Lieutenant Day, who's had fifteen years of experience in screening potential troopers, there is a "typical" highway patrol applicant. The average cadet, says Day, is a white male, twenty-two years old, and a high school graduate (though an increasing number are college-educated). He often has conservative political opinions and a prior connection to law enforcement.

The psychological test that applicants undergo is followed by a basic reading and writing exam, then a two-hour physical skills course (also designed by Wollack) that stimulates on-the-job experiences, from changing a flat tire while being timed to removing an "injured" person from a burning vehicle.

Until 1983, the North Carolina Highway Patrol had height requirements that excluded anyone under five feet six, a requirement that eliminated otherwise qualified men and women. Part of the reason for this restriction was the patrol's belief that a smaller person, particularly a female, could not physically handle the job. The other part was pure public relations: since 1929 the patrol had built its "don't-mess-with-me" reputation on the size and toughness of its men.

"When I was growing up, no one in their right mind would jump on a highway patrolman, because they knew he'd be a good-sized fella," said a trooper who bemoans the change in standards. "Now it happens all the time. Size may not have anything to do with a person's ability to do the job, but I think it does have something to do with the patrol's image."

Others disagree and say the concept of the "big, bad patrolman" was due for a change.

"It used to be that the meanest kid on the block got the job because he could physically handle any situation," said a ten-year trooper. "So here you had these big, robust men who didn't have a lot of education, but who could box your jaws in a heartbeat if you stepped out of line.

"Today, we realize that we need more education and training so we can learn how to deal with people intelligently and avoid confrontations."

In an interesting aside, police studies have shown that short and medium-height officers demonstrate a *greater* propensity for aggression than their taller counterparts, refuting the argument that tall officers make better cops. The studies went on to conclude that despite being more aggressive, smaller officers have learned to hold such tendencies within acceptable bounds so that they don't reflect negatively on themselves, their department, or the law enforcement profession.

Men and women under five feet six were not the only ones barred from the highway patrol before the sixties. In 1967, there was only one black man on the force, Charles H. Johnson. Faced with dismissal for growing an unauthorized mustache, Johnson filed state and federal class action suits against the patrol in 1975 on behalf of all blacks, contending that in his seven years on the patrol he had been limited to the rank of trooper and denied promotion "in ways which discriminated against me solely on the basis of race and color." He also stated that a mustache was "symbolic to black tradition and culture," and that the highway patrol's policy on hair should be amended because it was unconstitutional.

As a result of the lawsuit, North Carolina was placed under a five-year federal consent decree in 1980, which stipulated that the patrol must reach a goal of 50 percent black applicants and 25 percent women in each training-school session. As of 1987, the goal had not been met, and the highway patrol remained under the federal order.

After the initial screening process, all applicants are scored in three categories. The psychological test counts one-third, as do reading-comprehension and physical-skill tests. The totals are combined to form a "T" score for each applicant. Starting with the highest "T" scores, the highway patrol administration proceeds down the applicant list to fill vacancies, making sure that a percentage of women and blacks are included.

But there's still more weeding to do before the fifty to sixty individuals who finally enter cadet school are selected. At this point, about 150 applicants remain of the original 500. Each must go before a five-member review board consisting of field officers from various parts of the state.

The panel examines each file, grills the applicant with questions pertinent to the highway patrol, and judges him or her on appearance, personality, and demeanor. At the end of the two-hour session, panel members vote "pass" or "fail" in various categories, thereby determining the candidate's fate. About half of the 150 applicants do not pass this part of the screening procedure.

The remaining seventy-five are given a thorough physical exam. Since most applicants are young and relatively healthy, few are turned down for medical reasons. When it happens, it can prove devastating to the applicant.

"Some people are so determined to get on the highway patrol, they'll pay their family doctor to provide them with a 'clean exam,' " said Lieutenant Day, "only to learn the patrol has its own physician on contract."

Once an applicant passes the physical, he's placed on the waiting list for school. The entire process—from the time an application is filled out until the physical is completed—takes about three months. If no vacancies occur on the patrol, it can be two years before an applicant enters training. With the exception of retirees and involuntary dismissals, few troopers quit the patrol. Employee turnover rate averages less than 5 percent a year.

Not only is it difficult to get into the North Carolina Highway Patrol, there's a tremendous cost involved in turning each cadet into a well-trained officer. Lieutenant Day estimates that the state spends $90,000 per person, including the expense of screening each applicant, paying for five months of room and board at school, covering cadet and instructor salaries, and providing uniforms, patrol car, and equipment.

"That's why we tell cadets, 'Be sure this is what you want to do. We've got a lot of money invested in you,' " he said.

It is a warm Saturday afternoon in midautumn at the North Carolina Highway Patrol Training Center in Garner, five miles south of Raleigh. Outside the brick-red administration building, on 357 acres, are sixty-two adults, including three women, who are arriving for the first day of the Seventy-Ninth Basic Training School. Here they will spend the next five months; and here, through 288 hours of instruction, they'll learn what it takes to be a North Carolina state trooper. For some, the experience will prove too difficult to endure. For those who stay, the training will provide them with strengths and challenges they have never encountered before.

Initiation into the patrol's paramilitary rules and regulations begins immediately.

"Any of you people want to be troopers?" yells First Sergeant Braxton B. Oliver, basic school commandant. "Then fall in line!"

He is tall, blond, and lean, and wears wire-frame glasses that give him an almost boyish look. Accompanying him are four officers, a line sergeant, a first sergeant, a lieutenant, and a major.

Squinting against the harsh sunlight, the group quickly forms three lines. Dressed in civilian clothes, hair ranging from collar-length shags to crew cuts, they are a motley bunch. One youth is wearing shorts and a bright-colored sport shirt.

Sergeant Oliver approaches and glares at him, nose to nose.

"Did you ever see a trooper wear shorts?" he growls.

The cadet shakes his head.

"Then put on some pants! *Now!*"

The boy races off to change clothes.

Another cadet, twenty minutes late, comes wheeling into the parking lot, jumps out of his car, and hurries to the line of people who are standing at attention. Despite the day's warmth, the atmosphere is decidedly cool.

"Where you been, boy?" Sergeant Oliver says.

The youth mumbles an excuse and Oliver, much to the boy's relief, moves on.

Circling the group, closely eyeing each cadet, are the school's instructors, four troopers assigned to mold raw recruits into professional officers during the next twenty weeks. It is these men the cadets will come to know, fear, and respect the most.

But it is Sergeant Oliver who has their attention now. His fingers tapping the clipboard that contains the name and address of each cadet, he launches into a speech. It is one he has given numerous times before.

"Our program isn't easy," he tells the group. "What it takes to get through this school is determination. And along the way you may find that you don't really want to be a trooper. Well, that's okay. This world has got to have something in it besides troopers. Just be honest and tell me. If you slip out of here at night like a dog—and I've had that happen—you'll never get a recommendation from me for a job in any state agency. If you stay, that's great. We need you. But we want you to be the best you can be. We're not going to put you on the highway if you're not prepared. I wouldn't do that to my felllow officers."

Next comes a grueling physical assessment that includes push-ups, pull-ups, hand-strength tests, and endurance runs. During the assessment, one cadet faints from the heat and another, deciding that an hour of patrol school is enough, resigns. The remaining recruits are marched to a classroom across campus for orientation. At each desk are seven manuals and three loose-leaf notebooks, containing subjects that range from college freshman English to highway patrol policy. The cadets, seated rigidly in green plastic chairs, are not allowed to speak without permission. A few, exhausted from the physical evaluation, appear dazed, like battle-scarred soldiers who accidentally wandered into an enemy camp.

What Trooper Randy Hammonds is about to say is not meant to make them feel better. A handsome, muscular Indian in charge of physical training, he strides purposefully to the front of the room.

"We only have one race here," he says bluntly. "And that's cadet. And only one color, confederate gray.

"I'm not gonna make you do anything during your training. But I'm not gonna do anything for you, either. I didn't send those acceptance letters to you—headquarters did. The only way you're gonna earn my respect, and the respect of your peers, is through a four-letter word. It's called *work*. If you're not familiar with the term, you'll soon learn it. 'Cause we're gonna work you from five every morning till ten every night. My suggestion is that you take it one hour at a time. And you just might, by the grace of God, make it."

Trooper Tommy Cheek, whose finely chiseled features are now sternly set, goes over the list of do's and don'ts.

"I don't want to see water, hair, shaving cream, or anything else in the dormitory sinks. Keep all towels out of sight. Dry all water spots on the hardware. Don't use the soap that's on display. Clothes are to be hung with shirts buttoned, sleeves across the chest. Shoes are to be polished, with laces tied. Dresser drawers are pulled out six inches for display, with all items secured by tape so that nothing rolls around.

"And woe be unto the first one who squirrels M&Ms in the ceiling or sets his alarm for 3:00 A.M. to sneak across campus for a Coke! If one messes up, you *all* pay.

"Line sergeants will be coming on campus for in-service training and they'll be eyeballing you," he continues. "Their first questions are gonna be, 'How are they doing? Who's the sharpest? How many have you lost?'

"You are reflecting us, so you better not let us down.

"*Crosby!*" Cheek suddenly barks at a sleepy-looking cadet. "If you don't open those eyes, I'm gonna come back there and open them for you! If you think I'm standing up here just to hear myself talk, you're mistaken! And get your arm off that prop. There won't be *any* propping in here!"

"We're gonna get you like you're *supposed* to be," Sergeant Oliver cuts in, "and that means no squared-off, jitterbugged haircuts, no beards, no mustaches. Sideburns will be rectangular in shape, with hair no longer than the top of your collar. That goes for you women too.

"If you forgot something at home, that's your problem. We told you what to bring. Phones are off limits till Monday. You'll be too busy for that. We'll have daily devotions in class. If anyone is opposed to that, you can sit quietly on the steps at the back door. Sinus headaches, sore muscles, ingrown toenails, stomach cramps are *not* gonna get you out of physical training. And God help you if we think you're trying to sandbag us. You'll get a rude awakening when your butt lands on the floor. We'll assist you if you have problems. But don't try to pull any wool over our eyes."

Later that day, a cadet is caught smoking and has to run two miles while puffing on a cigarette. Another is found sitting down when he should have been cleaning his room. For punishment, the entire squadron of cadets is sent outside to perform a hundred push-ups.

By the next morning, two cadets have resigned.

"Sergeant," one says mournfully, "I woke up this morning and couldn't see no mountains. I've got to go home."

Before the week is out, others will follow. The average dropout rate is five to ten cadets during the first two weeks.

"There's a tremendous adjustment required in the beginning," explained Sergeant Oliver, whose harsh manner is artificially induced. Away from his charges, he is a pleasant, easy-going man.

"For some of these young people, cadet school is almost like culture shock. They've never been exposed to anything like it. About the second week, they become acclimated and the rules and regulations begin to make sense to them. For instance, when they undergo physical training each morning, I make them look at the instructor because when they're out on patrol and stop a car, they better not be looking at the ground. They need to focus on the person who's talking to them and stay alert to their surroundings.

"They begin to realize the importance of the physical workouts when we explain there will be people depending on them to provide help. Or that they may be on their own, with no help except their own ability to handle the problem.

"We teach punctuality because if they're assigned to a traffic block on patrol and they don't show up on time, there'll be a major problem.

"But the main thing we stress is self-discipline. Once a trooper's training is complete, there's no supervisor with him on the road, so he must be self-motivated enough to do the job alone."

Initiative and "pluck"—elusive qualities that are more inbred than learned—are what the patrol looks for in a good trooper, says Oliver.

"When you're tired and disgusted and have no more breath in you, are you the type that will get back up?" said a former instructor at the school. "Those are the kind of people we want. Because if I call you to the scene of an accident to assist me, I've got to know I can count on you to back me up."

The hours from eight to five each day at school are filled with classes, introducing students to patrol history (the organization was established in 1929 with ten members), structure (the patrol falls under the state's Crime Control and Public Safety Department), and geographic makeup (there are eight troops statewide, divided into forty-two districts throughout one hundred counties). Other courses include law enforcement philosophy, English, the "10"-signal numeric communication codes used by the patrol, laws of arrest, search and seizure, and constitutional basics.

Juvenile laws, drug enforcement, crisis management, techniques of traffic enforcement, transportation of hazardous materials, criminal investigations, use and care of firearms, pursuit driving, accident investigations, motor vehicle laws, civil disorders, self-defense techniques, courtroom practice, and a tour of the highway patrol headquarters comprise the last half of the course.

Physical training continues daily, along with periodic white-glove inspections.

About halfway through the twenty-week course, says Sergeant Oliver, group psychology takes over and the individual cadets begin to think, feel, and act as a single unit.

"When it happens, you can see it. On the morning runs, they'll all end up together, patting each other on the back, proud of what they've accomplished. They are working together as a team, so that when someone slips up, the others will step in as a group and tell him to shape up. It's peer pressure and peer support, and it's more effective than anything I can do or say."

W. F. ("Butch") Whitley, Jr., twenty-eight, has a degree in business administration. He was a purchasing manager for a distribution company when he decided to join the highway patrol.

"My father was a fire chief, so I was brought up around law enforcement," he said. "I got tired of being a paper shuffler and wanted to do something where I could help people and be my own boss. I chose the highway patrol because they were considered the 'elite' in my area and I had a lot of respect for the organization.

"I thought I had a little advantage when I first entered school, because my best friend graduated two years ago and he told me what to expect. But it was nothing like that. You try to prepare yourself, but it's something you have to experience to understand. The biggest surprise was the environment—having someone standing over you all the time. You knew they wouldn't abuse you physically, but there's a mental pressure to 'make it.' At the same time, I looked forward to seeing if I could get through, seeing what I was made of.

"At first, everyone was extremely intimidated by the instructors. Later, the intimidation didn't ease up, but the attitude on our part turned to respect as we began to see that the instructors were trying to help us—not only as people but as law enforcement officers. I have a great deal of respect for them now. They had to suffer through this the same as we did—leaving their families behind in order to be here, getting up each morning before we did, working long after we went to bed.

"In the beginning, everyone helps everyone else. The first week, someone was caught sitting on a desk top and we were all called out. We had to run laps and everybody wondered why we had to pay for one person's mistake. Then we realized that not all of us are good at everything and we'd have to learn to pull together as a team. It helped us develop a sense of camaraderie. I know that no matter where I am in the state, I can count on another trooper to come by and look out for my family or whatever needs to be done. There's a lot of pride in 'looking after our own.'

"Some weeks were boring, with all the classwork. But I enjoyed the defensive tactics. Boxing was no fun at *all*. But this is where the group really began to jell. You're standing toe-to-toe with your roommate or friend and you have to fight him, physically hurt him. It makes you closer to that person. When it was over, there were hugs and tears.

"What I disliked most was getting up at 5:00 A.M. and starting the day all over again. That's when you hear the moans and groans.

"If we had a theme through school, I guess it was to carry the same discipline we've learned onto the road. We have a responsibility to live up to certain standards so we don't tarnish the image of the patrol. I think it's that kind of integrity that makes a good trooper. Being fair to people, doing what's right. I like to think that's the kind of trooper I'll be. I get along well with people and try to be understanding. I'm not hard-nosed, but I have enough self-confidence to know I can handle myself if someone turns on me. The main thing I worry about is remembering the basic skills I've learned and not slipping up, making stupid mistakes."

Arthur ("Artie") Branch, a former fire fighter from

Lumberton, was thirty-two when he switched careers to become a state trooper.

"I was at an age when I knew I had to make a decision. My wife told me about six years ago she'd never be married to a highway patrolman, but we got divorced after that anyway, so I went ahead and joined.

"I had grown up around the patrol because my father was head of communications at Troop B in Lumberton. I was always impressed by troopers' professionalism and their sense of public service. And I thought the pay was pretty good.

"The worst part of school were the first few days—the academic work load, the physical training, and no time to do it all. I had been out of school a long while and it was a strain to keep up with the ones who had a degree or prior law enforcement experience. Like everyone else, I thought about quitting.

"School is rough, there's no doubt about it. Some cadets said if their wives had told them on weekend leave not to go back, they wouldn't have. I experienced that too. But now I feel I'm in the best physical shape I've ever been in, and I'm ready to go out on the road. I know I have a lot to learn and I'll be nervous until I get it down pat, but they've prepared us well. I'm ready for whatever happens.

"I guess what I liked best were the firearms training and the pursuit driving. Putting on the uniform for the first time felt good too. You put on your 'Smokey Bear' hat and look at yourself in the mirror and it's just a real proud feeling."

Uniforms are issued the last week of school. Each cadet receives six gray, long-sleeved shirts, three pairs of black shoes, six pairs of gray pants, a yellow raincoat, a foul-weather fur-collared jacket, an "Ike" coat (named after President Eisenhower, who made waist-length jackets popular during World War II), one summer and one winter hat, plus accessories—nameplate, tie tack, whistle chain, neckties, belt, badge, handcuffs, holster, and firearm—all at a cost to state taxpayers of more than $900 per cadet.

Troopers are allowed a yearly clothing allowance to

replace lost or damaged items, but the total must not exceed $300. Each officer is responsible for keeping his uniforms clean and sharply pressed.

Through the years, the patrol has learned that troopers who exhibit a good appearance help bolster the organization's professional image. That's why even in summer, long-sleeved uniform shirts are required. Shoes, belts, and holsters have a "clarino" finish designed to resist scuffs and keep a permanent shine. Pants are made of a wrinkle-resistant wool and polyester blend, while the campaign-style hats lend an air of authority.

Though cadets enjoy donning the uniform for the first time, it is getting the patrol car that really enthralls them.

Two days before graduation, the Seventy-Ninth Basic School cadets are scheduled to ride a bus across town and drive their patrol cars back to school. But it has snowed the night before—an almost unheard-of sixteen inches in Raleigh—and instead, they are shoveling snow and ice from the walkways outside the training center.

As a measure of how far the class has come in terms of discipline, no one complains about the delay. By late afternoon, Major Robert Barefoot, administrative director of training, and his staff decide the patrol vehicles can be brought to the school after all.

They arrive in procession, a steady stream of black-and-silver cruisers, Ford Crown Victorias marked "State Trooper," each sporting the distinctive blue-and-gold state seal on the front door panels. Behind the wheels of the forty-two cars are forty-two excited cadets, some of whom can hardly contain their enthusiasm.

"This is a good ole car. I'm tickled to death with it," says one soon-to-be rookie. "Can I sleep in it tonight, Sarge?"

Despite the inclement weather, the cadets vigorously wash and wax the vehicles, fiddle with the radios, the blue lights and sirens, and check and double-check to see that everything's in working order.

In the early days, North Carolina troopers rode motorcycles. An officer who stopped someone had to find a safe place to park, drive the arrested person to jail in the individual's car, then hitch a ride back to his machine. At wreck investigations, all he could do to help victims was locate a phone to call an ambulance, or flag down a motorist and ask him to take the injured party to the hospital.

By 1939, the patrol realized motorcycles were impractical and dangerous (several troopers were killed in motorcycle accidents while on duty) and replaced them with Ford sedans. One-way radio receivers were installed so a patrolman could receive messages from the dispatcher. But he had no way to acknowledge, nor could he communicate with other troopers.

Things improved only slightly during the next decade. "My first patrol car was a '49 Ford with 95,000 miles on it," recalls a retired trooper. "It was in pretty good mechanical shape, but the inside was raw. It had a small heater in it on the passenger side, so if you rode with another officer, you took turns getting your feet warmed. We had no blue lights so we bought these big spotlights and flashed them out the window at people we wanted to stop. There was no extra equipment available—nothing to fix a flat, just a tow chain, a shovel, and an axe. If there was anything else we needed, we had to pay for it ourselves."

Today, North Carolina patrol cars each have an electronic siren and public address system. Speakers are mounted under the blue light. Standard equipment includes shotgun and ammunition, axe, riot baton, booster cables, broom, clipboard, crowbar, dosimeter for measuring radioactivity during nuclear spills, first-aid kit, flares, fire extinguisher, gas mask, rain leggings, steel tape, tire chains, tire-tread depth indicator, shovel, wrench, and other assorted tools.

All of North Carolina's patrol cars feature high performance 351 engines with a speed capacity of 110 mph. Supporting the electrical equipment is a 100-amp alternator which runs the siren, radio, and blue light, and allows the vehicle to idle safely for up to two hours. The cars are mounted with standard radial tires and are serviced every

6,000 miles. After 70,000 miles, they are turned in and sold to other state or local agencies.

The patrol also has a fleet of unmarked cars, including Ford Mustangs and modified LTD Crown Victorias.

But the Seventy-Ninth School cadets are more than happy with their cars marked "Trooper." Each has already been assigned a permanent call number and a duty station. Within forty-eight hours, they'll shed their cadet status and be sworn in as North Carolina highway patrolmen.

It is a goal they have worked towards for five months, and an occasion that none of them will ever forget.

Friday, February 21, 1987, dawns clear and bright. It is still cold, but much of the ice and snow has melted, allowing families and friends to arrive at the school safely. Some have traveled to Raleigh from the farthest reaches of the state.

By eight-thirty that morning, people are milling around the auditorium on the training school campus, though the ceremony doesn't begin for another hour and a half. There will be standing room only, for the occasion draws not only relatives and friends of the cadets, but the commander of the highway patrol and other high-ranking officers, as well as troopers who've come to meet the rookies they are assigned to train.

"Dressing for graduation was like getting ready for a high school prom," recalled a former cadet. "There's a lot of primping and making sure the uniform and the shoes and hat are just right. Everything has to be perfect. You feel good, and there's a lot of pride involved. But you're also a little sad at leaving your friends. These are people you've lived with and shared a bond with for the past few months."

Shortly before 10:00 A.M. the cadets file in and take a seat, a solemn, polished-looking group of young rookies, far different in appearance from when they arrived on campus five months earlier.

"Your job won't be easy," says Joseph Dean, Secretary

of North Carolina Crime Control and Public Safety, addressing the forty-two graduates.

"You'll get cold, wet, tired, and frustrated. There will be drunks who'll want to fight you and people who want to give you lip. But your responsibility is to justice. Be just in the way you enforce the law. Do it fairly, to rich and poor alike, black and white, residents and nonresidents. Testify fairly in court. I've been a lawyer and the best testimony I've seen comes from highway patrolmen. Their cases are the hardest to break, their reports the most concise and factual. That's not an accident. It reflects the training you've gotten here. Do justice to it, to your fellow officers, and to the highway patrol. It is the family to which you now belong."

Other speakers follow, whereupon the cadets stand for the oath of office. By noon, the ceremony and a welcoming tea sponsored by patrol auxiliary wives are over. The cadets, now official members of the North Carolina Highway Patrol, are free to leave. All are scheduled to report for duty within a week at various stations throughout the state.

Like hundreds of graduates before them, they are eager, earnest, intent on applying the skills they learned, anxious to begin their careers as state troopers.

For some, it will be years before the fever wears off. Others will quickly come to see the highway patrol as just another job. A few will rise through the ranks to lead and teach their fellow officers. And a handful will never make it past the first few stages in a trooper's career.

But they are ready, as one cadet said, "for whatever happens on the road."

3
War Stories

> "The scary times are when you chase someone for twenty minutes and you get to their house and everybody comes out cussin' and raisin' Cain and wanting to kill you. You've walked right into a hornet's nest. There were times when I wouldn't have given a plug nickel for my life."
>
> —*A thirteen-year veteran of the patrol, now disabled from injuries sustained on the job*

It doesn't take long for rookies to learn that patrolling the highways can be hazardous to their health. Working late at night, sometimes alone in counties where help is an hour or more away, a state patrolman is an easy target for people running from the law, drunken crazies, and others who use the road to escape their problems or vent their anger. As a result, nearly every officer is confronted by danger at one time or another during his years on patrol.

Few troopers welcome a fight, even when the odds are in their favor. But fewer still back off when a physical confrontation occurs. Most are prepared to take whatever action is necessary for self-protection.

The following true experiences are told in troopers' own

words. In each incident involving violence or verbal abuse, the trooper maintains he was simply doing his job and the perpetrator was—well, you be the judge:

I was on duty in Murphy one night and a man's wife came up to the jail. He had beat her like a drum, so she took out a warrant for assault. Out there, the highway patrol was everything. We served more warrants out of our patrol car than any other law enforcement agency because the county officers had to buy their own vehicles. A lot of times, the deputies would just ride with us. It helped us, and it helped them too.

We set off to serve a warrant on this husband, just me and a deputy. When we got there, the guy wouldn't come to the door. He wanted to be belligerent about it, calling us names and saying "Come on in and get me, chickenshit!," stuff like that.

I told him to come outside and we'd talk. Then I went back to the patrol car to call for help. A few minutes later, I walked up to the kitchen window, raised up to look in, and saw him get a gun. I hollered back and told the deputy, "Larry, he's got a shotgun. He's going back through the house. Watch him! He just jacked the shell in the chamber."

The guy was roaming from room to room—hunting us, I guess. I went back to another kitchen window, chinned up, and looked in—and there he stood with the gun pointed right between my eyes, less than ten feet away.

I dropped down and headed back to the car, crawling on my belly. I figured he'd kill me for sure. When I got to the car, I radioed for the sheriff to come up and bring several officers. I told them to bring some tear gas too. Nine times out of ten, that stuff sets a house on fire—when it hits the curtains and carpets and all—but we kept shooting canisters into the house anyway. We filled the whole damn valley with tear gas, till we were just sitting there crying and gasping for breath. We even had to evacuate neighboring houses—and here it was three o'clock in the morning!

Finally, he came out the back door, vomiting. He still had his weapon, but only for a minute. He was staggering around cursing, drunk. We wallowed around for a few minutes until I fell into the creek fighting with him. It was just a nasty scene.

The guy got seven years in prison for that little trick.

I caught a bank robber one time and I wasn't even working in the area. I had transferred reports from one county to another and heard about this bank robbery and kidnapping on the scanner. They gave out a description of the vehicle—a light blue Chevrolet Chevette.

This boy had robbed the bank, come out, jumped in his car, and instead of putting it in forward, threw it in reverse and went down an embankment. Then he got stuck. Just as one of the bank tellers was about to go to work, he came up behind her, put a gun in her ear, took her hostage, and got her car. He put her out down the road, but when we picked her up, she was so shook up she couldn't even give us a description of her own vehicle. She said it was light blue, and it turned out to be black.

I met a line of cars and saw a black Chevy Chevette. Just on a hunch, I decided to turn around and follow it. I had already made the remark back at the station that I was gonna go out and catch this bank robber. The first sergeant had laughed and said, "If you do, be sure to give me a call."

After I turned around, the Chevette cut down a tobacco path and I thought, "No, it can't be him." But I went down there anyway—it was just a little narrow, dead-end road where two cars couldn't pass. I had to get off on the shoulder. He had gone on up the road and turned around. In a minute he drove right by me, threw up his hand, and waved. I threw up my hand and waved.

When he got past me, I saw the tag and knew it was him. So I wheeled around and turned the blue light on. He jumped out of the car and started to run. Then he stopped, put his hands up, and said, "I dun figured you got me. The money's on the seat."

I never even had time to call in and tell anyone where I was. After I got him handcuffed, I looked in the car and there was money all over the place. I got him back to my vehicle and thought, "Now, before I call in, I've got to calm down. If I get on the radio right now, they'll think something bad has happened." I just waited a couple of minutes until I settled down. When I called in, I didn't say anything except, "Is the first sergeant still in the office?"

They said yes and I said, "Well, tell him that bank robber he was talking about—I've got him right here."

In a few minutes I heard a siren and here comes the sergeant just as fast as he could come. I called the Jacksonville police department and told them to bring a crime lab down. They interrogated the boy and told me to take him back to the magistrate's office in Jacksonville.

This kid was only about nineteen, black, his father in the Marine Corps, a career marine. We still don't know why the boy robbed the bank.

On the way to the magistrate's office, he said, "Would you do me a favor? Before I go to jail, I want to eat one last good meal."

I said, "Okay, what have you got in mind?"

"Pull in here to McDonald's and I'll buy us all a hamburger." (We had a detective with us.)

"With your money or the bank's money?"

"My money!" he said. So we pulled into McDonald's and bought three Big Macs and Cokes, and ate them on the way to the Jacksonville jail.

Loggers and marines can be especially hard to handle. They've usually got arms on them the size of your leg. It took a while to learn about the marines. They'd come out of Camp Lejeune four or five at a time, all drunk. Most of the time they wouldn't say a word. But once in a while you'd get a mouthy one. So what you did was just grab the biggest, mouthiest one first. And when the others saw him go down they didn't say anything. Authority—that's what they understood best.

I was driving an unmarked car one night and met a gray Volkswagen with a male driver. His vehicle had no headlights, so I turned around to stop him and he took off. I chased him in my patrol car to an apartment complex, where he stopped and got out and ran.

As I jumped out of the car, I undid my seat belt, not realizing I had accidentally unsnapped my holster at the same time. I started running after the guy, but fell, and my gun slipped out onto the ground. Even then I still didn't realize what had happened.

This guy was big—six feet six, 240 pounds. As he ran into one of the apartments I tackled him. We both went through the screen door, then a wooden door, just busted them all to pieces. He started cussing me and telling me I wasn't gonna take him to jail. So it became a knock-down-drag-out fight. At one point I threw him into a wall. About that time, a woman tapped me on the shoulder and said, "What the hell are you doin' in my house?"

I said, "Get on the phone and call for some help!" And she says, "That's my man. You leave him alone!" Then *she* proceeds to tackle me. Her boyfriend, The Hulk, rises up to get me too, so I reach for my gun. But it's not there. I had my flashlight and my blackjack and I used them on both him and her. I had to literally knock the woman out to get her to leave me alone. I got the man handcuffed and arrested and was trying to get him out the door when he starts going crazy again. He was grabbing hold of the carpet and everything else he could get his hands on to keep me from moving him. Then I looked up and there stood my sergeant in the doorway.

"Damn, I'm glad to see you!" I said. Outsidc, where I'd parked, were about twenty patrol cars. Other troopers had heard me call in the chase and came to help. We went back to the car and there were about three hundred people from the neighborhood standing around watching us. Fortunately, nobody spotted my gun in the leaves, so I found it pretty quickly.

We transported both the man and the woman to jail. He had stolen the car he was driving, had no insurance, and was an escaped felon out of Charlotte. She was charged with assault, resisting arrest, and harboring a fugitive.

After it was over, I looked down and saw blood all over my uniform. I thought I'd been hurt, but it turned out to be the guy's blood. During the scuffle, I had broken his nose in three places and knocked some of his teeth out.

That's the worst fight I've ever been in and I hope it's the last one.

A trooper I know stopped a car in Greensboro with a New York license plate. The officer had been notified that this same car carried an occupant who was wanted for armed robbery and murder. The trooper got the guy out of the car and looked in the man's coat.

There was a gun in the pocket. Another one on him. One in the back seat. After he got him down to the jail the trooper asked him, "Why didn't you try to shoot me?"

And the guy said, "With the reputation of the highway patrol in North Carolina, I knew if I took a shot at you and missed, you'd get me. Or if I did shoot you, I'd never make it across the state line. So I figured I'd just take my chances."

I was down east near the South Carolina line and jumped a boy on Labor Day night. I started chasing him on U.S. 17. We ran all the way into the state line, weaving from one lane to another.

The sheriff's department had a bunch of warrants on him, plus the boy had wrecked two or three cars in the process of the chase. I was granted permission to proceed into South Carolina, then right through North Myrtle Beach on Ocean Drive. It was about 5:30 or 6:00 P.M.

I thought, "This is real good. Here I am in a North Carolina patrol car going through Myrtle Beach at 90 mph, traffic all over the place."

We got just out of North Myrtle Beach and there was a bypass. I saw two South Carolina troopers sitting there and I thought, "Something's gonna happen."

In a minute, something did. They pulled their patrol cars out in front of that boy and it was all over with.

When we got downtown, they asked the boy if he wanted to stay at the Myrtle Beach jail or go back to North Carolina with me. He said, "Back to North Carolina, *please*."

I still think most people are decent and honest. But I'm not as trusting as I once was.

That January day I was supposed to get off duty at 4:00 P.M. A city policeman was at the town square and I stopped to talk with him. Then someone called and said there was a problem across town. A boy was causing trouble. That's all they told us.

We were expecting to find a fourteen-year-old kid, but when we got there, we found a forty-year-old man with a knife in his hand.

As it turned out, I knew the guy, and thought I could talk to him. He was an intelligent person who had suffered a nervous breakdown, lost his job, and was having a lot of problems. In all the years I'd known him, he had never hurt anyone.

I walked up behind him as he was beating on the police officer's window—with the officer still in the car. As I approached, he heard me and wheeled around. I backed up, trying to calm him down, but he lunged at me, slashing back and forth with the knife. He didn't seem to recognize me.

"Come on, you son of a bitch," he said, "I'm gonna kill you!"

I drew my gun and started to shoot, but there were so many people around I was afraid a .357 bullet would go through him and strike somebody else. So I put the gun back in my holster.

I had forgotten to pick up my flashlight or nightstick and had no other weapon on hand. The police officer jumped out of his car and I called to him, "Hurry! Hand me something!"

The officer grabbed a broom from the trunk of his car and threw it to me. It wasn't much, but it was better than nothing.

The man lunged at me again and I struck him with the broom. I thought he had missed me, but he hit my arm.

I seized him, put him on the ground, and started to cuff him. But I had no strength in my arm. I looked down and saw blood squirting from my jacket. Someone helped me get the cuffs on him and arrest him.

By the time I got to the hospital, I had lost two pints of blood. As a result of the incident, I was out of work two months. Today, I still have trouble with my arm. The guy who cut me is in a mental institution.

I thought I knew him and could predict what he would do. But I didn't. It changed my attitude towards people. Now, if something similar were to happen, I wouldn't hesitate to shoot.

It was about 2:00 A.M. on a Saturday in Lincoln County. I saw a tractor trailer come out of a little side road and wondered, "What is a tractor trailer doing here?" When you "trooper" in a small county, you get to know everybody's husband, wife, kids, and dogs. I knew nobody who lived there was a trucker, so I got the tag number and had the communications center check it for me.

The truck came back from a different location than the trailer and that made me more curious. An ABC (Alcoholic Beverage Control Commission) officer happened to be around and he said, "I don't know about the tractor but that trailer belongs to some liquor boys. Do you want to go with me and we'll look around? We may find a still."

I checked off, changed clothes, and rode with him to a place where we parked and just sat, waiting. At daylight we heard a noise. We got out, looked around, and located this outbuilding in the middle of a pine thicket. It was made out of tin put on two-by-fours and nailed up, supposed to be disguised as a hay barn. We went inside, moved some of the hay around, and found a trapdoor. It was a false floor, with a tunnel inside and an underground still. They had the mash running out through vents to a small creek. No one was around. So we just left everything as it was.

The next afternoon Frank called me and said, "You want to go back with us tonight? We've got some federal and state boys coming too."

About 1:00 A.M. we walked in there and surrounded the place. They had backed the truck in and were loading gallon milk jugs filled with moonshine. We arrested six people. When we came in, one of them said, "Got us. How'd ya know where we were?" That's all the resistance we encountered. You don't generally get any trouble out of those people. All they wanna do is make a few bucks.

I stopped a pickup truck one time after a guy tried to drive across a six-lane highway. I chased him a pretty good ways, then he cut off into the woods. We both jumped out of our cars and I ran after him until I reached the end of a thirty-two-foot tunnel, where I fell and lost him. I had to go to the hospital for treatment, but after I was released I went back to look for him. Never did find him.

The next morning, I got a call saying someone had found him in the woods. The man had run himself to death, just fell over dead. The NAACP investigated it because they claimed I had killed him, beat him to a pulp. But they did an autopsy at the hospital and couldn't find the cause of death.

I still don't know what really happened to him.

There's no telling how many times you walk up to a car and somebody's sitting there thinking about shooting you. And maybe another person in the car has talked him out of it. It just makes you realize how often you play Russian roulette with the Grim Reaper.

Some crazy had stolen an armored truck from Fort Benning, Georgia, containing a bunch of Claymore mines. I don't know that much about Claymore mines, but people have told me they can wipe out half a football field.

I was positioned at a roadblock where this guy was supposed to come through. So I'm standing there thinking, "This is gonna be great. Here I am waiting to get blown away and there's nothing I can do about it." That's the worst kind of situation for me because I have no control over it.

The scariest type of situation for me is a car chase. Not so much for myself, but I'm afraid I'll hurt somebody else. You're speeding around curves on the wrong side of the road and you can just see somebody's family coming. You're in a bind because if you don't stop that person, he might go down the road and kill someone. If you continue chasing, you could hurt an innocent bystander. So it's real touchy when to cut it off.

It was pouring down rain that day when I got called to investigate a simple wreck. This boy, a construction worker in a truck with an out-of-state license, had rear-ended a lady. So I went ahead and filled out the wreck report in order to get her on her way.

I had the boy sitting in the back seat. He said he knew the wreck was his fault, and that he didn't have his driver's license with him. Said he had an Ohio license. I was about to write him a ticket for rear-ending this lady and picked up the radio to check his license when he said, "What are you gonna do?"

"I'm gonna call in and see if you've got a valid license."

"There's something you need to know before you do that."

I thought maybe he had a suspended license or something. But he said, "I'm wanted in Ohio for armed robbery."

Then he said, "Well, I thought I'd go ahead and tell you before you found out. I've been down here six or seven months and I'm tired of running. I'm homesick. I wanna go back."

So I called and sure enough, they confirmed he was a felon. He got to go back to Ohio all right—back to jail.

Years ago, before we had overtime, you could stay out all night and watch the sun come up if you wanted to. Then everybody would meet somewhere, work as a team to make a lot of arrests, or just talk and have a good time. One night we were standing around in this parking lot. Our patrol cars were backed in so that we were blocking each other. Then a car sped by at about 100 mph. Tommy—the only one who could get to his patrol car—took off running, jumped into his car, and reached for the steering wheel. Except he was in the back seat.

We just died laughing. Not only because Tommy had made a fool of himself, but because we knew the driver was so far away by now none of us would ever catch him.

We were told it was a felony stop—a couple from Seattle wanted on child abuse charges—but didn't know if the people had guns or anything. Me and another trooper stopped the vehicle, got the couple out, handcuffed them, then went up to the car. When we got there, we saw two little kids in the back seat. One of them had second-degree burns all over his body and cigarette-lighter burns on his arms. The other kid had bald places on his head where the hair had been jerked out.

We stood there choking back tears. I don't know what's going to happen to the children, but I'm gonna make damn sure that couple goes to prison.

It worries me when all these guys get into fights. I learned early on that you can talk a man to jail quicker than you can whip him to jail—and it's a whole lot easier.

I had a guy buck up on me one night in a place with a bad name. He said, "You don't know where you're at, do you? You're in Whittemore Branch."

And I said, "Well, that's in North Carolina, isn't it?"

"Yeah."

"Then you're under arrest for drunk driving."

"Son," he said, "I never went to jail without a fight and I ain't going tonight."

"You look like an awfully nice guy to me," I told him. "Too bad you're gonna have to go to the hospital."

"What are you talking about?"

"I'm gonna put you in the hospital—fractured skull, broken collarbone, the whole nine yards. You're gonna be laid up for at least a week, 'cause I'm gonna hurt you bad. And you're just too nice a fella for me to have to do that to."

He thought about it for a minute and finally he said, "Can I make a phone call before we go?"

So you *can* talk them down. In fact, some of my best friends [now] are people I've arrested in the past.

I worry about making mistakes. What if I kill someone through an error? I also have a recurring nightmare—I'm in a shooting situation, I draw my gun, I'm squeezing the trigger, and it won't move. I remember having a toy gun when I was a kid and I'd squeeze it and it wouldn't work. Maybe that's where the dream comes from.

My line sergeant and I were investigating an accident near the Tennessee border at Wolf Creek, and we were waiting on the wrecker to come, sitting there with the blue light going, shooting the breeze.

All of a sudden we heard a shot—then another—that seemed to be directed right at us. I said, "Hell, sergeant, somebody's trying to shoot us!"

So we bailed out, hunkered down behind the car, and called for assistance. I grabbed my .357 Magnum, opened the trunk, and pulled out a shotgun too. About five minutes later, a woman came by, driving very slowly. She had a young boy with her and when she got out of the car she was very excited. Said she lived on the hill across the road and that she was the one who'd been shooting at us.

When we asked her why, she said her husband—who was a known drug dealer—had been killed in her front yard recently and she didn't want anyone coming around. She'd been drinking, so I'm not sure if she was playing with a full deck or what.

We charged her with driving while impaired, but never brought charges against her for the shooting because none of the bullets struck the car. Plus she refused to make a statement saying she had been using a gun.

Later on, as I thought about it, I realized we could have been killed over something that didn't even make any sense.

After one of our troopers was shot, we were looking for the two guys who did it. There were so many law enforcement officers around—everyone armed to the teeth—that it's a wonder somebody wasn't shot accidentally.

We were told the two fugitives had spent the night in a deserted barn, so our job was to go in and search the area.

I remember crawling up into a hayloft. The first two steps were broken off, so to keep my balance, I'd hand my shotgun to the person below me, take a step, then take my gun back. When I got to the top, I had to stick my head up into the hayloft, shine the flashlight, and look around to see if anyone was there.

The place was empty. But I'll never forget that sitting-duck feeling. I guess that's the most afraid I've ever been.

A trooper in Cleveland County stopped a motorist one night and was attempting to place him under arrest for drunk driving when one of the guy's friends drove up. He didn't like the idea that his buddy was about to go to jail so he walked up and stabbed the trooper in the back with a four-inch blade. I was called to assist and was the first one to arrive on the scene.

When I got there, I checked the trooper out and determined he was in no imminent danger. I was trying to get the guy in custody, when his father arrived and tried to stop us from arresting either of the two boys.

We scuffled around for a while and the guy with the knife started lunging at me. I took my pistol out, cocked it, and told him if he tried it again, I was gonna kill him. About that time, all three of them ran into a store and we had to go in and get one at a time. More troopers had arrived to help us.

We charged one guy with assault with a deadly weapon with intent to kill. The father was charged with assault and interfering with an arrest. The driver was charged with drunk driving and interfering. It could have been a simple arrest, over and done with in a few minutes. But the others had to turn it into a free-for-all. That's when I begin to think people are their own worst enemies.

One of the most dangerous drunks I ever had was a big rascal who wanted to fight all the way to jail. I wrestled with him, struggled with him, and finally had to pull my blackjack out and beat him down. Every time I'd hit him, he'd shake his head and say, "I'm gonna kill you, you son of a bitch!"

I hit him so hard the blackjack fell apart in my hand, but he was still shaking his head and coming after me. So I'm wondering, "What have I got here?" Finally, I got him down enough to put the handcuffs on him.

About that time, I spotted what he was after. He had a sawed-off shotgun laying in the seat and he was trying to get to it.

I guess I would have been within my rights if I'd shot him. But I just couldn't do it.

I ran a man into his driveway one time and he got out and pulled a gun on me. I talked him out of it. The judge gave me the shotgun and gave the guy six months in jail.

In Thomasville, a man had robbed an oil company just as I was driving by. I saw a city policeman and a State Bureau of Investigation [SBI] agent standing out front with guns drawn. They motioned me to pull over and bring my shotgun. When I got there I said, "What's going on?"

"This place is being hit and we're gonna be ready for them when they come out," said one of the officers. Just then, a man comes out the door with one hand down and one hand holding a bag. I was standing on the far left, the SBI agent and the city cop beside me.

Without saying a word, the man's hand came up with a gun and he shot at us. The city cop was hit in the foot. I took aim and was ready to fire when this same police officer dived forward, knocking me off balance and nearly causing me to accidentally shoot him in the head.

The robber took off running. Other officers had arrived by then and were shooting at him. Three .45 slugs struck him in the shoulder but he kept going, still firing at us. I saw which way he went and ran around the other side of the building.

I was getting ready to blow him away when he saw me and threw down his gun. Another officer yelled at him to put his hands up.

"I can't, I can't," he said, "I've been shot!"

"Well, you better *can,*" said the officer. And he did—put his arms in the air with three bullets in his shoulder.

While this thing was going on, it didn't seem so bad. But later, as we began talking about it, every one of us got shaky.

Most people sense if you have the right presence about you. Your voice will be authoritative, you'll have a certain look in your eyes, and the way you stand will denote authority.

But let's face it. Troopers are human beings too. None of us want to get our ass beat.

The bottom line is whether you, the violator, think you can "take" me and get away with it. If you see an authority presence in an officer, you know he's not a good "take."

That's why we've been taught to appear professional, serious, and like we can handle ourselves at all times. It's a way to avoid a lot of confrontations.

That night, it was quiet in the communications center. I was working as a telecommunicator and Peter Peterson was on duty at the McDowell County line on Highway 221, talking to another trooper. Pete was known as a "Super Trooper," the kind of officer who went strictly by the book. No one thought anything bad could happen to him because he always knew exactly what to do.

At 6:08 P.M. he called me.

"Cecil," he said. "Have you heard any radio traffic from Rutherford County?"

I told him I hadn't heard a thing.

"Have you heard anything about anyone getting shot down there? We keep picking up things on our scanners but we can't figure out what it is."

"Nope," I said. "Don't have anything on it. But I'll check it out with the Rutherford County sheriff's department."

A few minutes later, Peterson called back.

"Cece," he said, "Something is going on down there. I think I'll ease on down 221 South and see what's happening."

I sent a total of five messages on the computer to the sheriff's department. But I never got an answer. Now the other troopers were starting to hear things on their radios about a white '68 Ford.

I told the other telecommunicator, "There's definitely something going on because now I'm hearing things about two officers getting killed. And here we sit knowing nothing. To hell with this!"

I contacted the Rutherford County sheriff's department again and got a deputy on the line. "This is the highway patrol in Asheville," I said. "I've sent you five computer messages. Can you tell me what's going on?"

"We've had two deputies shot and killed."

He then described a white '68 Ford and said it was last seen on Highway 221 heading north. The driver was wanted in connection with the shootings.

Later, I learned they had a dispatcher on the radio when the killings took place, but she had fainted. The deputy found her passed out on the floor and had to take over the radio without knowing how to work it. That's why he hadn't answered my messages.

I radioed all the troopers in the area and said, "Look, they're after a 1968 white Ford. Hutchins is the guy's name. He shot and killed two deputies tonight after they were called to his house over a domestic squabble."

About three minutes later, Peterson, who was traveling south on Highway 221, came back on the radio.

"Cecil," he said, "I've spotted him. I'm going after him."

I turned to the telecommunicator beside me.

"Now it's on," I said.

There were all kinds of dirt roads and turnoffs in the area so the chase continued for quite a while. In the meantime, other patrol cars were listening to the radio transmissions. Even the troopers on the South Carolina line were heading up this way to see if they could help.

Peterson came on the radio again.

"Cece! I've got him!"

Those were his last words. He had spun around a

curve and stopped in the road. Hutchins was standing there with a shotgun, and fired. Peterson never had a chance.

I didn't realize then what had happened so I radioed the other troopers.

"G-239 just told me he got Hutchins, but I can't get him back on the radio."

Trooper Spears arrived on the scene first. Hutchins was gone, but he found Peterson slumped over in the patrol car.

Spears came on the radio and said, "Cece, I think he's dea . . ."

He was trying to say "dead," but his voice kept breaking.

I knew then we had a serious problem.

We began to mobilize. It was suppertime and lots of off-duty troopers had their scanners going. They had heard the transmission and were already checking on.

Meanwhile, Hutchins had gone down the road after shooting Peterson, parked his car, and run into the woods, where he stayed all night.

Troopers from everywhere were calling in, asking, "Do you need some help? Can we come?"

The officers surrounded Hutchins, but for hours it was a standoff. Even the radios were quiet. About 5:00 A.M., two shots rang out.

The troopers returned Hutchins's fire but missed him.

At nine-thirty that morning he gave himself up. It was just as well. He had more than 400 law enforcement officers around him—and a lot of them were Peterson's friends.

[James W. Hutchins was executed on March 14, 1984, for the 1979 slaying of two deputies and highway patrolman R. L. ("Pete") Peterson in Rutherford County, North Carolina. Hutchins was the first person to die by lethal injection in North

Carolina after the state's death penalty was reinstated in 1977.]

I don't like fights. I've been in law enforcement eight years and have been in only three or four physical skirmishes. I don't hit a man unless it's a last resort.

But—and here's what they don't teach you in school—you stop a car and a man *this* wide in the shoulders says he's not gonna be arrested.

Do you take him right then or let him make the first move? When do you react? When do you take control of the situation?

It's something you've got to learn on the job. And if you don't act quickly enough, you stand a chance of getting hurt.

The court wants you to wait until he resists. But if you do, especially with someone that size, how do you regain control? You can't shoot him. So you've got to physically grab him and tell him he's under arrest. By that time, it's too late to go back to your radio for help.

That's why I try to talk people into coming with me peacefully. I also try to stay in shape—lift weights, run regularly—for the confrontations that may not end well.

I was stationed in Lincoln County, had been on my own about two or three months, and was still green as I could be. There was a place I often patrolled called "Hog Hill," all dirt roads, miles from nowhere, one of the roughest sections I've ever been in.

We'd go up there, two or three troopers together, and arrest drunk drivers by the carload. One Saturday night I was working by myself and had just gotten to Hog Hill when I hit a bump in the road. I looked down and realized the lights were off on my radio. It was no longer working.

I thought, "Damn. I just got up here and I hate to

leave. But a man's a fool to be in Hog Hill without a radio."

I was debating whether to stay or go when I came around a curve and got behind this old beat-up car.

"There's a drunk for sure," I thought. "I'll arrest him and get the hell out of here."

I turned on the blue light, pulled the guy over, and asked him to step out of the car. He was the biggest man I'd ever seen. I'm a big fella myself—six feet four, 225 pounds—but this guy was at least six feet eight and must have weighed more than 300. He was *huge*.

When I saw him, I said to myself, "Mac, if he wants to fight you, he's gonna kill you, there's no doubt about it. And you don't even have a radio to call for help."

"Let me see your driver's license," I said. He showed it to me and I noted his name.

"Mr. Smith, you've been drinking some, haven't you?"

"I've had right at a fifth of liquor," he replied. "But I'm a big man and it takes a lot to get me drunk."

Then he asked me who I was. I told him. I also told him he was under arrest.

"Trooper," he said, "I don't want to go to jail."

My heart rate suddenly doubled. And there's no telling where my blood pressure went. I knew if I backed down I might as well hunt a new career because technically, I had already arrested him. On the other hand, I thought what a dumb attitude that was—because this man was gonna beat me to death.

"Well, Mr. Smith," I said, "it's like this. I'm sure you don't want to go to jail. But I have arrested you and I'm gonna try to take you. If you manage to get away from me, you'll have to hurt me to do it. And if that happens, there'll be about ten of my buddies who will come and get you. So why don't you come along peacefully?"

He hung his head and shuffled those two big feet.

"Officer, you misunderstood me. I wouldn't give you no trouble at all. I was just asking you not to take me."

As he got in the patrol car, he was as meek and mild as he could be.

That's the most terrified I've ever been and I was in absolutely no jeopardy at all.

I've been so scared that I couldn't write a ticket because my hands were shaking so bad. Or I couldn't remember my call number.

But after a while, you learn to accept the fear and the possibility that you might get hurt or killed while doing your job. It's just something a trooper learns to live with. Otherwise, you lose your nerve and can't go on with everything else you have to do.

4
Working the Wrecks

"Mister, would you get this bus off of me?"

—A young boy's plea to a trooper after a bus crushed the car his mother was driving

Among the most heart-rending duties a trooper must contend with on duty is investigating wrecks.

Nationwide, it's been estimated that every twenty-three minutes, someone loses his life on a U.S. highway. In fact, motor vehicle accidents are the single greatest cause of death among Americans aged five through thirty-four. About 150,000 automobile accidents are reported in North Carolina each year. Most are minor in nature but, sooner or later, every trooper investigates his share of serious wrecks.

Major car crashes bring with them traumatic scenes—bodies broken, dismembered, or crushed. A relative, spouse, or friend gone forever. Lives permanently changed in a single, sudden moment. Auto accidents involving children are the worst, touching even the most hardened troopers. Some officers—recalling wrecks they investigated years ago—still cannot recount the details without displaying emotions. Others refuse to discuss those accidents that affected them most deeply.

"I remember every single fatality just as though it happened yesterday," said one patrolman. "It's the kind of thing that stays with you."

Yet when a trooper arrives at the scene of an accident, he must put aside his feelings and assume the role of authority figure.

"You have to be the one to take charge, the one who knows what to do," explained a training officer. "I tell my cadets, if you don't know what you're doing, *act* like you do. Take an authoritative stance and look serious. People will think you're sizing up the situation, even if on the inside, you're saying, 'Oh shit, look at this mess. Where do I start? What do I do?' "

Another trooper, with eight years' experience on the patrol, says he's worked out a system to convince a watchful public he has control of the situation at hand.

"There may be dead bodies all over the place, but I'll get out my notebook and start scribbling," he said, "or I'll pull out the tape I use to measure skid marks—anything to stall for time until I figure out exactly what to do."

Once a call comes into the highway patrol's telecommunications center that an accident has occurred, a trooper in that assigned area is notified by radio and sent to the location. He generally has few details about the wreck and may be receiving second- or third-hand information, relayed by another law enforcement agency before it reaches the highway patrol office.

"I've had a telecommunicator tell me that a car was on fire and I've raced to the scene only to discover it was an overheated radiator," said a trooper. "Other times you're told when there is property damage involved or a personal injury. But you still don't know what to expect until you get there."

When he arrives at the accident, the officer's first responsibility is to check for injured. All troopers are trained in first aid, and a growing number of officers are certified emergency medical technicians. In most cases, ambulance personnel arrive before the trooper, freeing him to begin investigation of the mishap.

Basically, his job is to determine what happened. Who was driving? How fast? Any witnesses? Were the car's occupants wearing a seat belt? Had anyone been drinking? Have any laws been violated? Who's at fault?

Physical evidence must also be collected in order to support any charges filed. Skid marks are measured, auto damage recorded, and signs of alcohol or drugs noted. The trooper draws a rough diagram of the accident, gets a statement from the driver (or drivers) involved, and puts this information, along with other details, on an accident form which he fills out by hand at the scene. A copy of the report must be mailed to the Division of Motor Vehicles in Raleigh within twenty-four hours. The trooper retains a copy of the report, and a third copy is sent to the highway patrol district office. If an arrest is made or a citation issued, the officer must include that fact on his report as well. An additional report is filled out if the accident is caused by a fallen sign or damaged roadway, and the Department of Transportation is notified. The trooper also has to get traffic flowing freely again around the accident scene. Poor weather conditions can make this part of the job miserable.

"I remember directing traffic one night on the interstate after a bad wreck," said a western North Carolina trooper. "It was snowing and sleeting and the windchill factor had the temperatures down to about thirty below. I couldn't stand in one spot too long because my feet would literally freeze to the pavement. My face was uncovered and I got so cold that my eyelashes froze and I couldn't blink. I finally had to go sit in the patrol car and get warmed up so I could continue working."

Sometimes figuring out exactly what caused an accident is difficult and frustrating.

"I was called to an accident scene in Haywood County on Interstate 40," said another trooper, "and when I got there the car was sitting in the eastbound lane smashed to pieces. There were three girls in the vehicle, all badly injured. They had been on their way to college at Western Carolina University. One was pinned under the dashboard and later died. I went to the hospital and interviewed the two who survived, but neither could remember what happened.

"One of the girls said she thought she recalled seeing the back of a tractor trailer just before the crash. But there were no skid marks, no witnesses, and very little physical evidence at the scene. Whoever the girls hit, didn't stop.

"It bothered me a lot because, as investigating officer, it was my responsibility to explain what happened, and I couldn't. I even put an article in the paper asking for information. I also contacted tractor-trailer firms to find out if any of their carriers had reported a recent accident. But I came up with nothing.

"To this day, I don't know what happened. It was the strangest wreck I ever investigated."

When all else fails, veteran troopers say they use the SWAG method to determine what happened at an accident—"Scientific Wild-Assed Guess."

Accidents involving alcohol occur in about 50 percent of all fatalities reported. As a result, many officers develop a low tolerance for drunk drivers, having seen firsthand the destruction an intoxicated driver can inflict on himself and others.

"I don't get personally angry at drunk drivers," explained a trooper with twelve years experience, "but I don't take any crap from them either. What pisses me off is when they say, 'Man, you're taking my license away and I'm gonna lose my job, etc.' The way I see it, I'm not doing a damn thing except trying to protect the public. Whatever damage is done to the drunk driver is damage he brought on himself."

After investigating numerous accidents where innocent people were killed as a result of a drunk driver, this same trooper says he has given up social drinking and will arrest anyone—from a relative to a fellow law enforcement officer—for a drunk-driving offense. That kind of attitude helps explain why North Carolina ranks among the top three states in the country for number of drunk driving arrests.

State law dictates that an individual with a blood alcohol level of 0.10 or above is considered intoxicated. Punishments for convictions of DWI (Driving While Impaired) are harsh by national standards, including fines of up to $2,000 and two years in jail. Get arrested for drunk driving in North Carolina and your driver's license is automatically suspended for ten days, at which time the court determines your fate. Anyone who refuses to take a DWI test can have his or her license revoked for a year.

Yet drunk drivers continue to drive, making up the largest percentage of violators arrested by North Carolina state troopers. On any given weekend, it's not unusual for a highway patrolman to spend the majority of his shift in the breathalyzer room at the local courthouse, administering breathalyzer tests to DWI violators he has arrested.

The number of drunk driving arrests varies greatly from trooper to trooper. Officers who are "high arrest" men average anywhere from twenty to thirty drunk drivers a month, depending on the area in which they are working and other factors such as weather conditions, what shift they're on, and the number of special assignments they pull that take them away from the road.

One of the toughest assignments any trooper encounters on patrol is breaking the news to family members that a loved one has been killed or injured in an auto accident.

"I try to get relatives to come to the hospital without telling them anything specific," said one officer. "Of course, the first thing they want to know is the condition of the victim. I tell them what I can, but I'm not qualified to pronounce people dead, even if I'm sure that's the case. My duty is to notify the family and then be there to answer questions and provide support."

In certain cases, notifying relatives can prove especially painful, as it did for this trooper:

> It was about one o'clock on a Sunday morning. The driver had gone down a rural road at about ninety miles per hour, run off the shoulder and hit two trees. The car exploded and caught fire with the driver pinned inside. He was burned beyond recognition.
>
> When I pulled up to the scene, the fire truck was already trying to extinguish the flames. I attempted to get the information I needed by talking with different people and getting the tag number off the car, but even it [the tag] was burned pretty bad. In fact, you could hardly tell what kind of car it was. The wheels looked like they had come from a Dodge, Chrysler, or Plymouth. The metal was still so hot we couldn't touch it, and we knew the boy inside was dead.
>
> I was getting skid measurements to fill out my report when one of the firemen came up to me and said, "Can I talk to you for a minute?" I told him I was kinda busy, but if he'd wait I'd be glad to talk to him shortly.
>
> "I really need to talk you now, in private," he insisted.
>
> "All right. Come on back to the patrol car."
>
> I picked up the radio and told the wrecker where to come to the scene, reported what I had to the dispatcher, and turned to the fireman sitting next to me.
>
> "Would you do me a favor?" he asked. "Would you run me up to my house? It's only about a mile from here."
>
> "Well, I'm kinda busy right now," I repeated. "I can take you in a few minutes if you can wait."
>
> "I really need to get there right now," he said. "You see, when the fire alarm went off, I jumped up, put on my clothes, and raced to get here. I didn't look

to see if my son was home. He's twenty years old and I didn't check on him."

Then he pointed to the burned vehicle.

"What kind of car is that?" he said.

"I don't know. It's hard to tell. It looks like a Chrysler."

"Those wheels sort of look like the ones he had on his car."

So I backed up, left the scene, and drove towards the man's house. All the way there, I kept trying to reassure him that his son was probably home safe and sound. But when we pulled into the driveway and looked around, the boy's car wasn't there. At that point, the father began to cry.

"Just try to relax," I said, "and we'll go back to the scene. Are there any identifying things about your son—a ring, for instance, or a particular kind of wallet he carried?"

"Yeah, my boy had on a high school class ring and wore a belt buckle with his initials that one of his uncles had given him."

By the time we arrived at the scene, the wrecked car had cooled down. Not knowing any other way to get the information I needed, I crawled into the front seat. There was nothing left of the boy except bones, scraps of cloth—and a class ring that I found on the floor. The belt buckle, with the boy's initials on it, had fallen off, but I found it on the floorboard and wrapped it in a handkerchief. Then I went back to the patrol car.

The fireman was waiting for an answer. I knew I had to tell him the truth. There's no way to sugarcoat that kind of thing, so I just handed him the belt buckle and said, "It's him."

Then he asked me if I'd go back to the house and help him break the news to his wife and younger son. I remember going into the home and the man waking up his family. It was three-thirty in the morning and they were startled, of course. State troopers don't normally appear at your house in the middle of the night under happy conditions.

I tried to tell them, as gently as I could, what happened. The mother refused to believe it at first, and the little boy went all to pieces. Apparently, he was very close to his brother.

I got choked up telling them about it because I could feel for them, what they were going through. When I had crawled into that car I had wanted so much for it *not* to be their son.

I stayed with the family till daybreak, just sitting there talking with them. The mother grew calm after she began to accept the fact her son was dead. The next afternoon, when I checked on duty, I returned to the house to offer my sympathy and find out if I could help them make funeral arrangements.

That wasn't my first or my last fatality, but it was my most memorable.

How do I cope with bad accidents? When it's over, I just want peace and quiet. I don't want to talk to anybody about anything. I'll read, go back through some of my scrapbooks, or sit and think. Later on, I'll talk about it with someone I know. But there's no certain way to deal with the pain. You do what you have to do and go on to the next one.

Teenagers who drink and drive bother me the most. I've got kids of my own and every time I investigate a wreck involving teens, it reminds me of my own children and what can happen to them.

I once investigated a wreck where two cheerleaders —daughters of a doctor and a lawyer—turned their car over and were thrown fifteen feet from the vehicle. One of the girls had been hanging out the window and was decapitated. I found her head in the middle of the road. It reminded me of a mannequin wearing a wig, with every hair in place.

There was a question about both girls drinking

because they had just come from a party—a party given by one of their parents. Here was a young girl with a promising future, whose life ended tragically because of drinking and driving. It was also the twenty-third of December, and I thought of all the unwrapped gifts she'd never see and what her family must be going through. That upset me. They buried her the day after Christmas.

People told me that Indians don't cry; they keep their sorrows to themselves. But when it comes to losing our children, we're all the same. I remember investigating a wreck on the Cherokee Indian Reservation in which four boys had hit a tree at more than a hundred miles per hour. They were killed instantly.

I went to the funeral and one of the mothers came up and asked me what happened. As I began telling her, she didn't say a word, but big tears rolled down her cheeks. It made me realize that underneath, we're more alike than we are different. We just have so many damn hang-ups, we can't always see it.

I was in court one day and got called out to investigate a wreck at a nearby intersection. Three women in a pickup had hit a logging truck head-on. All of the women were killed. It took two or three hours to extract them from the truck. We were about to tow the pickup truck away when we heard a strange noise.

One of the guys said, "That sounded like a cat."

I said, "Hiram, there can't possibly be a cat in that truck. It was smashed flat."

But we cut the top off the truck and looked under the seat anyway. There lay a baby, about nine months old, crying but unhurt. Somehow, it had landed in the cavity under the seat and wasn't harmed, just scared. That entire incident still seems incredible to me.

What bothers me most about working wrecks is to see a little kid hurt. If there's anything left in the world that's innocent, it's a child. I've stood at the scene of an automobile accident involving kids and cried. Then I went home and couldn't sleep. Seeing a dead or injured child is something I'll never get used to, though I know it's part of the job.

There were two kids riding in the back of the truck. The father, who had been drinking, was driving. The truck hit a bank, overturned, and threw both the children out. One child, a ten-year-old girl, was pinned between the rear wheel and the fender and was lying in the dirt when I got there.

She was still alive but the truck was on top of her chest, wedged between two trees, and there was no easy way to get her out. We hooked cables to a wrecker and tried to move the truck, but that only made the pressure on the little girl worse. She began to cry and said she couldn't breathe.

The medics had arrived by then and gave her oxygen but the truck was still across her chest. I was getting desperate, trying to think of the best way to help her. I even climbed a tree to attach a cable so we could haul the truck straight up, but that didn't work either. We couldn't cut her out from under it because it was too dangerous to use a blowtorch around the gas line. I didn't know *what* to do next. I thought she was dying. It was the most helpless feeling I've ever experienced.

As a last resort, we decided to dig her out. I took off my gun and blackjack, got down on my knees, and began digging in the dirt with my hands. Everyone pitched in. We just kept going until we were finally able to pull her to safety.

Amazingly, after we got her to the hospital we found she wasn't too seriously injured. The dirt beneath the truck was soft enough to create a slight crevice and that small space is what saved her life.

It was cold that morning, with fog so thick you could barely see past the hood of your car.

I got called to a wreck on a rural paved road about eight-thirty that morning near Interstate 40. When I reached the bridge that spans the interstate, it was lined with people. Ahead, I could see the top of a Trailways bus. The remainder of it was covered in fog.

I walked down the bridge abutment and saw a man lying on the shoulder of the road. He had a broken arm and cuts on his head. Other people from the bus were nearby, many of them complaining of injuries.

When I went around the bus I discovered it had landed on top of a car. Under the front wheel was a nine-year-old boy. As I went past, he looked up, grabbed me by the arm, and said, "Mister, would you get this bus off of me? I can't breathe."

His mother was in the front seat, impaled by the gear shift. There was a small child on top of her. Both were dead.

In the fog, the mother's car had rammed a tractor trailer and bounced backwards, causing the bus to run over top of her.

I talked to the little boy and told him I would do what I could. But I wasn't sure what to do. The wreck had caused a seven-car pileup and the interstate was completely blocked.

I walked to the other side of the bus and stood there thinking. I am not a long-distance runner, but suddenly it came to me that I should run down the highway. I didn't know what I was looking for, but I was sure it would come to me soon.

About a mile from where I left the bus, I saw a wrecker. The driver spotted me as I came toward him and he climbed out of his truck to unload the vehicle he was towing. Together, we got the wrecker through the traffic and back to the scene of the accident.

It took two and a half hours, but we finally got the

bus lifted off the little boy. After we moved him, we found his seven-year-old brother beneath him on the back seat, dead.

The nine-year-old boy was the only survivor in the car. Later, I found out that his father was alcoholic, and so he really had no family left at all.

That was one accident that will stay with me for the rest of my life.

The public astounds me with their desire to see blood and bodies. I worked a bad wreck one time, and within fifteen minutes after I arrived, there were two hundred people milling around. The rescue squad couldn't get through for the crowd.

I got so pissed off that I tried to set up a barricade with a rope. But people kept coming through. I couldn't even *push* them back.

Finally I yelled "You S.O.B.'s get out of the way!"

It made me furious because I believe that at a time like that, everyone should show a little respect.

You never forget your first fatality. That night, I had turned onto the Blue Ridge Parkway and met a brown Mercury coming off a ramp. The driver was an elderly man and the passenger was his wife. As I went across a bridge, I heard the sound of air horns blowing on a tractor-trailer rig. I turned around and was heading [back] in the direction I came [from] when I saw the back end of the tractor trailer sitting in the middle of the road. The front end was over a bank.

The old man and woman had pulled out in front of the rig and been hit.

I jumped out of the patrol car and, using my radio, called the police and told them to get us some medical help *fast*.

The truck driver had gotten out of his rig and was running toward the couple when I got to them. We found the old man under the steering wheel, dead. The woman was leaning toward him. The impact had crushed the car against her side.

When I moved her away from the steering wheel, I could tell she was hurt real bad. As she looked up, you could almost see the words, "Help me, help me," in her eyes.

I called to the truck driver, "What can we do?"

He shook his head.

"I don't know," he said.

Neither of us had the equipment or the skills needed to save her. I knew the ambulance would be there, but *when?*

I held on to her for about five minutes, talking to her, trying to reassure her. She was looking up at me the whole time. Then all of a sudden she closed her eyes and went limp. She was gone.

That accident happened twenty-five years ago. But I still remember every single detail. And it still bothers me whenever I think about it.

Sometimes, the accidents troopers investigate are their own. Because of the nature of their work, they are at higher risk for auto accidents than many of the people they arrest. Since 1980, more than 225 North Carolina troopers have been involved in motor vehicle accidents while on duty. Some were seriously hurt or killed. These two officers were lucky:

It was raining hard that night and I was almost ready to get off duty when I saw one car coming around another one and begin to spin. The first thing I thought was, "Boy, that looks just like a race car spinning out of control." My next thought was "Oh no, he's gonna hit me!" I didn't even have time to look and see if anyone was behind me.

When the vehicle struck, my patrol car felt like it did a cartwheel, but actually it bounced up in the air and came down hard before sliding to the shoulder of the road.

I knew that drunks often survive an accident because they go limp, so I forced myself to slump down into the seat. When the patrol car came to rest, the window was gone and the rain was pouring in. Then I looked down and saw blood streaming from my face.

I thought, "Damn, I've broken my nose. Now I'm gonna be ugly for the rest of my life!"

About that time, an old man reached into the window, got me by the shoulder, and said, "Are you all right?"

"Yeah, I think so."

"Well, do you know so-and-so?" he asked, starting up a conversation. I couldn't believe it. Here I was bleeding to death and he wanted to gossip.

Fortunately, an ambulance had passed earlier, seen the car spinning out of control, and turned around, in case there was an accident. I was bruised, had cuts in my mouth and other superficial wounds, but wasn't injured too bad. The driver of the other car was unhurt. I charged him with no insurance or registration, driving on slick tires, and driving on a license that had been permanently revoked. He also had to pay me $250 for damages to personal property. I recovered with no problem but was out of work for a week. I could have stayed out longer but I wanted to get back on the road.

My accident happened the first night I was on patrol after my six weeks of training. I should have been home but I decided to work a few minutes past my shift.

I had pulled a car over for having no taillights and was about to get out of my patrol car when a drunk driver hit me from behind.

I remember my car door slamming back onto my leg

and the next thing I knew, I was slumped over the steering wheel. I thought I had fallen asleep. I could hear people talking around me. Someone told me later that I kept asking if it was my fault. Was the accident my fault?

I had a fractured leg and a few other injuries. I was in the hospital a week and out of work for more than a month. The lady who hit me broke her leg, and the man in front of me hurt his back. She was charged with driving while impaired and having no insurance. But she never paid the fines because she skipped town. That's why I despise drunk drivers.

Not all accidents are caused by alcohol or carelessness. Many troopers believe that fate often plays a part, as it did in this case involving a young girl:

She was driving a new 300ZX and went off the road in Haywood County over a bank with a 125-foot vertical drop. A passing motorist saw the wreck and called the rescue squad.

By the time I arrived, there were three doctors at the scene. They worked hard to save her—she had a fractured neck, broken leg, internal injuries. We had a helicopter there from the local trauma center waiting for us to get her out of the wreckage.

When we put her on the chopper she had a weak pulse, but things had gone well, it seemed, and we were beginning to think our efforts had paid off.

I radioed the local police department to send someone to the girl's home and notify her parents there had been an accident. Then I drove to the hospital so I could meet them there.

When they walked in the first thing the mother asked was, "Is my daughter alive?"

"At this point she is," I said, "but she's very seriously hurt and it's touch and go."

I attended the same church as this family so I spent the next few minutes telling them to have faith in God, that everything was in His hands.

They seemed to be comforted from what I was saying. Then the emergency room doctor walked in and told them, "I'm sorry. She didn't make it."

I thought, "What do you do? You try to console people and tell them everything is going to be all right, but you know it's *not* going to be all right. All you can do is be there for them."

That night, I didn't sleep. I kept thinking of all the drunks I've seen who will never amount to anything, but who walk away from wrecks. Then someone like this girl—young, intelligent, with a promising future—gets wiped out. I know we should value all human life, but it's sometimes hard not to make judgments about those who live and those who die.

I've seen troopers laugh and make jokes about fatalities. I've done it myself. But it's a defense mechanism, a cover-up to disguise what we're really feeling. When you get home, that's when it hits you. You try to sleep and you can't, because what you've just seen—a person's death—goes through your mind over and over again.

I attended the girl's funeral. I guess I needed to be there to make it clear in my own head that it was over, she was gone. I was standing at the back of the church, trying not to be noticed, when the mother looked up and saw me.

She came straight toward me, put her arms around me and hugged me. People turned and stared. I kept wishing I was somewhere else because she wouldn't let go. I didn't know what to do, so I put my arms around her.

"Thank you," she said. "Thank you for doing everything you did to help save my daughter. I hope God is always with you in your work and keeps you safe."

She did more to help me in those few seconds than I was ever able to do for her. We didn't save a life, but we tried. And that's what being a public servant is all about—doing the best we can for the people we represent. Having people appreciate what we do—appreciate that we try—can make up for a lot of the bad things that happen on the road.

5
Strange Encounters

"Well, I'll just prove that I'm not drunk. I'll stand here on my head in front of the courthouse!"

—*Sixty-four-year-old man on his way to the breathalyzer room with a trooper*

Not everything that happens on patrol involves trauma and tragedy. Sometimes the job has its humorous, though somewhat bizarre, moments. Experienced troopers even come to expect odd behavior from people they encounter on the road. Many highway patrol veterans say that nothing surprises them anymore. One patrol officer, a trooper for seventeen years, puts it more bluntly. "People are just damn crazy," he says.

All of the following incidents are true:

Me and another trooper were riding down the road one night when we passed a pickup truck. We thought we spotted a child in the vehicle with an axe sticking out of its back.

I said, "Jesus Christ, Ron, they've killed a kid!"

"Aw, come on, it's Halloween," said Ron. "It's got to be a prank."

"Let's stop them and make sure."

So we got them to pull over and I walked up to the driver. About the time I got to him, he jumped out of the truck, raised his arms, and bared two white fangs at me. He had on a black cape, white powder on his face, and this red stuff squirting out of his mouth. It startled me so much that I drew my weapon and told him not to come any closer. Then I heard someone in the truck laughing. Turns out that both her and "Dracula" were sheriff's deputies on their way to a Halloween party.

We made jokes about it all night, but I'll have to admit, it scared the hell out of me at the time.

I clocked the car speeding at eighty miles per hour, walked up to the driver and said, "Ma'am, can I see your driver's license?" I noticed that she was wearing a miniskirt, hose, high heels, and makeup. But when I looked at the license, it had a man's name and picture on it.

Sitting next to the driver was a male dressed in a suit and tie. I asked the driver to come back to my patrol car. As "she" got out of the car, I realized "she" was a "he." By that time I was totally confused.

I put him in my vehicle and proceeded to write the ticket.

"Why do you do this?" I asked.

"Do what?" he said.

"Dress like that."

"Because my mother dressed me like this all my life," he replied.

"And who's the man riding with you?"

"Oh, that's my date," he said.

"I see."

Later, when he came to court, he was dressed the same way. Neither the judge nor the people in the courtroom were surprised, but the whole thing was a shock to me. That was years ago. You see more of it today. In fact, I no longer expect people to come across a certain way. Now I just ask "what's normal?" and go on about my business.

People will use any excuse to get out of a speeding ticket. I stopped a man on Interstate 85 and asked him what his hurry was.

"It's my dog," he said, pointing to a large animal riding next to him. "He needs to go to the bathroom."

"So why didn't you pull over and stop on the side of the road?"

"You don't understand, officer," he said. "This is a three-hundred-dollar dog and he won't go to the bathroom just anywhere. I've got to get to the next rest stop."

"Well, take him on down there," I said. "But meanwhile, dog or no dog, I'm gonna write you a ticket."

And that's exactly what I did.

I got a call one night about a drunk woman sitting on Interstate 85 at the South Carolina line. There was a question about which state she was in, so when I arrived a South Carolina trooper and a police cruiser were there. One of the officers had put her in his car and she had taken off her shoe and was trying to beat the back window out of his cruiser. By the time I arrived, they were tired of her high jinks and were glad to be rid of her.

I got them to help me handcuff her and I put her in the front seat so I could keep an eye on her. We had just gotten on the road when she started kicking and screaming and trying to bite me. I struggled with her as long as I could, but finally couldn't control her any longer.

I called my sergeant and he agreed to come and help me. As soon as I stopped the patrol car to let him in, the woman got real calm and quiet. We put her in the back seat and the sergeant got in front.

"You might as well get in the back with her, Sarge," I said, "because as soon as I start this car, she's gonna raise hell."

"No she's not." Then he turned in her direction. "You're gonna be a real sweet little lady, aren't you?"

She just looked at him.

Sure enough, when I started the patrol car, she went wild. The sergeant ended up in the back seat and he said it was like riding a bucking bronco. She fought him all the way to jail.

When we got there, we put her in a cell and left her by herself. When we went back to check on her, she was sitting in the middle of the floor—stark naked. She had stripped off all her clothes and placed them in a pile in a corner of the room. But at least she had settled down.

I remember that little episode every time I see a South Carolina trooper. Thanks a lot, guys.

This trooper had stopped to buy a drink and a candy bar, and left the door open as he got out of the patrol car. He came back a minute later, climbed in, closed the door, and took off. Just as he was coming into the patrol parking lot, we heard tires squealing and someone yelling. We raced outside to see what was happening and saw the trooper with his gun drawn, pointing it toward the back seat of the patrol car.

Said he'd been driving along and felt something nuzzle his head. When he had left the door open, a dog had jumped in the back seat and put his nose on the trooper's neck.

That sure came close to being one dead dog.

I stopped a girl traveling ninety mph one night. Walked up to the car and saw right away that she didn't have a stitch on. All of her clothes were on the seat beside her. She was good-looking too.

I said, "Uh, lady, I need to see your driver's license. I clocked you at ninety mph. I suggest you get some clothes on while I write this ticket."

I took my time writing out the ticket so she could dress. Then I went back to her car and handed her the citation.

"By the way," I asked her, "where were you going in such a hurry?"

"I've been at my boyfriend's house," she explained. "But my husband called wanting to know where I was. So I have to get home right away."

I have no idea what happened after that, but every now and then I see her in the shopping mall. She smiles as we pass. And I smile back.

It was a Fourth of July and another trooper and I were working late shift when we noticed a car driving erratically in the middle of the road.

I said, "He's drunk. Let's pull him over."

I walked up and shined the flashlight, saw a well-endowed girl trying to get her clothes on, and the driver pulling up his pants. She turns out to be his wife, but they were doing more than celebrating the Fourth. The car was full of Valium, Quaaludes, marijuana, and other controlled substances they had obtained illegally.

To beat it all, he was a pharmacist and really should have known better.

I was working the interstate in Gaston County one day and noticed a hitchhiker on the road. It's illegal to thumb a ride on North Carolina's interstates, so I stopped him and gave him a warning ticket. When I asked for his identification he said he didn't have any.

I patted him down, took him back to the patrol car, and attempted to find out who he was. He handed me a slip of paper and told me to call this number in Washington, D.C.—collect.

"They'll tell you who I am," he said.

I got the telecommunicator in Newton to put the call through. A minute later she came back on the radio and said she had the White House on the line and who did I want to talk to?

The guy said, "Tell them to ask for President Carter." Then he gave his name and added, "He knows who I am."

The telecommunicator relayed the information and was instructed to have me stay put. There would be someone from Charlotte arriving at my location shortly. About fifteen minutes later, two unmarked cars pull up and two men jump out and flash their badges, showing me they are Secret Service. Then they take the guy into custody.

Seems my hitchhiker had been to the White House on a protest march and gotten inside the private quarters where the president and his family lived. Some personal items were missing. While no one actually said the man had stolen anything, that was the impression I got. He was also a former mental patient.

When I caught him, he was passing through North Carolina on his way to Texas to see Lady Bird Johnson. Said he had been in phone contact with her and wanted to pay her a visit.

Later, I got a nice letter from the two Secret Service agents. They explained the man posed no threat, but was a real nuisance, and they appreciated my help in apprehending him.

Right before he got into the car with the agents, the guy came up and shook my hand.

"I'll see you later, Trooper," he said.

And the next time he hitchhikes through North Carolina, he probably will.

It was Sunday afternoon in Jackson County and I stopped a guy for what I thought was a drunk-driving violation. When he got out of the car, he didn't shut the door completely and this big Persian cat jumps out.

As the fella was handing me his driver's license, the cat ran across the road, rolled under a car, and got hit. Then it took off across a golf course and into the woods.

Next thing I know, the driver is chasing after the cat, yelling, "Fur-Ball! Fur-Ball! Come back here!" while I'm holding his driver's license and wondering what to do.

By this time, several people had stopped to see what the commotion was about. To their right they could hear someone in the woods yelling, "Fur-Ball! Fur-Ball!," and to their left, see me standing there looking stupid.

Finally the guy comes out of the woods carrying the cat in his arms, brings it to the car, and lays it across the front seat.

Then he walks back to me with tears streaming down his face and says, "Fur-Ball's gonna die. Now, what do *you* want?"

I shook my head, said, "Not a thing," and handed him back his driver's license. What else could I do?

I was in Bryson City when I got a call that a guy was shooting at cars.

He was standing there facing me with a shotgun when I stepped out of the patrol car. I pulled my weapon and looked at him. No one said a word. For several seconds we just stared each other down, like in a western movie. Then he turned around, got in his truck, and drove off.

I thought, "What the hell am I supposed to do *now*?"

So I went after him. He stopped, got back out of the truck. I stopped, got out of the patrol car. The same thing happened again.

Now we're about twelve feet apart, facing each other. I told him to drop his weapon. He looked at me like he didn't hear me and kept coming. He could have easily shot me before I had a chance to pull the trigger.

He kept approaching and I'm thinking, "You need to shoot him. You need to shoot him." But my instincts were telling me otherwise—that I wasn't threatened enough yet to take a human life.

Now he's eight feet away and still coming. Then he suddenly stops. I was so damn mad at him that I walked up, took the gun away from him, punched him in the mouth, and said, "You stupid son of a bitch! Don't you know how close you came to getting killed?"

I took a chance that time and I won. But I could have lost just as easily.

It was a Saturday afternoon, about suppertime. I was patrolling north of Robbinsville and had turned around to head back to the house when I met an old pickup truck with an expired inspection sticker.

I thought, "Well, I'll give one more warning ticket before I take a break." So I turned around to follow him. But he picked up speed and went down a dead-end road called Cat Eye Hollow.

Being a rookie, I was too inexperienced to know the guy was running from me. I just thought he wanted to see Cat Eye. When I got there, he had wrecked his truck in a pile of dirt and I figured I had a drunk driver. He jumped out and ran, so I jumped out and followed him. Didn't take a flashlight, nightstick, nothing. Didn't even call in to let the telecommunicator know where I was or what I was doing. Just acted like a dumb rookie.

I chased the guy about half a mile into the woods. He was a big fella, a lumberjack, and drunk as a hoot owl. At one point he fell and I jumped on top of him, pulled his arm around his back and said, "Gotcha!"

He looked up and said, "Oh no you don't."

Then he brought his other arm around and grabbed me. I knew I was in trouble when he threw me across the woods. As soon as I fell, he was on top of me, reaching for my gun. He put it to the side of my head, cocked it, and said, "I've got *you* now."

"Yeah, I guess you do."

I didn't really think he would shoot me on purpose, but I was afraid he might slip or accidentally release the trigger. So I used the only trick I had left—my gift of gab. I struck up a conversation with him right there in the woods, with the gun at my head.

We'd been talking for a while when he said, "By the way, why'd you stop me?"

When I told him it was because of an expired sticker, he said, "But I can't read. How was I supposed to know it was expired?"

I thought about that for a minute and said, "Aw, don't worry about it. A lot of people can't read."

We talked a few minutes more and then he got an idea.

"I tell you what," he said. "You handcuff yourself to that tree."

I said, "Do what?"

"Handcuff yourself to that tree," he repeated.

"Aw, come on. Let's not do that."

He put the gun back to my head and said, "Put the handcuffs on."

I put 'em on.

Then he changed his mind, decided that wasn't such a good idea after all and asked me to drive him to his brother's house instead.

On the way to the car, he explained why he ran from me. Said he was scared of being arrested and locked up.

"I just die when I get locked up," he said. "I can't stand it."

When we got to the patrol car, he showed me his driver's license and I began to call him by his first name. I drove to the top of the road, where he got edgy again, put the gun to my head once more, and said, "Did you call any more law?"

I said, "No way, man."

"You know if you called any more law and they're sittin' up there, you're dead. They'll kill me, but I'll kill you first."

"Yeah, I know that, but I haven't called anyone." The whole time, I was praying we wouldn't see any officers.

We got to his brother's house without incident and he started to get out of the patrol car with my gun in his hand.

I said, "Now, Ed, you've got to give me my gun back."

"No, I'm not gonna do it."

"Come on, give it back. I can't leave without it."

"I'll give it back to you if you promise not to use it on me," he said.

"I promise."

To make sure I kept my word, he emptied out the bullets and threw the gun down on the seat. Then he hightailed it up to his brother's house.

Meanwhile, I'm sitting there wondering what to do about this situation. I went home, changed clothes, and drove to another trooper's house. I think I was in shock.

As I pulled up, the trooper came out of his house and I was about to say, "Let me tell you what happened," when all of a sudden I hit the ground. Just passed out cold in the driveway.

Ed eventually got eleven years in prison for kidnapping me and I got transferred out of the county. The patrol thought I'd be too easy a target for anyone wanting to try the same thing. It took me a long time to live that one down.

I investigated a wreck one time in Chapel Hill where a car had turned over and thrown the occupants out. Two people were hurt, so I sent them to the hospital for treatment.

I was looking for evidence near the scene when I spotted what appeared to be a full-face Halloween mask. Only it wasn't. It was the embalmed head of a cadaver.

The driver of the car that wrecked was a resident in oral surgery at the University of North Carolina-Chapel Hill and had taken the head home with her. I put it in a plastic bag and delivered it to the medical examiner at the hospital.

The next morning the dental school called me wanting to know where to find their cadaver's head. I assured them I didn't have it, didn't want it, but would certainly tell them where to find it.

There's a T-shaped intersection at U.S. 52 and U.S. 74 that connects right after you pass the crest of a hill. To warn drivers of what's ahead, the highway department installed a flashing red light and a sign before you reach the top.

One night an elderly lady from South Carolina came speeding through the intersection in a Buick, left the road, and crashed her car through the window of a real estate office. She wasn't hurt, but there was considerable damage to her vehicle and to the building.

The trooper who investigated the accident asked her point blank, "Lady, did you not see those flashing red lights when you came up the highway?"

"Yes, sir," she said.

"Then why didn't you stop?"

"Well," she said, "I thought it was a railroad crossing and I wanted to beat the train!"

I was patrolling the Cherokee Indian Reservation one night when I arrested a drunk driver and put him in the back seat of my car. I had a Cherokee police officer with me in the front. We were talking to each other when I noticed the drunk driver trying to open the car door. He had been mouthy ever since I had picked him up and was mumbling something about "getting out of here."

"Go ahead and get out," I told him, jokingly. We were traveling about 35 mph at the time.

Sure enough, the door opened and he started to jump out. I slammed on the brakes, and when I did he fell out of the car and rolled into a ditch. I stopped, backed the car up, and put my headlights on him. There he was in the ditch, handcuffed, not moving. I thought he was dead.

I got on the radio and called for an ambulance. Then I walked over to check on him. He was addled, but otherwise seemed okay. We felt kind of sorry for him, in the ditch, in the cold, so the Cherokee police officer took off his coat and covered him up.

By the time the ambulance got him to the hospital he was mouthing off again, threatening us. They stripped him down, took his wet clothes away, and made him put on a hospital gown—one of those skimpy things that open in the back. We were told to step outside in the hall and wait for the doctor. As the physician was telling us about the man's condition, the guy climbed out a window and escaped.

We never caught up with him, but I would like to have seen him running down the road in that hospital gown.

I seldom believe any of the reasons people give for speeding, but once I stopped a little old lady who was so sincere I couldn't help but think she was telling the truth.

"Sonny, do you know why I was going so fast?" she said.

"No ma'am, I don't."

"My husband put high-test gas in this car for the first time," she said, "and I've never driven on high-test gas before."

I gave her a ticket, but her explanation made more sense to me than all those excuses we hear about going to the bathroom.

I was in Burke County one night on my way home when I got behind a Mustang II weaving across the road.

I flipped on the blue light but the car kept going. Turned on the siren, but the car kept going. So I radioed Asheville and told them I was about to engage in a pursuit down Salem Road and if possible, send me some assistance.

The car finally stopped and I made my approach. About the time I got to the rear window, I heard a woman calling, "Rape! Rape!" I put my hand on my holster and unsnapped it, wondering, "What have we got here?"

I tapped the glass on the driver's side, shined my flashlight into the car, and told the guy to step out with his hands in plain view. Beside him was a naked woman.

The man got out and I patted him down to make sure he had no weapons. Meanwhile, the woman climbed out of the car on the passenger side and started walking down the road. She was the ugliest female I'd ever seen in my life—weighed about four hundred pounds—with rolls and rolls of fat and a huge scar running down her side.

I said, "Woman! Get back in the car and get some clothes on!"

I led the man back to my patrol car, advised him of his rights, and sat him down in the front seat. I looked back and there was the lady walking down the middle of the road again.

"Woman!" I yelled. "Get in the goddamn car and get some clothes on!" I met her at the driver's side of the car and cussed her till she followed my instructions.

Then I went back to the patrol car, climbed in, and looked at the guy.

"What the hell is going on here?"

He said, "Fella, you won't believe it."

"Try me."

"I'm drunk."

"Yes, I can see that."

"I don't have any idea who that woman is," he said. "I was coming through town and stopped at a red light beside the courthouse when she jumped out from behind a bush and got into my car."

"When did she take her clothes off?"

"I don't know," he said, "she didn't have any on when she got in the car."

"Well, damn, I would have locked the door if I'd seen *that* coming," I told him.

"I was too drunk to think that fast, officer."

By this time, the woman had started to get out of the car again. I rolled the window down in the patrol car and stuck my head out.

"Woman, don't you get out of that car till you get some clothes on!"

"I ain't got no clothes!" she screamed.

"Stay in the goddamn car then!"

The fella convinced me he was telling the truth. I mean, hell, who wouldn't believe him after getting a look at her? Then I got to thinking, "What's the story here?" I knew there was a mental hospital nearby. I figured she must have escaped, walked into town, and was trying to catch a ride with the first person who came along.

I had an obligation to do something about it but I wasn't sure what. I did *not* want her in my patrol car. So I got on the radio again and called the telecommunicator in Asheville.

"Did you get in touch with the Burke County sheriff's department?" I asked. They said yes.

"Then how about sending someone down here. I've got a woman who says she walked away from Broughton Hospital and would like a ride back." (At this point, I was making up the details.)

A short time later, a deputy pulled up beside my car.

"Whadda ya need, Mac?" he said.

I told him I had a guy under arrest for drunk driving and was ready to take him to jail.

"But there's a lady in the car up ahead who needs a ride back to Broughton. Would you mind taking her?"

"Sure," he said, "I'll be glad to."

He put his car in reverse, backed up to the Mustang, took one look at that 400-pound naked woman, and let out the worst cussing I ever heard—just as I was driving away.

He transported the woman to Broughton, but it took them all night to figure out she wasn't one of their patients. Nobody knew where she came from and I made a point of never finding out.

A disturbed man used to call our communications center in Currituck County. They'd hang up on him, but he'd always call back.

He'd tell them, "Aliens are bombarding my residence with radioactivity. I've covered all the windows and storm doors in my house with tinfoil. And I've completely wrapped my body in it. What else should I do?"

The trooper who investigated the case told him that

Saran Wrap would repel radioactivity waves even better, so the man said he would try that too.

I guess it worked, because he finally stopped calling us.

We get a lot of strange calls from the public. Some drunk will dial our number, say he's Johnny Cash, and to prove it, sing "Folsom Prison Blues" over the phone. Or people tell us they're getting radio signals from their refrigerators and want to know if UFOs have landed.

It gets worse after midnight. That's when the real nuts come out.

I was coming down U.S. 70 when I saw a car sitting in the middle of the road. A lady stood beside it and the hood was up. I assumed she was having car trouble. So I pulled in beside her and asked if she needed any help.

"There's someone under my car," she said.

"You mean you've run over somebody?"

"No, no," she said. "There's someone under my car. Can't you see his legs sticking out?"

I backed up, parked the cruiser behind her, and walked up to where she was standing.

"Where?" I said. I couldn't see a thing except the concrete pavement under the car.

"He's right there. Don't you see him?"

"No, I really don't. Let me get my glasses."

I thought if I stalled for time, I could figure out what was going on. I went back to the patrol car and picked up the radio. But I didn't know what to tell the station. So I gave them the woman's name and license number and asked them to run a check on her.

Meanwhile, she got back in the car and started to leave. She hadn't committed a crime that I was aware of, but I thought she was too crazy to be driving. I went after her on foot, reached into her car, and grabbed the keys.

"You sit right here," I told her.

When I returned to the patrol car, the radio station notified me that her license had been revoked.

By now, she had left her car again and was walking towards the woods. I ran after her, got her by the arms, and handcuffed her. Then I took her to jail. On the way, she told me her car was controlled by demons and the town where she lived was possessed.

"Yeah, lady," I said. "It's possessed with people like you."

She stayed in jail for a couple of days, then was sent to a mental hospital. A few days later, she was released.

When I talked to the hospital officials, they explained they couldn't keep her because even though she was crazy, she wasn't "crazy-crazy." In other words, she wasn't certifiably nuts and no one would sign a statement to that effect.

Except me. I *knew* how crazy she was.

I clocked a white station wagon at eighty miles per hour, pursued it, and noted a woman driving. When I turned on the blue light, I got no response. Turned on the siren. No response. I pulled in right behind her and she swerved all over the road.

Suddenly I saw a large black head come up from the back seat and move from side to side.

I thought, "This woman has been kidnapped and there's a man in the back going berserk!"

Finally, she pulled over and stopped. Needless to say, I approached the car with great caution.

Before I could reach her, she jumped out and ran back toward me. I pulled my gun because I thought the next person coming out of the car would be the perpetrator of this terrible crime.

"Officer!" the woman cried. "You've upset my chimp!"

It seems the animal was sound asleep in the back

seat until it heard the siren on my patrol car. Then it went crazy and started biting her on the neck, nearly causing her to run off the road.

I walked up and looked in the window. If you want to see something fierce, try eyeballing an angry chimpanzee.

And you know what? I forgot all about giving her a ticket.

We had a terrible snowstorm in Haywood County one year, with roads blocked for up to fourteen hours. I came across two ladies stranded on the interstate, pulled in behind them, and got out to see if they needed help.

"I really need to go to the bathroom," said one.

"Ma'am, I'm afraid there's no rest room around here," I told her. "Why don't you bail out over the guardrail?"

As I drove off, I looked in the rearview mirror and saw her get out of the car, step over the guardrail—and disappear!

That's when I remembered there was a twenty-foot drop over the railing, hidden by a mound of snow.

I stopped the cruiser, jumped out, and ran back to see if she was all right. As I shined the flashlight over the bank, I spotted her hanging on to a tree, pulling herself upward inch by inch.

"Are you hurt?" I asked.

"I'm just fine, officer," she said, reaching the top of the bank.

"In fact, now that I'm soaking wet, I feel a whole lot better."

6

"Call Me Ma'am"

"I'll pull a car over and the guy will say, 'What'd you stop me for, man?' Sometimes it doesn't bother me, but if I'm in a bad mood, it'll fly all over me and I'll come back with, 'Call me *Ma'am!*' "

—*Female trooper*

In North Carolina, meeting up with a female highway patrol officer can seem like a strange encounter all its own. At present, the state has fewer than twelve women troopers. That's less than 1 percent of its entire work force. As a result, it takes a special kind of woman to overcome professional barriers and succeed in this still male-dominated career field.

Elizabeth ("Dee") Parton is one of those unusual people. At twenty-seven, she is North Carolina's most senior female officer, having joined the patrol in 1981 as one of the first women cadets in the state. A handful of women before her had tried to become troopers, but failed. Dee not only made it through patrol school with flying colors, but along the way gained the respect and admiration of her fellow officers.

"The whole time I worked here, I wondered how she'd be if we needed her," said Trooper Rick Terry, stationed in Madison County. "Then one night I pulled a car over at the county line and got the driver out. I informed him he was under arrest and searched him. As I looked up, I saw the passenger coming out of the car towards me. I didn't have the first man handcuffed and was attempting to get the second man back into the car without turning loose of the driver. At that point, I didn't know what was going to happen. Both guys were drunk.

"Then Dee came by in her patrol car, saw that I needed help and said, 'I'll take care of him, G-153.' And she escorted the passenger back to the car and made him get in. That one incident gave me a lot of respect for her because I know that in a tight spot, she'll at least try to help. And that's the main thing."

At five feet five, Dee is slender but sturdy, with light brown hair and a no-nonsense approach to life. Growing up as a tomboy in the small town of Waynesville, North Carolina, she was naturally athletic, and played sports through high school before attending East Tennessee State University, where she earned a degree in criminal justice.

"I knew I wanted to go into law enforcement, but at the time North Carolina didn't have any female troopers," she said. "So I realized it was going to be a big challenge."

And a challenge it was.

"We were up at five-thirty every morning doing push-ups, sit-ups, jumping jacks, and a four-mile run. If you failed one academic test in a major subject or two minor tests, they sent you home. Two girls flunked out because of that. The remaining girl went through school for ten weeks, then failed the firearms test because she couldn't hold on to the gun."

That made Dee the sole woman among thirty-seven male cadets.

"The guys could have given me a hard time," she said.

"But they were basically good to me. I'd help them study, then we'd go out and get a drink or sit around and talk. It was like having thirty-seven brothers. There was still an underlying feeling that women didn't belong on the patrol, but I wasn't treated any different from any other cadet."

Her first—and current—duty station was Buncombe County, where she immediately gained the distinction of being the only female trooper in the western part of the state. Since so few women were in the highway patrol, the only uniforms available were those designed for men.

"I'd tuck my shirt in and the pocket would go down into my belt. Then the neck would hang out. I was in the patrol office one day and a major looked at me and said, "You got any more shirts?" I told him no. "Well, I want you to go right now and order something that fits," he said. She now wears tailor-made shirts and a bulletproof vest adapted to female curves. Everything else about her uniform is standard, including the heavy-soled lace-up shoes, black socks, gray pants, and campaign-style hat.

Public reaction to a woman highway patrol officer ranged from unspoken acceptance to disbelief.

"The first day on the job I arrested a man for drunk driving. I put him in the back seat and his response to my questions was, 'Yes, sir, no, sir,' until I finally said, 'You might want to take another look, mister. I'm not a sir. I'm a ma'am.'

" 'Oh, I'm so sorry!' he said. 'In that case, can I kiss you? I ain't never seen a female patrolman before!' And he started coming over the front seat. My training officer, sitting beside me, burst out laughing. He was enjoying every minute of it.

"Another time, I arrested a sixty-year-old man for drunk driving and he drew back his arm like he was going to strike me. I said, 'Buddy, I don't think you want to hit a police officer.'

" 'I wouldn't hit you,' he said. 'You're a lady. Besides, you might shoot me.' "

It's Dee opinion that female officers have an easier time

on the road than male troopers because of men's more aggressive natures.

"A drunk starts cussing a man and it's instinct that he wants to fight back," she said. "But I don't have any macho image to protect, so if there's any way I can avoid a fight, I'm gonna do it."

Which doesn't mean she hasn't faced life-threatening situations on patrol.

"One night I had a guy draw a sawed-off shotgun at me. Then he changed his mind and threw it down on the ground. When I picked it up I noticed it had a shell in the chamber. It didn't bother me too much at the time, but later I thought, instead of throwing that gun down, he could have killed me! That's when I got scared."

Like other troopers, Dee works swing shifts, rotating days, nights, and weekends. The erratic hours, plus the fact that she's a female highway patrol officer, puts a damper on her social life. She has never been married.

"When men find out I'm a trooper, they say 'You? You mean, *you* are? Boy, you must be tough.'

"I've tried dating people in law enforcement," she said, "but the only thing we do is talk about our jobs." In the future she hopes to marry and start a family, but says she'll choose "a banker, lawyer, or construction worker," rather than a cop.

For now, Dee wants to complete her master's degree in sociology and climb the promotional ladder in the highway patrol. It's a good career, she maintains, despite its ups and downs.

"I have a lot of freedom and I enjoy that. I can go anywhere I want to within my assigned area and stop whenever I want to. Our main responsibilities are the state highways, but most accidents occur on rural roads, so that's where I like to patrol. I also get to know a lot of people in the country, people I can wave at or talk to regularly. These are the folks who can make you or break you when you need help serving a warrant or getting directions. I also like the satisfaction that comes from helping people. Once I found a boy sitting by his car because he didn't know how to fix a flat. So I did it for him.

"I pick people up when their car runs out of gas, or call a wrecker for them when they need it. Or I'll stop and talk to kids and answer their questions about my gun, my uniform, anything they want to know. I love that part of the job."

Her advice to other women considering a career in the highway patrol is to first get all the education they can.

"My only regret is that I didn't finish my master's degree before I came on the patrol. I don't think anyone can have too much education. There's always something new in the world to learn."

What Gail Cloer learned when she joined the highway patrol in 1986 was that she had more gumption than she thought.

A single parent with a nine-year-old child to support, Gail was going nowhere in finding a career until her mother suggested she try law enforcement. So one summer she joined the Sylva Police Department as an intern and found that she loved the work. Afterwards, she enrolled in a technical college and earned a degree in criminal justice.

"Until I worked at the police department, I had no prior contact with the highway patrol," said Gail, a tall, striking blonde. "But as I got to know different troopers, I realized how professional they were and I thought, 'This is for me.' From then on, it got into my blood and joining the patrol was all I thought about."

Getting in was fairly easy for Gail since the patrol was recruiting females and minorities. Staying in was difficult.

She began cadet school when she was twenty-six, in January, 1986. She stills rolls her eyes at the memory of those first few weeks.

"People tried to tell me how hard it would be. But it's something you can't explain to another person. The biggest adjustment was stepping out of the world where I had control and going into one where I was told what to do and when to do it. I was in shock for two weeks. The first night I was there, I thought, 'What in the world am I doing here? What have I gotten myself into?' "

At first the men cadets paid little attention to her and to the two other females enrolled. But toward the end of school the women began to hear taunts and chauvinistic remarks.

"They'd say things like, 'You have no business being here,' " said Gail. " 'You should be at home.' Some of it was joking around but some of it was serious too. The men tried us. But if we came right back at them, they accepted us. They just wanted to see what we were made of."

One of the women cadets excelled in physical training, but struggled through parts of the book work. Another breezed through the academics and had difficulty with the physical training. Gail was somewhere in between. But none of it was easy.

"I learned that to become a trooper you have to want it more than anything else in the world. There were times when I had to really reach inside myself to get through. If it wasn't for my family's support I'm not sure I could have done it."

For Patricia Anne Poole, a twenty-four-year-old cadet, the sense of comradeship she expected from the highway patrol was sometimes hard to find.

"I'm not saying I didn't get support from the other cadets, because I did. There were times when I wondered if I'd get through another day and someone next to me would say, 'Yes, you can.' But if an instructor talked to me, some of the guys said I was kissing up to him, which was the furthest thing from the truth. I'm in this job for my career and myself. I didn't come here to see how many troopers I could get. But because I'm a female, that's what a few of the cadets thought."

Her family opposed her decision to become a trooper, partly because of her diminutive size. At five feet five, she weighs just over 121 pounds.

" 'You're gonna get killed,' they told me. 'It's not a place for a woman.' But when I hear things like that, it makes me want to do it even more. So I told them I was going to join whether they liked it or not. I want to be happy in a career. After that, they were all for it."

"I admire Poole," said W. F. ("Butch") Whitley, one of her classmates. "There were a lot of guys who couldn't cut it, while she progressed."

During Gail Cloer's first few weeks on the road she learned lessons that never came up in school.

"My training officer and I were called to a wreck one night at a place named Hanging Dog, a rough section in Cherokee County. I arrested the driver for driving while impaired, a big man about six-three, 250 pounds, rough-looking. I put handcuffs on him and took him to jail while my training officer stayed behind to write out the report. The man lost his temper a couple of times on the way but I talked to him and calmed him down. Later, my training officer asked if I had any trouble and I said, 'No, he seemed to be a pretty nice guy.' Then he starts telling me how this man was once arrested for kidnapping a social worker and how many fights he had been in, that he was into drugs, etc.

"And I thought, 'My lord, I really let my guard down. Anything could have happened.' But the experience stayed with me. I became more aware that people can appear to be one way and turn out to be something entirely different."

One of the biggest misconceptions female troopers encounter among people they work with is that women law enforcement officers are homosexual.

"A deputy in my county was trying to fix me up with a male friend," recalled one lady trooper, "and I kept telling him my social calendar didn't need any help, but he kept on. Then he said, 'I've been hearing some things from my friends who are asking some questions.' I knew what he was getting at so I just looked at him and said, 'Every female who comes on the highway patrol has been called a lesbian at one time or another. That doesn't bother me. I've been expecting it. But we're not lesbians. And we're not out to prove anything. We just want to do our jobs and be accepted.' He didn't say anything more about it after that.''

Often patrolling alone in isolated parts of the county, Gail is not afraid to admit she worries about her safety.

Her greatest dread is stopping a van with tinted windows.

''You can't see inside those darn things and there's no way to know what's going on.''

She handles fear by setting it aside till later.

''I deal with it after I get back in my patrol car, especially after I've been in a chase. I don't always realize I'm afraid until I get out of the car and find that my knees and hands are shaking.''

At the same time, she's prepared to protect herself.

''I don't have any problem with drawing my gun whenever it's necessary. I like myself too much to get hurt.''

Still in the process of proving herself as a new trooper, Gail has built up a sense of trust among her co-workers by ''doing my job the best way I can.'' Along with Dee Parton and the handful of other women troopers across the state, she hopes that eventually female patrol officers won't be such a novelty in North Carolina.

''Unfortunately, not so many women want to be troopers,'' she admits.

That wasn't the case with Leah Weirick.

Interested in law enforcement since she was a teenager, Leah was influenced by an uncle who was a city cop and an aunt who was a detective.

''I'd see her name in the paper whenever a drug bust occurred and I guess that impressed me.''

She chose the highway patrol for a career because she considered it ''top of the line'' in law enforcement. After graduating from cadet school in 1986, she was sent to Bryson City, a remote mountain town in the westernmost part of North Carolina. She was twenty-three and single.

Athletically built, with cropped brown hair, clear gray

eyes, and a pretty smile, Leah was stunned when she heard about her new assignment.

"I couldn't believe it," she said. "I had been told that no females would be put in this part of the state because people in this area just weren't ready for women or minorities. It was like the patrol wanted us to come out here and prove ourselves. There's not always a backup trooper readily available either, so I worked lots of times completely alone in places where help was an hour away."

As the new trooper in town—and a female at that—Leah felt she had to work twice as hard to prove herself. Community reaction to "that lady trooper" was mixed at best.

"I'd walk up to investigate a wreck with my training officer, carrying a clipboard to take notes, and people would ask if I was a secretary. Or they'd call me 'Honey,' and I'd have to look at them a certain way until they backed up and said 'Excuse me, I mean 'Ma'am.' "

Dressed in uniform, bulletproof vest, and wearing a hat and sunglasses, she is often mistaken for a male officer.

"The vest makes me look thirty pounds heavier (she is five feet seven, 140 pounds) and from a distance it's sometimes hard for people to tell that I'm a woman. Men will get out of their cars and say, 'What's the problem, sir?' I don't even correct them anymore. When I do, it comes as a shock to them that I'm not what they thought."

As a rule, she finds women drivers more difficult to deal with than men. Other female troopers have said the same.

"I've had women drivers crying their eyes out because they think they're going to get a ticket. Then when I walk up to the car and they realize I'm a female officer, the faucet turns off just like that [she snaps her fingers]. I've found that most women don't like to be told what to do by other women. When Bob [Leah's training officer] stops them, its 'Yes, sir,' and they go pay the ticket. I can stop that same female and she'll argue with me about it."

Another female trooper tells of an incident where she

stopped—and surprised—a young woman who was speeding.

"As I pulled up behind her in the patrol car, I saw her primping in her rearview mirror—putting on lipstick, combing her hair. I'm sure she was hoping to flirt her way out of this one. You should have seen the expression on her face when she turned around and found a lady trooper. Her whole attitude went from sweet to sour in about ten seconds."

According to women officers, more than half the complaints they receive on the job come from other females.

"I think I've already proven to law enforcement people I work with that I can do the job," said Leah, "but it takes longer for people in the community to accept you. I still run into individuals who say, 'So *you're* the one I've heard about.' "

Not only her sex, but her size has worked against her.

"I stopped a man one time who was absolutely one of the hugest people I've ever seen and he was pissed when he got out of his truck. He came stalking back to me just glaring. The only thing I could do was stare him in the eyes to make him think he didn't bother me. That kind of situation puts me on the defensive and I don't like it."

Those who argue that women are too small to handle the job physically fail to remember that since height requirements no longer apply in the highway patrol, there are dozens of men troopers who fall into the same short stature category as women. In addition, women must pass rigid physical requirements to get into patrol school and learn the same defensive tactics as men. If that fails, they can resort to "the great equalizer"—their .357 Magnums.

Nevertheless, there are some situations on the road, says Leah, that no trooper—male or female, large or small—should tackle alone.

"When you pull up behind someone and several people get out, you'd better get back in your patrol car and call for help. Because whether you're a man or a woman, you can't handle four potentially dangerous individuals."

What bothers her more than fear on the job is the way women troopers are perceived socially, especially by men.

"When we wear the bulletproof vest, it hides our shape, so people don't always realize we have one. I've had guys walk up to me in the health spa and say, 'Hey, you're thirty pounds lighter than I thought!' But they still won't ask me out because they are intimidated by what I do. And the fact that I make more money than a lot of them is a problem too. The 'big' salary in this county is $13,000. I make more than that and they know it. They also know I live by myself, take care of myself. I'm independent. Some men are still threatened by that."

She sees herself getting married, having a family, and staying on the patrol in the future, but only if she finds someone "who can deal with it." So far, that hasn't happened to the handful of North Carolina female troopers currently on the patrol. All are single or divorced.

Despite the drawbacks, there is a force that attracts and binds women like Weirick, Cloer, Poole, and Parton to the highway patrol.

"All of our reasons for joining are about the same," said Leah. "We're interested in law enforcement. It provides something different every day. We don't have to sit behind a desk. We are our own bosses. We can go anywhere on patrol at any time. And the work is a challenge—just as getting into the patrol is a challenge."

She says the first thing a woman who is interested in becoming a trooper should do is talk at length with other female officers.

"I talked with Dee before I joined but I still didn't realize what it was like. You must be physically fit. But you also have to be psychologically prepared. One officer asked me how I put up with getting screamed at during cadet school. I grew up with it—my dad was a screamer—so I was used to it. But if you're not accustomed to being cussed at or told that you're useless, etc. [all basic training tactics at cadet school], you don't need to be there. Because you won't make it."

"I know what's it going to be like," said a female cadet fresh out of patrol school. "I'll be the only female stationed in my area, so I'll be in the limelight. Some of the people I'll be working with have never even seen a trooper before. So I'm gonna be watched. I'll do the best job I can, but I'm nervous about it."

"Right now," said another female trooper, "it's still a man's world on the highway patrol. You're the lowest there is. As a result, you must have more confidence in yourself than you've ever had before. And you have to grin and bear it—no matter what."

While a growing number of male troopers are beginning to realize that women patrol officers will add to—not detract from—the overall strength of the North Carolina Highway Patrol, there are still plenty of hard-core antifeminists in the organization who are unhappy with the new direction the patrol is taking.

"There's a place in law enforcement for women, but I don't think it's on the road," said one fifteen-year veteran. "I haven't accepted the fact that we must have female officers. There are too many dangers they simply can't handle—physically, mentally, or emotionally. If I call for help, I want someone who can deliver when they get there, because I don't call for help unless it's a bad situation. When it happens, I don't want someone with me I have to wonder about—can they handle it or can't they?"

"The thing that concerns me about women officers," said another male trooper, "is their safety. Because of a woman's physical makeup, a group of men are more apt to resist arrest and give them trouble. I also worry about a female trooper getting raped on the road and having it reported in the newspapers. That wouldn't look too good for the patrol."

Interestingly enough, both men admit they've never worked with a female trooper and have heard nothing but praise for the three women officers who patrol in their district.

"If we're going to put women on the patrol, let's help them do well," said a retired highway patrol captain. "I think it's bad management, for example, to send them to isolated rural places where they are not easily accepted and have no backup help. There are numerous other areas where they could do a good job and be happy. I'm not saying it's deliberately done by the entire patrol but it's likely there are one or two people in management who've said, 'Let's throw them out there and they'll quit.' "

Whether the patrol likes it or not, however, female troopers are here to stay. In 1972, Title VII of the Civil Rights Act outlawed discrimination in employment on the basis of race, sex, color, or creed. Congress then extended the law to include state and local agencies. Police forces around the country—many with deeply embedded attitudes about male superiority—could barely contain their distaste for the new ruling. Yet, as upholders of the law, they were forced to comply.

In 1979, a recruiter position was established in the North Carolina Highway Patrol to enlist females and minorities. Currently, there is one member in each of the patrol's eight troop districts whose specific role is to seek out qualified applicants.

Leah has already been informed that, along with her regular duties as a trooper, she'll be required to spend two days a week traveling throughout her district for recruiting purposes. She says she will do her best to explain the job, its risks, its hazards, and its rewards, as realistically as possible.

"What people need to realize most is that, as women troopers, we're just doing our job," she said. "We're not trying to prove anything or be something we're not."

A little more tolerance and understanding from the general public would go a long way in helping all women law enforcement officers gain the respect they deserve, adds Trooper Dee Parton:

I stopped a lady on the interstate one morning for speeding.

"What'd you stop me for?" she snapped.

"I clocked you at seventy-two miles per hour in a fifty-five-mile-per-hour zone."

"Well, that's really something. Here I am on my way to an Equal Rights Amendment rally and I get pulled over by a lady officer! Can't you give me a break?"

"No, ma'am."

"You mean, I'm trying to stand up for your rights and you're still going to write me a ticket?"

"Yes, ma'am," I said. "Because, just like you, I've got a job to do."

7
Badgers & Skirt-Chasers

"There's an international signal for meeting a woman on the road. She taps her brakes twice and if the trooper has been on patrol more than a year or two, he knows to return the same signal. Then he stops and waits for her to come back."

—A veteran trooper

Aside from women officers, there's another, entirely different type of female who's part of the highway patrol. Troopers call them "badgers," an unkind term used for women who are so drawn to men in uniform they'll use any ploy to gain an officer's attention.

Not that highway patrolmen are unwitting victims who go kicking and screaming into the arms of predatory females. Quite the contrary. In fact, troopers have long harbored a reputation as womanizers. Old-timers tell of "breaking in" patrol cars by engaging in sex in the back seat, keeping tallies on the number of women they encounter on the road, and illicit meetings both on and off duty between troopers and willing females. A few women have their own stories to tell about getting stopped and propositioned by a highway patrolman.

However, today's trooper believes the image of the highway patrol officer as an indiscriminate ladies' man and the availability of "badgers" are vastly overplayed. More than a few patrolmen say that many of the tales involving sexual shenanigans on patrol are exaggerated versions of somebody's wishful thinking.

The truth is probably somewhere in between. Realistically, troopers are no more likely to be involved in back-street affairs than bankers, lawyers, or anyone else who works daily with the public. In all fairness, many highway patrolmen are conservative, family-oriented individuals who flatly refuse to engage in any type of misconduct on the job and resent it when troopers as a whole are categorized as "skirt-chasers."

Yet there's no denying that a combination of low supervision on the job, law enforcement's macho reputation, and the clean-cut appearance of a well-groomed trooper in uniform help attract the opposite sex.

There's also no denying that certain women, in certain situations, can spell big trouble for a highway patrolman.

The warnings begin in cadet school.

"We're told that if the skirt rises higher, you can look," explained one rookie, "but you better keep writing that ticket."

"They pump it into your head that every woman you stop is going to make a pass at you," said a trooper with two years on the patrol. "I'm still waiting for that to happen."

When it does, the propositions are seldom explicit. But it doesn't take a genius to read between the lines.

One trooper remembers his sense of discomfort when faced with such a situation:

I stopped a girl for speeding on her way back from the beach. It was a summer day and she was wearing a bikini. I asked for her driver's license and registration.

"You're not gonna give me a ticket, are you?" she said.

"Yes ma'am, I am."

Then she told me she worked for a group of attorneys and asked if I had ever heard of them.

"No, I can't say that I have."

I instructed her to sit there for about five minutes while I returned to my patrol car to write up the citation. When I went back to hand her the ticket she had taken off her bikini top.

"Would this make a difference?" she said.

"No, not right now, ma'am. Would you please sign this citation?"

She did, but left in a huff. At that point, she was probably embarrassed. I know I was.

Troopers who yield to advances on the job—or who instigate them—run the risk of automatic dismissal if knowledge of the incident makes it way to highway patrol headquarters. Rules regarding an officer's conduct are clearly defined and strictly enforced.

An incident too serious to be handled on a local level, such as an officer making sexual advances to a female he has arrested, is turned over to Internal Affairs and a full investigation conducted. The officer in question is notified and offered a chance to give his side of the story. If the evidence warrants disciplinary action, the trooper is either fired, suspended till further notice, or—in some cases—hastily transferred to another county or district.

Another factor that makes fooling around especially risky for highway patrolmen is the lack of privacy inherent in their jobs. Within the community in which he lives, there's no such thing as an anonymous trooper.

"If John Q. Public gets caught having an affair with his secretary, a few of his co-workers may know it," said one officer. "But if a trooper gets caught, it makes front page news."

By its very nature, however, law enforcement attracts people who thrive on risk and excitement. And people are fallible, especially where sex is concerned. As a result, when opportunity meets with temptation on the highway patrol, troopers are just as human as the rest of us:

> You're away from the house at night, you're always meeting new people, and you don't have to explain your time. Then there's the uniform. It's an icebreaker.
>
> You can say almost anything in uniform and get away with it. Things you can't say in civilian clothes because you'd look like a jerk or like you're trying to pick up a girl.
>
> You say things and she doesn't know if you mean it or not—but you really do. She also knows you're "safe," not some weirdo she's likely to catch a disease from.

> There are many reasons women go for the uniform. I think the main one is because they believe there's something macho about men in uniform. Also, men's dress and demeanor have changed in the past decade. We're an organization that promotes a clean-cut, neat appearance and a lot of women no longer like men with beards, long hair, and unkempt clothes.
>
> And who else is out in the middle of the night other than the milkman and a patrolman? Besides, a woman knows the trooper won't tell anyone about it because if he does, he'll lose his job.

> Badgers are worse in small counties. If you're a young trooper, the women literally chase you around. I've had mothers, daughters, mothers and daughters *together* after me. In places like that, where there's

nothing else to do for entertainment, the women will run you crazy. You realize it's the uniform they like and after a while you learn to accept it as part of the job.

The opportunities are out there, no doubt about it. You get the phone calls, the remarks, the flirtatious looks.

A girl I had given a ticket to kept calling my house. Finally, my wife answered the phone and told her, "If it's the uniform you want, he has six hanging in the closet. I'll be glad to give you one."

I remember one woman in a rural county who always came through our traffic checks with her blouse pulled up. Another was so bad about wanting to get stopped by a trooper that she deliberately busted the headlights on her car. When we'd walk up to ask for her driver's license, she'd show us a picture of herself in the nude. Her husband would fix the headlight but next time she was out, she'd bust it again so she could keep getting stopped. She just loved us to death.

I know a first sergeant who was always telling me, "If I see you on duty with a woman, I'll fire you or have you transferred."

Then one Friday night he was speeding through the county and wrecked. He had a woman with him.

My point is that troopers aren't the only ones who get into those kinds of situations. It happens throughout the ranks. At meetings you'll hear supervisors stand up and say, "All right, boys. If you're gonna do anything, be discreet. Don't get caught with your zipper down."

He is addressing his remarks to everyone in the room, including himself.

You could always tell when a trooper had had a woman in his car. You looked in the back and—

hell, it hadn't rained in two months—but there's his raincoat on the seat. That's what he'd use to hide his girlfriend.

I know a trooper who got caught with a woman after another officer walked up on them.

"I'll have your job for this," the officer said.

So the trooper went home and woke up his wife.

"Honey," he said, "I just found the prettiest piece of property you ever laid eyes on. Let's go look at it right now."

It was the middle of the night, but somehow he convinced her to go with him. He took her up to the place where he'd been caught a few minutes earlier.

When the complaint came through, he told his superiors, "But that was my wife! I took her to show her some property."

As far as I know, he got out of that one and is still on the highway patrol. But I don't know if he's still married.

I don't think the "womanizing" is as common as it used to be. Some of the older troopers, for instance, would say that if you got a new patrol car, it was bad luck if you didn't break it in with a woman. I'm sure a lot of that was idle talk.

But now, we stay so busy you wouldn't have time to do anything like that even if you wanted to. I've set things up while I was working—arranged to meet someone later—but I've been too scared to actually try anything on the job. It's just not worth the risk.

I met a girl who worked with us in law enforcement. She'd flirt with all of the troopers but most of them just let it slide. With me, though, she kept on and on. I finally agreed to see her one night while I was on duty.

We arranged a meeting at a deserted pull-off near the beach.

I'm not very big on doing things like that in the car because I knew somebody could come along. So I said, "Let's pretend you're stranded and I'm helping you." She put the hood up on her car and I unhooked my blue light so it wouldn't attract attention.

Then we had another problem. She was wearing slacks. I knew that wasn't going to work because you can't have your pants off if someone drives by.

So I told her, "Here, I've got a pair of pull-on shorts in my gym bag. Put those on."

After that, we proceeded to have a big time—kind of on the car, over the car, so we could watch for anybody coming by.

I met her two or three times after that. And I worried about it.

I thought, "Somehow I'm gonna get caught. And if I get caught, I'll be fired." Because I probably would have. It was stupid. A stupid thing to do.

You overhear a trooper tell a story about a woman he met on patrol and the next week you hear another officer repeating the story to someone else, only he adds a few details. That's how one little incident turns into a big deal.

I'd say women are definitely a main subject among troopers. The guys will say, "Hey, have you been by so-and-so's store? There's a good-looking girl working there."

We pass tips like that along to each other. But we try to keep it respectful. Most of us have a high regard for women.

I was called to witness a breathalyzer test one night for a young woman. The first test went over the legal limit and the arresting officer left the room to wait the required time for the second reading.

This girl, early twenties, very attractive, came over to the cabinet where I was standing and said, "Isn't there something you can do?"

I played dumb and said, "What do you mean?"

"Well, I know you guys can manipulate these tests to make them read whatever you want. I'll do anything, *anything*."

By now she was standing three inches from my face and looking right at me. I knew exactly what she was talking about.

I was tempted, but I remembered what my training officer told me when I first came on the patrol.

"This badge can get you a lot of women," he said. "But it just takes one piece of ass to get the badge."

When I first got to Robbinsville, I was twenty-three, single, and almost every teenage girl in the county would call me or knock on my door. I was the "new blood" in town.

But I'd just gotten engaged and thought, "Well, this is a place where everybody knows everybody else, so if I do something now, I know that before long, it'll be all over town."

That's what kept me straight.

Another trooper and I were working one night and decided to go by my house in order to meet two girls. At the time, we were the only two patrolmen on duty in any of the three counties around us.

We turned on the TV, fixed some popcorn, and were waiting on these girls to arrive when we heard a car pull into the driveway.

"I guess they're here," I told the other trooper, and went to the door.

There stood two troopers from two counties away, out of their district, who were also on duty.

They had sneaked off the job, knew where to find

the key to my house since we were friends, and came by to see if *they* could meet two girls.

So they caught us and we caught them.

Several years before I came on the highway patrol, there was a young woman I wanted to date. I thought she was beautiful but she wouldn't give me the time of day. I tried a number of times to get to know her but she wouldn't even say hello to me.

I'd been on patrol about three years when I clocked a car one night running about seventy miles per hour.

I walked up and asked for a driver's license. There sat this same girl—with her blouse opened all the way down to her waist, nothing on underneath.

She didn't recognize me at first, just thought I was another trooper.

I took her license number, went back to the patrol car, and positioned myself at the front of it, so she could see me writing the ticket. By the time I got back to her and handed her the citation, she had that blouse buttoned all the way up to her chin.

I said, "You don't remember me, do you?" as I gave her the ticket. "I tried to go out with you years ago and you'd have nothing to do with me. Now here you sit, exposing yourself, when you don't know me from Adam."

She left after that, with very little to say.

Two troopers on duty met two girls one night at an abandoned road near a railroad crossing. They parked parallel to the railroad, one behind the other.

The trooper in the back heard a train coming, panicked, and got out of his patrol car with nothing on but a T-shirt and a hat, went up to the other patrol car, and began "checking" for a license.

Afraid somebody on the train would see him fooling around in the car, he wanted to make it look as "official" as possible. But all he managed to look was ridiculous.

I know a trooper who had a girl with him when her husband drove by. As the man was turning around to come back, the trooper put the girl in the trunk of his car. About that time, his first sergeant called on the radio and told him to meet him, so he had to take off. The poor woman had to stay in the trunk until the conference with the sergeant was over. Fortunately, it was winter. So at least she had a warm place to hide.

I've found this to be a good policy. If you're going to stop a woman who's alone, be sure to write her a ticket for something, even a warning ticket. Don't give her a verbal warning, because if she files a complaint, accuses you of coming on to her, or anything of that nature, at least you'll have some evidence to back you up.

Women will chase you, but only if you want to be chased. I know a trooper who met a girl at the same time every night. Me and one of the local deputies would hide and watch them. We weren't spotted because we were smarter than they were.

He never got caught and we never told on him. There are a few things I would tell on a trooper, but that's not one of them. I don't care what he does on the side, as long as he leaves my wife or girlfriend alone.

It's more image than anything else, this whole idea of women coming on to men in uniform.

It makes some troopers go crazy. Swells their head. Sends them on an ego trip. They've come from nobody out on the street, then they get in this patrol car, rub shoulders with attorneys, judges, politicians, and other big shots who might not otherwise give them the time of day.

A lot of them begin to think they are "Mr. Wonderful." Then they find out it's just the uniform that people are impressed with, and that's when they take the big fall.

8
Wives & Widows

"If anything happened to my husband, it would be hard for me to marry another trooper. I've gone through so much with him and the patrol, I'm not sure I could do it again.

—Highway patrol wife, married four years

Worrying about "badgers" is only one of the problems highway patrol wives face once they marry a state trooper. Many of them learn to accept the idea that other women are attracted to their husbands in uniform and don't allow it to disturb them. Others have more immediate, day-to-day concerns that must be dealt with first: who's going to care for the couple's sick infant, for instance, when she has to work and he needs to sleep after a night on patrol. How to explain attending her son's high school graduation alone. What to do when the basement floods and he can't be reached. Then there's the scheduling; she's working days and he's working nights. When he wants sex, she's dead to the world, and vice versa. She wants to go out and he wants to stay in. On weekends she's off, but he's still on duty and won't be free till the middle of the week. So little time, so many demands.

Even in the strongest of civilian relationships, conflicts are inevitable. But in trooper marriages, the pressures are likely to be greater and the discord more intense. That may explain why highway patrol officers, along with law enforcement personnel in general, have one of the highest divorce rates in the country.

"We know there's resentment among wives and families because of what we do," said a ten-year trooper. "In my opinion, this isn't a job for a married man. If you are married, you've got to have a really special relationship just to keep it going." He says out of his half-dozen closest trooper friends, all but one are divorced.

Yet wives have always been and always will be an integral part of the highway patrol. In the organization's early years, trooper wives were expected to wash, starch, and iron their husband's uniforms because there was no money allotted to the officers for dry cleaning. They also served as secretaries, relaying messages between the highway patrol and their husbands. Often they were awakened in the middle of the night to cook meals when a trooper brought his colleagues home to unwind. Moving from town to town whenever their husbands were transferred, these women not only reared their children virtually alone, but managed a household on trooper salaries that seldom exceeded $500 a month—even as late as 1966.

Today, there's a "new breed" of trooper wife. The modern highway patrol wife is more independent, less involved in her husband's work, and more likely to have a career of her own which, in its own way, may be just as stressful as his. Unfortunately for her, she still carries the major share of responsibility for running the house and rearing the children.

"It's the daily routine that gets to you," said a full-time teacher who's been married to a trooper for seven years.

"Sometimes I feel like I have to do everything, from organizing birthday parties for the kids to getting the car fixed."

Nor does she feel free to call her husband on duty whenever a problem arises. In seven years, she's phoned him only four times on the job.

"People I work with can pick up the phone and call their spouse any hour of the day for any little thing. But when I call Jim, I can't talk to him directly. I have to contact the telecommunications center and leave a message to have him call me back. So I feel like everyone who has a radio scanner in our part of the state knows my husband is supposed to call home. It makes me hesitant about calling him on the job, even when it's important."

The biggest adjustment for most of these women, however, is the loneliness.

"It began immediately," said a highway patrol wife recalling her days as a newlywed. "I'd come home from work at four-thirty and if he had to begin patrol at three that day, our paths never crossed for a week at a time. Having just gotten married, it was really hard for me. It's still hard, but we have the kids now and I've found a lot of things to do that keep me busy."

Before the federal government passed a law in 1985 limiting the number of hours certain public employees could work, it was not unusual for troopers to patrol seventy hours a week with no overtime pay, a situation that did little to improve conditions at home.

"We were stationed in Wilkes County," said a trooper wife, married twenty-five years, "and there were lots of times he would be called out on patrol when he was off duty. One night was particularly bad. Every time he'd get into bed the phone would ring and he'd be sent out on another wreck. It was near daylight when the phone rang for about the fifth time. He was trying to put his socks on when I said, 'Honey, are you sorry you joined the patrol?' I could tell he hadn't slept and was dead tired.

" 'Hell, no,' he said. He finished dressing and went out the door."

This same wife admits there were times through the years she asked her husband, "Do you love the patrol better than me?" And he'd always say, "I married you, didn't I?" Eventually, she realized she'd have to settle for that.

One young trooper told his wife point blank that the highway patrol was the number one priority in his life, he was number two, and she came in a close third. Then something happened that changed his way of thinking.

"I had to go to a bridal shower that day," his wife recalled, "and he was supposed to get off at 5:00 P.M. I fixed his supper, put it in the microwave, and left. I got home about eleven-thirty that night and he still hadn't come in. I hardly ever call the station but I was worried about him, so I called the highway patrol office and asked 'Where's Terry?'

" 'Who is this?' the telecommunicator wanted to know.

" 'It's his wife.'

" 'I'm not sure where he is.'

"I knew something was going on and my heart was nearly jumping out of my chest.

" 'But he got off at 5:00 P.M.,' I said. 'Now where is he?'

"She put me on hold, then came back on the line and told me Terry was on his way to the sheriff's office and should be home soon. I went to bed but couldn't sleep. By 1:30 A.M. he still wasn't home. Finally, at two, he came in, shaking all over. I'd never seen him like that.

"He'd been on a routine traffic check when a pickup truck went by at a high speed. Terry went after the truck in his patrol car but the driver veered into a cornfield and he had to get out and follow on foot. A young boy was driving. As he saw Terry running towards him, he turned the truck around and tried to run over him. He made two or three attempts, nearly hitting Terry each time.

"Terry pulled his gun and shot at the tires until the boy gave up and wrecked. Other officers arrived to help make the arrest, and that's when Terry learned the guy had just killed his mother and stepfather and was running from the scene of the crime. The boy kept saying, 'I wanted to kill that trooper,' referring to Terry. And we know that he would have.

"After that, I had trouble sleeping until Terry got home from work. It took me two or three months to get over it."

Nearly losing his life—plus the shooting death of a fellow officer (Trooper Giles Harmon)—made Terry realize that something could happen to him on patrol. He began to rethink his priorities.

"Now he tells me that God is first in his life," says his wife. "I'm second, he is third, and the highway patrol comes fourth."

Another patrol wife recalls seeing a television station flash the news that a trooper had been shot and killed in the same vicinity her husband was patrolling. No names or details were given.

"I was on the couch when the news report came and I got so scared I couldn't move, even to get to the telephone. In a situation like that, you just lie there wondering what you're going to do if this or that happens. Then you hear the back door open and he comes in. And you want to wring his neck for not calling."

Some women are familiar with the risks and problems associated with a trooper's job before they marry into the patrol. But it doesn't seem to stop them.

She is the epitome of the cool, elegant blonde. He's the classic "tall, dark, and handsome." They met in the emergency room where she was a nurse and where he, as a trooper, accompanied accident victims. On her part, it was hate at first sight.

"I didn't like him at all. I thought he was arrogant, showy, and into numbers when it came to women."

For months, she refused to date him.

"I was at a low point, having just broken up with someone, and wasn't really interested in getting involved.

Then a friend invited me to a birthday party and that's where David and I finally got to know each other. I was surprised at how intelligent and sensitive he was. I guess I was intrigued by him. And I had respect for the patrol. I knew those guys were real professionals."

Within a few months they were engaged. Both were twenty-seven, but she says he still had some growing up to do.

"He was immature," she says, "and because of it got into a few problems on the job. For one thing, he was too aggressive. At times, I wasn't sure who was right—him, the patrol, or the public. A month before we got married, he got into a nasty fight. I was working that day and had gone to the cafeteria for lunch. Halfway there, I got paged to go back to the emergency room. There was David, bleeding, his clothes torn off.

"He had gotten into a motorcycle chase and a fight and as a result was accused of police brutality. It was all over the TV that night and in the newspapers. It was awful. And I thought, 'Is this what I'm in for?'

"But David was having a hard time too. His sergeant came to the emergency room, walked in, and without saying a word to me, asked David what happened. He wasn't the least bit sympathetic. Just seemed worried about how it was going to look for the patrol."

Now married seven years, this wife says she has no regrets about her decision and has come to appreciate the highway patrol and the service it provides.

"It's getting to be a good career," she said. "But I think it takes a special breed of man to be a highway patrolman and a special breed of woman to be married to one. I don't mind being put in that category."

Not everyone shares her view.

"The highway patrol almost wrecked my life," maintains a thirty-year-old trooper wife.

She met her husband at a college dance in 1978. By the time they were seriously dating, he was considering the highway patrol as a career.

"I was hoping he'd go for a nine-to-five job," she recalls, "and I really didn't think anything would come of this patrol business." When it did, she was already emotionally involved in the relationship and says it was "too late" to back out. They were married after he graduated from patrol school and sent to a small town in the western part of the state.

She disliked both the people and the area.

"I had a degree in nursing, but the place didn't have a hospital or a doctor's office, so I had to drive an hour to and from work in order to keep a job."

Her husband often patrolled the region's back roads alone, with little or no help if trouble arose.

"During that time, I had a lot of nightmares about him coming into the hospital on a stretcher."

On the few occasions when their schedules allowed them time together, there was nowhere to go and little to do in the isolated town. Restaurants and theatres were sixty miles away. So were most of their family and friends.

Then he was transferred to a large city and things improved. She moved up in her career field and he found troopers who welcomed him into their circle. They bought a house and settled down.

Two years later they had a child, and new problems emerged.

"After the baby was born, I realized that if something happened to my husband, I'd be a single parent. So the possibility of his getting hurt became even more frightening. But the worst part was the hours. The highway patrol doesn't budge on the hours a trooper works, so the wife has to accommodate to his schedule. That means when I was working opposite shifts from him, or his hours changed suddenly, I had to find someone to keep our little girl. And it caused a lot of problems."

In a fit of anger, she insisted her husband do something about it.

"I told him he would have to speak to his sergeant and explain to him that I can't always be the one to call work and ask them to change my hours, or excuse me from the job because of child care. After all, I went to school and was trying to build a career too. The highway patrol doesn't seem to understand that. So it got to the point where we argued a lot about who was going to keep her and who was going to get up early and take her to the sitter, etc. I felt like he was leaving too much of that responsibility to me."

She also resented his staying out past his regular shift—especially when it involved no overtime pay.

"If he wasn't home when he was supposed to be, I couldn't sleep, wondering if he was hurt or where he was. Then I'd have to get up at 5:00 A.M. and go to work."

To trade off baby-sitting chores, this couple worked opposite shifts for more than a year, seldom seeing each other except in passing. Not surprisingly, they grew further and further apart.

"You lose a sense of communication and that's when the family breaks down," said her husband. "If you don't see each other long enough to even talk about your problems, it's hard to work them out."

They were on the verge of a separation when she was offered a job that gave her better, more stable hours, alleviating some of the pressure. Today, she still isn't crazy about the highway patrol, but she realizes her husband wouldn't be happy doing anything else.

"I would never ask him to quit, because he loves it so much. And even if my marriage doesn't work out in the future, I wouldn't trade these years for anything."

Every trooper wife, young or old, must live with the possibility that she could suddenly become a widow. Some women have resigned themselves to the fact their husbands face special risks on the job and refuse to dwell on it. Others take a philosophical attitude and decide that whatever happens will happen, and there isn't much they can do about it. Then there are women who never get over the worry.

Edna was one of those wives.

"If he's an hour or two late, you walk the floor and wring

your hands because you know something's wrong. Even after I was a trooper wife for many years, I didn't get to the place where I accepted it. I knew he was out there working with criminal elements and that something could happen anytime."

She would be proven all too right.

Dean and Edna Arledge had been married ten years when Dean became a trooper. A former hosiery mill employee, he had always admired the highway patrol and would, while driving, remark to his family, "If I was a trooper, I'd pull that guy over." At age thirty-one, he joined the organization. If he'd waited another year, he was told, he'd have been too old to qualify.

Edna had mixed reactions to her husband's newfound career. During an interview as part of Dean's acceptance into the patrol, she was questioned by a sergeant who asked if she agreed to her husband becoming a trooper.

"No, not really. I wish he wouldn't," she said.

"Well, at least you're honest," he replied.

"At that time [1951], the troopers weren't paid for going to school," she recalled, "so it was financially tough. We had two school-age children and I had to work to help support us. I only saw him once during the entire summer he was in training. He did okay in school, but it was harder than he thought. Two nights before graduation he called and said they had sent two boys home.

" 'I don't know if I'm going to make it or not,' he said. 'Maybe I'll just catch the next bus out of here.'

"I knew he was worried and tired, but that if he gave up, I wouldn't be able to live with him.

" 'Honey,' I said, 'if you get on that bus, don't get off here in Tryon. Just keep going.'

"He was all right after that and finished the course. We went down for graduation and I remember seeing him in his uniform for the first time. It was a disappointment. They couldn't afford to issue new outfits, so everybody had to wear old uniforms that had been turned in. None of them fit right and they had slick spots on the knees.

"Then we learned where we were being assigned. When they announced, 'Ronda, North Carolina, in Wilkes County,' I looked at Dean and he was shaking his head. I didn't know where Ronda, North Carolina, was, but I had a sneaking idea it was somewhere we didn't want to be."

Edna says the highway patrol knew what they were doing, however, for Ronda was a one-horse town between Elkin and North Wilkesboro that desperately needed a trooper.

"The town had requested a patrol officer and I think Dean's superiors recognized that with his even temper and fair-minded ways, he would be a good person to send."

A sturdy man who stood six feet tall, Dean was well regarded by everyone who knew him.

A friend remembers him as the type of person "who could give his own grandmother a ticket and make her like it."

Edna admired his fun-loving nature and zest for living.

Not that everything was peachy-keen during their thirty-four-year marriage. Edna refers to her husband's first duty station as "the town where I served my sentence."

In the early fifties, Ronda was a wide place in the road with a church, a school, a general store, a filling station, and a chair factory. Locals grew tobacco to earn a living, and opportunities for women were as rare as the visitors who moseyed through town.

"I finally landed a job working for an attorney in the county courthouse," said Edna, "but I had to drive twenty-five miles each way."

With her husband's salary barely topping $225 per month, and two young children to help support, she had little choice but to work.

New at being a trooper wife, Edna was startled by the attitudes she encountered.

"I was the same ole gal I had always been, and Dean hadn't really changed. He had just learned to be a law enforcement officer. But people suddenly didn't like us because we were 'the law.' "

The long hours and crazy shifts brought troubles too.

"We couldn't do things together as a couple, so if I went to a church social, it was always, 'Where's Dean? What's going on with you two?' It was hard to get it through their heads that he was working."

Even worse, Edna says, were the reactions her children experienced.

"There were kids who didn't want to play with our kids because there was a lot of 'Your daddy arrested our uncle for so-and-so.' You could tell they didn't want any part of us. And you didn't have time to really cultivate friendships or be a part of everything going on in the community."

Since Dean was the only patrol officer stationed in the county, Edna also lacked the support another trooper wife could have provided.

Still, she struggled through, and in 1955 Trooper Arledge and his family were transferred to Buncombe County. Dean was promoted to sergeant, and Edna became active in the North Carolina Highway Patrol State Auxiliary, an organization for trooper wives that bears the motto, "The Women Behind the Men Behind the Badge."

Though she had learned to deal with the frustrations of being a trooper wife, Edna never conquered her fears for her husband's safety.

"Dean wouldn't talk about his work because he wanted to protect me. And I had sense enough not to ask."

Saturday, October 5, 1974, began as a normal day for the Arledges. Their daughter, Charlotte, now grown with a baby of her own, was staying the weekend, much to the delight of her parents.

About 3:00 P.M., Dean began preparing for work while Charlotte put the baby down for a nap. An immaculate man, he always waited till the last minute to slip on his long-sleeved uniform shirt so he wouldn't wrinkle or stain it. Besides, he had one more thing to do before he finished dressing.

Slipping into the baby's room, he leaned over the crib,

picked up his sleeping grandson, and carried him into the living room.

"This is my boy," he said, patting the infant's back. He turned to Edna and handed her the baby.

"Here honey, you take care of him for me."

A few minutes later, as he was leaving, Edna asked what he wanted for Sunday dinner.

"Charlotte loves round roast," he answered. "Why don't you fix that?"

Dean then kissed her good-bye, and went out the door. It would be their last conversation.

"His supper hour was between 7:00 and 8:00 P.M. and we had an understanding that if he wasn't home within half an hour of the time he was supposed to be, not to look for him," she said. "So as it got closer to 7:00 P.M., I waited. I began thinking about the leftovers I could fix for supper. Charlotte's husband was planning to fly to Washington the next day and she had gone home for a while. I decided to go to the store and pick up what we needed for Sunday dinner. As I was heading back, I noticed a patrol car behind me and thought, 'Good, Dean's coming home after all.' I pulled into the carport and the patrol car pulled in too. Then I saw another one. And a third one.

"I was standing there with a bag of groceries in my hand and was just about to say, 'What do you think we're running here, a motel?' when I saw the lieutenant step out of his car.

"I remember saying, 'How bad is he hurt?' and thinking, 'I want to go help him wherever he is.' They were trying to tell me he was dead, but it took them the longest time to convince me it was true."

In a daze, Edna entered the house and called Charlotte at home.

"As I was talking to my son-in-law on the phone, I could hear Charlotte crying in the background, 'Not my daddy! Not my daddy!' By the time she got to the house, several troopers were here. My other daughter, Deanna, arrived later. The officers stayed through the evening. The man who shot Dean was still at large so the patrol made a point of protecting us."

Dean had stopped a fifty-four-year-old man on Interstate 40 for drunk driving shortly after 7:00 P.M. About ten minutes later he arrived at the Buncombe County courthouse in Asheville and took the driver, identified as Edward Collins Davis, into the breathalyzer room, where fellow trooper Lawrence Canipe was to administer the test.

No one knows exactly what happened next except that three loud noises sounding "like doors slamming" were heard around 7:50 P.M. When the troopers failed to report their whereabouts, another officer went looking for them and found the door to the breathalyzer room locked. He got a key, turned the handle, and stepped inside.

What he saw appalled him.

Dean was kneeling against the desk. Trooper Canipe was facedown on the floor, his .357 Magnum missing from its holster, along with a watch that had been jerked from his wrist. Both men had been shot in the back at close range. (Later, the defense would argue that Dean had been killed accidentally when he interfered in a struggle between Davis and Trooper Canipe over the officer's gun.)

Davis, who had fled the building on foot, was captured the next morning. Five months later, he was sentenced to death by a jury who found him guilty on two counts of first degree murder. The execution never took place. Instead, Davis's sentence was commuted to two consecutive life terms, leading to a final twist in the case that left Edna and her children understandably bitter.

"I started getting letters from Davis in prison," she said. "Even his wife wrote, wanting to come and see me. They were looking for my sympathy, but all it accomplished was to make my adjustment to Dean's death even harder. Imagine his wife wanting to see me. What could we possibly have in common?"

Through highway patrol efforts, the letter writing was stopped, while troopers and their wives offered Edna moral support.

"They did everything they could to help me."

Today, she is still a steadfast member of the state auxiliary for trooper wives and lives alone with her memories of Dean and the highway patrol.

"It's lonely," she admits. "I don't expect it to be otherwise."

Her advice to a young woman about to become a trooper wife is simple and direct.

"You must have plenty of love, understanding, and stamina. Because he's probably going to be married to the patrol. So the bottom line is that you have to love him enough to put up with it."

Other trooper wives—all with stories of their own—agree:

> There are two things you have to do to survive as a highway patrol wife. First, you don't think about the bad stuff, the dangers, the women, and all. And second, you learn to build your own life. You get involved with your children and their lives. You get a job, make your own friends. Because if you don't, the patrol will eat you up.

> The worst part for me is all of the abuse my kids have gotten because their father is a highway patrolman. My son has been in several fights because someone called his daddy "pig." We've even had people come into the yard and slash the tires on the patrol car, or come to the door unannounced to ask questions. And when we all go out together in public and he's in uniform, we get looks, as though people are saying to him, "You're not supposed to have a family." It's like troopers aren't human or don't have feelings. It's not a normal way to live.

> What surprised me most about the highway patrol was the closeness troopers feel for each other when there's a crisis, and the pettiness they show over silly

things. There are certain times in the year when an unmarked car comes around [for the troopers to use] and it's always a matter of "Who's gonna get it this time? Who's pulled the right strings? Who's the favorite child?" They're like little kids fighting over a new toy.

People want to look at you as Trooper So-and-So's wife. That doesn't set well with me because I know who I am and how I want people to know me. I have my own friends who are not associated with the patrol. And I am not active in the auxiliary—which I've avoided on purpose. I got into it at first but I lost too many friends through divorce and once you're divorced on the patrol, it's like no one else is supposed to be friends with you anymore. So I separate myself from all of that and lead my own life.

If any woman tells you she's never felt threatened by the fact that other women are attracted to her husband in uniform, don't believe it. It's a very common reaction among trooper wives, and one of the more aggravating things we have to deal with. When I was young, it upset me something terrible every time my husband got phone calls from girls he had given tickets to. One time it went on for days on end. Now it's more of a nuisance than anything else.

I've always said of the women who come on to him, I wish they could see him first thing in the morning. Or do his laundry for about a week. Maybe then they could see past his uniform.

It seems like the public goes out of its way to see if they can catch a trooper doing something wrong. I was coming home from my mother's one day and my husband stopped me. He was standing there talking to me on the side of the road, and the next day, we found out someone had called the station and filed a complaint. Another time, he used his supper hour in order to attend a Christmas event for our daughter, and that got back to the patrol station too. So you have to constantly be on guard.

I'm proud of my husband's role as a highway patrolman, especially the things he does the public never knows about. One night he called from the courthouse at 2:00 A.M. and wanted to know if he could bring a teenage girl home. I asked him what happened.

"She's a runaway," he said. "And she's only fifteen. If I don't take her somewhere she'll have to spend the night in jail."

So I told him to bring her home, and I made a bed on the couch. We fed her and took care of her until her parents came to pick her up the next day.

Another time, a boy from Ohio wrecked his car coming through Mrytle Beach and had only five dollars in his pocket. He had spent all his money at the beach. We put him up until his parents could wire him the funds to get home.

Unfortunately, the public never learns about that part of a trooper's work. They only hear the bad things.

What I like about being a trooper's wife is when your kid gets a ticket, at least you know how to handle it.

When my daughter got a speeding ticket, she asked me, "What's Dad going to say?"

"He's going to say, 'Fifty dollars,' and make you pay it," I told her. And that's what he did.

What I dislike most about being married to a trooper is that we have no privacy. We go out to eat and people recognize him and come over and sit down. The next thing you know, they're spending the entire evening discussing the highway patrol. I resent that.

What I like most is that if I'm late for work and I'm speeding down the road and see a trooper I know, I just wave at him because I know he'll give me a break.

I don't worry too much now about other women coming on to my husband. But it was a problem at first. He's very talkative and flirtatious and it took time for me to learn to deal with it. We discussed it—not very calmly either—because I'd rant and rave.

"I'm not doing anything!" he'd say. And I'd come back with, "Well, it doesn't look like it to me!"

We fight like cats and dogs but overall, we've got a good solid marriage and I trust him.

Some troopers worry more about their wives having affairs than the other way around. I can understand how it happens because the guys focus so much of their time and attention on the patrol, it leaves their wives out of the picture. When it does happen, the women usually go outside the patrol, because this organization is a hotbed of gossip. You can't get away with anything and not have somebody find out about it.

My husband and two other troopers went out to a club one night and I got a phone call.

"Do you know where your husband is?" the caller said.

"Yes, I do."

"I don't believe you know what he's doing though. He's having a big time here, dancing and carrying on."

I thanked her and hung up. Then it got to be midnight and I thought, "Where *is* he?" About one-thirty in the morning I heard him tiptoeing in with another trooper. They admitted they had been dancing, but only with some friends of mine from work.

I said, "Look. Number one, I'm not gonna put up with this nonsense. And number two, it looks bad on you guys and the patrol."

They were also accused of getting into a fight that same night. That part of it turned out not to be true, but it shows how closely troopers are watched and judged, even off duty.

I don't like that aspect of the patrol. And I don't want to have to worry about getting any more calls.

My father thinks that because I'm married to a trooper, we can get anything done for him. When my brother got into trouble, my dad called us wanting my husband to get him out of it. He couldn't understand why his trooper son-in-law couldn't "fix it." And it caused some hard feelings. As a result, my husband and my father don't get along anymore.

People don't realize what troopers go through. They say, "Oh, your husband's a highway patrol officer. Rides around all day in a car and hands out tickets."

I lost one of my best friends because she said she wouldn't have anything to do with someone who issued citations and arrested people.

At work, I've heard others say it's unfair that my husband gives out tickets in an unmarked patrol car. But that's not the main thing he does. He's in that unmarked car to catch drunk drivers and to help protect the public. I wish people understood that.

He gets phone calls from girls just wanting to speak to him. It got so bad we finally had to buy an answering machine to screen them out. You can't have an unlisted number either, or take the phone off the hook, because the patrol might need to reach you. It's a pain, but you learn to live with it.

My husband's really honest with me. If a woman comes on to him, or some incident happens, he'll tell me about it—just in case someone else tells me first. I trust him totally because I know it's against his ethics to do anything wrong on the job. So I really don't let the patrolmen's reputation with women bother me.

But I think more things happen than what he tells me.

I don't really know my husband as a trooper on the road. I just know what he's like at home—kind and gentle. But I realize what it's like out there. I have a police scanner and I listen to it because the patrol is such a big part of our lives that I want to be involved in what he's doing, even when it's hard to deal with.

To make a trooper marriage work, you have to be patient, be a good listener, and most of all, be there. When he comes in at midnight, it's like he's getting off at 5:00 P.M. and you have to understand that he needs to relax and unwind.

You're always apprehensive. You do a lot of praying and have a lot of faith the patrol has trained its officers as well as possible. And you come to realize that troopers are not there for any other reason except that they like what they're doing. It gets in their blood and it stays there and there's nothing you can do about it.

It's a perilous thing to love a man in the highway patrol. Because every time he walks out the door to check on duty, it's like a piece of yourself goes with him.

Then one night you're watching TV and a bulletin comes across the screen that a trooper has been shot. And your heart jumps clear into your throat. You don't know if it's him, but you can see him in your mind, lying dead or hurt somewhere. The fear becomes so great that you sit there, rooted to the chair. Even if it isn't him, the chances are good that it's someone you know, or have heard of within the patrol. So it's a very bad feeling either way.

When it's over and you know that he's okay, the cycle starts again. You are aware there'll be a next time and that when it happens, he might not be so lucky.

9

"Trooper Is Down"

"We tend to forget that law enforcement is a dangerous business and that it demands a devotion to public service beyond anything ever asked of most Americans."

—*James J. Kilpatrick*
Washington columnist

It is a trooper and his family's worst nightmare.

What begins as a routine patrol turns suddenly violent when someone pulls out a weapon. Moments later, the officer is down—wounded or dead.

Assaults on law enforcement officers are not uncommon. According to FBI statisics, nearly 62,000 city, county, and state police personnel were assaulted while performing their duties in 1985. Of those, seventy-eight were killed.

Within the North Carolina Highway Patrol, forty-four troopers have died while on patrol, either through accidents or assault. Seventeen of those deaths involved a shooting, three of which occurred less than six months apart in 1985.

When it happens there is shock, anger, and grief within the ranks, followed by a grim determination to find the culprit and bring him to justice.

"Everybody knows that individual better watch out," said one civilian who has no ties to the highway patrol, "because whenever someone does something injurious to a trooper, it's like turning loose a swarm of bees.

I

On March 5, 1985, in the early hours of the morning, 100,000 tons of rock thundered down a mountain in Haywood County some sixty-odd miles from Asheville, North Carolina.

The slide blocked the major east-west twin tunnels heading to and from the North Carolina–Tennessee lines. As a result, the highway was closed for eighteen days and traffic was slowed for months. Before the episode was over, the state would spend more than four million dollars to clean up the mess.

To provide access to and from the state line, a graveled U.S. Forest Service road that bypassed the tunnel was designated as a temporary detour. Department of Transportation (DOT) workers quickly paved the half-mile road, and debris was removed from the mouth of the eastbound tunnel. Westbound traffic was then diverted through the newly opened passage. A twenty-mile-per-hour speed limit was posted around the slide area and traffic began to flow again.

Since it was important to enforce the slower speed limit in order to prevent accidents near the rock slide, DOT requested that the highway patrol maintain two troopers on duty twenty-four hours a day—one moving east and one moving west. On March 20, 1985, troopers throughout western North Carolina were notified of the special assignment and rotating shifts were announced.

The following week, Trooper Giles Harmon received

word that he was scheduled for duty on this stretch of the highway.

Two states away in Lexington, Kentucky, Billy Denton McQueen, Jr., was having run-ins with the law. A volatile young man with a history of aberrant behavior, most of his troubles involved crimes such as burglary, trespassing, and criminal mischief stemming from problems with his ex-wife. After he was charged with kidnapping and harassing her, she moved to Statesville, North Carolina.

In early April, 1985, McQueen decided to pay her a visit.

On Monday, April 8, Giles Harmon began his special assignment at the rockslide in Haywood County.

"I'm so bored out there I can't stand it!" he told his wife, Melinda, that night. "All we do is ride up and down the highway. I want to *work.*"

At one point, desperate for something to do, he pulled onto the shoulder of the road, reread his motor vehicle manual, and thought back to the series of events that had led him to the highway patrol.

Ever since he was twelve years old, he knew he wanted to be a state trooper. Growing up in Brevard, North Carolina, he would watch for patrol cars to pass, hop on his bike, and follow the black-and-silver cruisers as far as he could go.

"He just had to see what was going on," said his mother, Bonnie, a petite, attractive woman in her early sixties. "There were lots of times patrolmen brought him home from the hospital where he had followed them. He'd sit in their patrol car as long as they'd let him, asking dozens of questions about the radio, the equipment, the work. I know he must have driven them crazy."

One day Giles disappeared and Bonnie got a call from someone at the courthouse.

"Your son is sitting in the back of the courtroom listening to a case that's being tried," said the caller. "And he's hearing things he probably shouldn't be hearing. I'm going to send him home."

An only child, he lived in an eighteen-room motel owned

and operated by his parents. It was here where he learned how to deal with the public, and here where his early values were instilled.

"We kept the cash register unlocked in the lobby, but he never got into it without asking me first," said Bonnie. "And we always insisted he work around the motel. He said there wasn't a kid in Brevard who made as many beds as he did, filled as many drink machines, or raked as many leaves."

A handsome boy with a sideways grin and a stocky build, Giles was adored by his parents and grew into a happy-go-lucky youth who struck an immediate rapport with almost everyone he met. Active in football, wrestling, and other sports, he maintained good grades through high school and could have been successful in a number of careers. But law enforcement remained his first choice.

To gain some initial experience, he joined the Brevard police department, working first as a telecommunicator, then as a part-time policeman. In 1980, he graduated with a degree in criminal justice from East Tennessee University. Now twenty-one, he was eligible to apply for the job of state trooper.

The only thing that worried him was his height (just over five foot seven) and his nearsightedness. He was afraid both would keep him out of the patrol. He'd already been turned down once because of his vision, but he persuaded a doctor to write a letter telling the patrol his eyesight was correctable by contact lenses and would not hamper his job performance.

In August, 1980, Giles learned that he had been accepted into the highway patrol. Like everyone else who entered cadet school, he found the going rough.

"One weekend he came home and told us about using tear gas during a training exercise," said Bonnie. "Since he wore contacts, the experience was very painful physically. But he wouldn't think of quitting. I told him it was okay to give up if he wanted to—that he had already proven himself by getting into patrol school."

" 'Mother, you *are* kidding, aren't you?' he said."

Once out of training, he was assigned to Buncombe County, where he proved an eager, exuberant rookie.

Patrolman Gib Clements recalls his first meeting with the irrepressible Giles.

"I had just been transferred to Asheville. I was doing a breathalyzer test one night, getting everything set up. There were several troopers in the room.

" 'Is this the way you do it?' I said, off-handedly.

"Giles jumped up.

" 'Here,' he said. 'Let me show you how we do it in Brevard.'

"And he'd only been out of school a week! I looked at him and thought, 'Who the hell are *you?*'

"After I got to know him, I realized he was sincerely trying to help. He was the type of person you couldn't stay mad at for long. If he had to fight a drunk while arresting him, they'd be buddies by the time they got to jail."

"Giles bubbled with enthusiasm," said patrol captain Charles Long, now retired. "He'd come into a room filled with soreheads and the place would light up."

Such praise would normally set the stage for intense rivalry among the tightly knit troopers, but Giles—who wore a smile you couldn't beat off with a hammer—had a way of turning people's attitudes around.

"He was so damned likable," said one officer, "even when he stayed on your ass about something.

" 'Man,' he'd say, 'you smoke too much.'

" 'And you grin too much,' I'd tell him. Which just made him grin all the more."

Tuesday morning, April 9, Giles slept in. Melinda had worked the night before and they had both stayed up late, talking, watching TV, and playing with their dog, a white miniature Eskimo spitz that was a gift from Bonnie.

The couple, married two years, seldom disagreed, but when they did, it always revolved around the highway patrol.

"He wanted to be the best trooper around," explained

Melinda. "It drove me crazy because I knew he was doing so well. But it was, 'I can do better. I can do better.' The first year we were in Buncombe County, he topped everyone else in the number of arrests he made. After that, he began to feel the stress of having to stay on top, which in turn, made him want to try that much harder."

It even affected their plans for the future.

Giles wanted to start a family, but because of his extreme attachment to the highway patrol, Melinda wanted to wait. They'd argue about it; at least Melinda argued. Giles, who hated confrontations, mostly listened.

"It was hard arguing with Giles because he didn't have a temper—which really bugged me. I'd get excited about something and he'd say, 'Don't yell! Let's sit down and talk.'

"He wanted everything to be perfect and smooth all the time. I think that's why he got into so few fights on the road."

Nor did he seem overly concerned with the dangers inherent in his work, though he and Melinda did discuss the possibility that he could be hurt or killed on patrol.

"If anything ever happens to me," he said, "please don't let anybody blame my job. Just tell them I was doing what I loved to do."

Gordon Conner, Giles's training officer, was at the weigh station on Tuesday when Giles drove past on his way to the tunnel. Now in his second day on the new assignment, Giles was scheduled to report by 3:00 P.M. It was already past two-thirty and there was still a long way to go.

"I saw him coming through," said Conner, "but he didn't stop, and I knew he was running late."

Then he heard Giles's voice come over the patrol car radio.

"You think I'm gonna make it?" he said excitedly. "I figure just about a mile a minute!"

Conner grinned. Knowing Giles, he'd be right on time.

The two had met up the night before, and Conner had playfully tapped him on the chest.

"You got that bulletproof vest on?" he said.

"Yeah," Giles answered.

"Well, make sure you wear the damn thing. And be careful."

Assigned to work with Giles Tuesday night was Kurt Casey, a young black trooper from Haywood County who'd been on the highway patrol for five years.

Less than a minute after Casey checked on duty, Giles was calling him on the radio.

"Are you en route to the special assignment area?" he said.

"I'm going by the patrol station to gas up first," replied Casey, "and then I'll be on down. I'll meet you there."

A short time later, Casey, parked next to Giles's patrol car, noticed a bulletproof vest sprawled across the front seat. Since there was no regulation requiring troopers to wear them during routine patrol, he gave it little thought.

The officers had been instructed to write mostly warning tickets because of the unusual traffic situation, so both began clocking drivers going to and from the tunnel. By 5:00 P.M., Giles had stopped a car with no tag, issued a speeding ticket to a Texan, and apprehended a drunk driver.

Later, over supper at a nearby truck stop, Giles explained his assembly-line technique to Casey.

"He'd stop a person for a warning ticket," said Casey, "then stay parked on the shoulder of the road with his lights out, waiting for another car with a violation. He'd catch them, give them a ticket, then wait for another one to come by. He said he wrote about twenty-five warning tickets a week. I averaged about ten, patrolling as most troopers do, by going up and down the highway."

Back on duty, Casey drove past the tunnel towards the Tennessee line while Giles patrolled the road in the opposite direction. Each time one saw the other with a stopped vehicle, he'd slow down to see if everything was all right.

At 9:12 P.M., Giles stopped a truck driver and issued a

warning ticket for a defective light. During the stop, Casey had driven past and Giles waved him on, reassuring him that all was well.

That April ninth morning, Billy McQueen, accompanied by Charles G. Barker, set off for Statesville. Five years earlier, after his marriage fell apart, McQueen had gone to work for Barker doing odd jobs around Barker's Kentucky farmhouse, which the two men shared. Despite McQueen's checkered past, Barker called him ''honest and hardworking.'' As the two of them made their way down the highway toward Statesville, McQueen would stop along the way to phone his estranged wife.

''I've got a gun and stick of dynamite and I'm ten miles closer to getting you,'' he told her. Further up the road, he'd call again, saying ''Now I'm five miles closer.''

''I followed another car, stopped it,'' recalled Trooper Casey, ''and gave him a verbal warning. Then I clocked another car—not running all that fast—but thought I'd follow it. So I turned around and went back through the tunnel going west. As I came out the other side, I rounded a curve and spotted Giles's patrol car on the eastbound side of the highway. It was still running, with the headlights and the blue light going. There was traffic backed up behind it. I saw someone lying in the emergency lane, almost on the white line, in front of the patrol car. I didn't think it was Giles but I didn't see him anywhere else.''

''Then I got closer and realized it was Giles. Knowing what a cut-up he was, I first thought, 'What is he doing? Is he acting or what?' I knew it wasn't anything to joke about, but I couldn't believe it was for real.''

Casey parked in the westbound lane, jumped out of his patrol car, and bounded over the three-foot concrete barrier that divided the highway. Giles lay flat on his back, arms and legs outstretched, his black summer hat still in place.

''He wasn't moving so I bent down and called his name. I felt his neck and arm for a pulse, but there was nothing. His eyes were open and he had a staring, puzzled look I'll never forget—almost as though his last thought was 'Why?'

"There were people standing around, and I asked them what happened. Maybe I was in shock and couldn't hear their response, but it seems like no one said anything."

Casey ran back to his patrol car and grabbed the radio.

Manning the Asheville telecommunications center that night were Cecil Pettit and Eddie Masters.

"I had my feet up on the desk," recalled Pettit, "and Eddie and I had just commented how quiet it was. As soon as we heard the emergency signal, we reached over and hit the transmitter at the same time. Mine opened up first."

"Ten-four, go ahead," Pettit said.

"This is G-541, Asheville. 10-33, 10-33! (Help me quick!) I need a rescue squad at the three-mile marker on Interstate 40. G-444 is down. Trooper is *down!*"

"What's the problem?" Pettit asked Casey.

"I don't know. He's not moving at all. I don't think he's conscious and I need a rescue squad as quick as possible."

To Casey, it appeared that Giles may have died instantly.

"I got a blanket out of the back of my car and covered him. It was the most helpless feeling I've ever experienced. I wanted to go after whoever had done this, but I didn't want to leave Giles."

With no policy to follow (the highway patrol had not yet developed a procedure for dealing with trooper slayings), Casey fell back on the training he'd had in cadet school.

"I knew my first responsibility was to take care of the injured or deceased, then get everyone away from the scene in order to preserve the evidence. I told people to move back and not touch anything. Then I got traffic moving again."

An emergency medical technician stopped and asked if there was anything he could do to assist.

Casey took him to where Giles lay. The technician checked for vital signs, stood up, and shook his head.

"That confirmed what I thought," said Casey. "I realized then that Giles was dead."

Afterwards, he questioned several witnesses, trying to

piece together what had occurred. A couple traveling from Tennessee said they saw the trooper bend over the window of a vehicle he had stopped, then stagger backwards as though he were attempting to return to his car. Someone else noticed that Giles's flashlight had fallen out of his hand and rolled under his patrol car. It was retrieved and brought to Casey.

Casey also questioned Gene Mull, a fifty-year-old trucker, who told him he was driving an eastbound tractor trailer near the blocked tunnel about 9:20 P.M. when he came upon a trooper standing in front of a car.

"I seen the trooper turn around," Mull stated later in a press interview. "Then he staggered, like he had tripped over something. I was afraid he was going to fall under my wheels so I hit my brakes. There was another trucker in front of me and he got on his CB radio and said a trooper had been shot."

Mull was the first person to reach Giles.

"I stopped in the road, ran to him, and unbuttoned his shirt. He was gasping and his lips were moving. That lasted a minute or two and that was the end of it. In my opinion, he never knew what hit him. The worst thing about it was that there was nothing I could do."

The trucker in front of Mull who had reported the incident tried to block the car as it sped away. But the driver stopped on one side of the truck, spun around the other side, and disappeared into the darkness.

Rescue-squad personnel arrived at the scene only to learn that it was too late to do anything to save Giles. One of them asked if Casey had started cardiopulmonary resuscitation (CPR), and he said no.

"It was like getting slapped in the face," said the trooper. "I was sure Giles was dead—and later the State Bureau of Investigation said he was probably gone before he hit the ground—but it made me wonder if I could have done anything. I didn't realize it, but the rescue squad's policy is to start CPR even if the person is dead."

By now, the scene was beginning to look like a TV

drama. Flashing blue and red lights lined the highway as patrol officers, ambulance crews, a State Bureau of Investigation team, and media crews converged.

For the next five hours, Sergeant Mike Overcash, Casey's supervisor, along with other officers called in to help, sealed off the area so the state crime lab could gather evidence. Then they directed traffic and set up a perimeter for the manhunt already under way. Television crews moved in and filmed Giles's inert body (the crime lab didn't want it moved until all possible evidence had been secured), whereupon the news began to spread.

Melinda Harmon was on duty as a dispatcher for the sheriff's department in Buncombe County.

"I was sitting in the office taking phone calls when I heard one of the deputies from Haywood County come over the radio and say a trooper had been shot in Haywood. I thought, 'My God, that's terrible,' but I really didn't connect it to Giles. A few minutes later, I got real shaky and this bad feeling came over me. I started to cry. One of my friends, a deputy, took me to a back room and sat down with me.

" 'What's wrong?' he said.

" 'I don't know, Steve. But I'm all to pieces.'

"He calmed me down and I went back to try and answer the phones. We sent a message on our computer asking for more information and received a message back telling us the shooting took place near the Tennessee state line."

"I looked at Steve and said, 'Where's the Tennessee state line?'

" 'Right near the blocked tunnel,' he replied.

" 'Oh my lord, Giles is working up there tonight!'

"I think I was in shock because I just remember sitting there and then looking up and seeing Sergeant Christopher from the highway patrol walking down the hall towards me. He didn't have to say anything. I knew by the look on his face that something had happened to Giles.

"I was contacted shortly after the shooting took place," said Christopher, "and told to go to the Buncombe County sheriff's department and stay with Melinda in case she needed anything. I didn't know then how bad it was.

"When I walked in, she was behind a desk. She stood up, looked at me, and said, 'Is Giles all right?' She was visibly upset but still composed.

"I explained to her Giles had been shot and we didn't know any more than that, but I would relay any information to her that I received. Then I proceeded to find out who Giles's parents were, and called someone from the Brevard police department to ask them to relay the news."

Bonnie Harmon had already gone to bed but was still awake in the upstairs apartment at the motel. Frank was in the office closing up for the night when the doorbell rang.

Immediately Bonnie sat up in bed, sensing something wrong.

"I heard them tell Frank, 'Do you want us to go up with you?'

"Oh God!" she cried, as they were coming up the stairs, "Don't let it be Giles!"

Giles's best friend, Joey Reece, was at home, half-dozing in an easy chair, when the phone rang.

Two years older than Giles, Reece had joined the patrol in 1978 and shared Giles's enthusiasm for patrolling. There were other similarities as well. Both were small, well-built men, with the same kind of clean-cut good looks. Both worked out religiously to keep themselves in shape. And both loved the highway patrol. Before long, they had become nearly inseparable, with Giles changing his days off to accommodate Reece's schedule. To Giles, Reece was a more experienced, low-key version of himself. To Reece, Giles represented the brother he never had.

The collect call came from Trooper David Miller, attending in-service training at the patrol school in Garner. Miller had heard through radio reports that Harmon was down, but wasn't sure how serious it was.

Reece hung up the phone and walked back to the living room, the color drained from his face.

"Shit," he said. "Giles has been shot."

"That can't be!" said his wife, jumping up from the couch. "Who would do something like that?"

Reece got back on the phone and dialed Trooper Gib Clements's number.

"We were watching *Coal Miner's Daughter* on television when Joey called," said Clements. "He asked if I knew anything about Giles getting shot."

Clements said no, then paused. "I'll see you in a few minutes."

Reece, Clements, and two other troopers arrived at the Haywood County line about the same time. Roadblocks were being set up throughout the area and the men were told to stay put until further notice. One of the four patrolmen there was Gordon Conner, Giles's training officer.

"A trooper called me at home and told me that one of our men had been shot, but he wouldn't say who," Conner recalled.

"After I arrived at the Haywood–Buncombe County line, the four of us began stopping traffic both ways. A few minutes later, a truck driver pulled up and walked over."

"I've got some information," the trucker said. "I came by the tunnel and that boy didn't stand a chance."

"What are you talking about?" Conner said.

"That trooper. He didn't live five minutes after he got shot."

"By then, we knew it was Giles," said Conner. "And it hit me hard. Just completely drained me. I didn't know whether to get mad, raise hell, or what to do."

As the other troopers absorbed the news, their reactions ranged from grief to shock.

Joey Reece left the group, went behind a nearby barn, and cried. Months later, more committed to the highway patrol than ever, he would tell his wife, "I'm working hard for Giles because I know this is what he would do if it had happened to me."

Gib Clements says he was too stunned to react immediately.

"I didn't cry or anything—at least not then—but I couldn't understand why it had happened. Why didn't he have his vest on? I had no anger because I didn't know who to be angry at. So it was more a sense of loss than worrying about capturing anyone. Giles was my buddy—regardless of the highway patrol—and now he was gone."

Melinda Harmon and Giles's parents were instructed to come to the Haywood County Hospital, where they were notified by the physician on duty that Giles was dead. Late into the night, patrol wives and troopers came to sit with the family and offer their support. They would remain a steady source of comfort throughout the days ahead.

For the men on duty, work took on a new meaning. Someone had killed a law enforcement officer—the first North Carolina patrolman to be slain since "Pete" Peterson's death six years earlier in 1979—and it was now the highway patrol's job to find out who had done it, and why.

Immediately after the shooting, Billy McQueen and Charles Barker sped up Interstate 40 in Barker's dark green 1969 Oldsmobile, taking the first exit into an area known, ironically, as Harmon Den. From there, they drove onto a U.S. Forest Service gravel road and stopped. McQueen, who was driving, got out, pulled the yellow stakes from the entrance to a side road, and backed the car into the woods—reinserting the stakes so that no one would suspect he had driven the car off the main road. He then cut some small trees, placed them over the Oldsmobile, and covered it with a quilt.

The Asheville Communications Center began receiving eyewitness reports describing the vehicle shortly after Giles was killed, but kept getting conflicting information.

Part of the problem was that Giles had not radioed in prior to stopping the driver. As a result, there was no quick way to track down the license tag number or registration. To back up their radio systems, some troopers carry a device that records vehicle information and then automatically signals the telecommunications center to send help if the officer fails to return to his patrol car within three minutes.

Giles had such a device and used it regularly. But that day, Tuesday, April 9, it was being repaired in the highway patrol's Asheville garage.

Meanwhile, the North Carolina patrol established a command post at the North Carolina welcome center, less than three miles from the tunnel, while the Tennessee state patrol blocked highways from Newport to the North Carolina state line. Troopers from as far east as Raleigh were mobilized and told to head for the mountains of western North Carolina.

By Wednesday, the area was saturated with law enforcement officers—from N.C. Department of Correction employees who brought their tracking dogs, to U.S. Forest Service rangers who evacuated campers and fishermen. The FBI, the SBI, wildlife officers, deputies from surrounding counties, Bureau of Alcohol, Tobacco, and Firearms agents, and nearly every top-ranking officer in the highway patrol were there. Those without a specific assignment sat around makeshift tables at the welcome center sipping coffee and speculating on why Giles had been killed.

Below the welcome center in Harmon Den, men were spaced every few hundred yards, watching and waiting for any unusual signs of activity. Overhead, National Guard and highway patrol helicopters, along with fixed-wing aircraft, scouted the dozens of logging roads that snaked across the rugged terrain.

But there was no sign of the dark green car or its occupants. All the patrol knew so far was that the fugitives could possibly be the same men wanted in connection with an armed robbery that had taken place earlier Tuesday in Tennessee.

Then a major break occurred in the case.

About 1:00 P.M. on Wednesday, less than twenty-four hours after the shooting, Steven Burns, a forestry technician with the U.S. Forest Service, was cruising an isolated road in Harmon Den when a car approached. The driver, who identified himself as Charles G. Barker, stopped and motioned to Burns.

Dressed in soiled, wrinkled overalls and looking like he hadn't shaved in days, the older man appeared scared and nervous.

"Help me!" he said.

"How can I help you?" Burns replied.

"I've been kidnapped, robbed, and shot."

"At first," said Burns, "I thought he was a nut. I figured he wanted money from me or some kind of favor. I didn't believe his story."

"Say you've been kidnapped, robbed, and shot? Well, why didn't you tell the patrolman stationed at the top of the mountain?"

"I haven't been to the top of the mountain and I didn't see no patrolmen," Barker said. Then he opened the car door and raised his right pants leg to show Burns an obvious gunshot wound.

"Help me," he repeated. "He shot that patrolman for no reason at all."

"You mean you saw that patrolman killed?" Burns asked, startled.

"Yeah. And he's gonna come back and kill me if he finds me here. He told me not to leave until after five o'clock."

"All I can do is turn you over to the highway patrol," Burns said.

"Okay. Just help me."

Burns instructed Barker to follow him out of Harmon Den but to stop and pull over when he got to Interstate 40. He, Burns, would then radio ahead from his Forest Service vehicle, explain what had happened, and have a trooper meet them there.

But the highway patrol refused the request. Certain they were on the right trail with the Arkansas fugitives, it appeared they could not be bothered with what they thought was a false lead.

Asheville Citizen-Times reporter Bob Scott remembers

seeing Barker and Burns arrive at the welcome center command post and try to approach several officers who all but ignored them.

"Everyone thought Barker was just a drunk who had wandered in," said Scott. "He looked rough, like he'd been behind a mule all day. There were two holes in his right trouser leg and some bleeding from what appeared to be a gunshot wound. I went over and started talking to him and he told me how this patrolman came up to the car and that his buddy, for no reason, had shot him point blank. So I went to Charles Chambers, head of the SBI, and said, "You need to talk to this guy. He claims he was with the fella who shot the trooper. And look at his car. It matches the description the truckers gave."

All of a sudden the officers realized they had an important witness in hand, rushed over to Barker and Burns, and shuffled them off to a room for questioning. Since Burns had accompanied Barker to the welcome center, both cars—Burns's light green U.S. Forest Service Jeep and Barker's dark green 1969 Oldsmobile were immediately impounded and searched for evidence.

Barker recounted his story that he had been kidnapped by his companion, twenty-five-year-old Billy McQueen, of Lexington, Kentucky, forced to draw sixty dollars out of a safety-deposit box, then brought to North Carolina, where he was robbed, shot, tied up, and abandoned on one of the back roads in Harmon Den.

After McQueen ran off into the woods, Barker managed to free himself and was attempting a getaway in his car when he spotted U.S. Forest Service employee Steven Burns. He either could not or would not explain why McQueen had kidnapped and abused him, but repeatedly told the officers that McQueen "shot that trooper for no reason at all."

It was a strange tale, but at least now the patrol had something to go on.

Barker was taken to a local hospital, where he was treated for his wound and brought back to the scene at Harmon

Den. Accompanied by highway patrol and SBI officers, he pointed out where his car had been hidden and added that McQueen had a .22-caliber pistol and a rifle with a scope. It was later established that the gun—which was never located—belonged to Barker. A .22-caliber shell casing was found in the car, along with bloodstains (apparently from Barker's leg wound) and several empty beer cans. Both men had been drinking heavily the night they were stopped by Giles Harmon.

With that, the search for McQueen began in earnest and intensified throughout Wednesday night and the next day. About 4:00 P.M. on Thursday, a motorist on Interstate 40, three miles from where the shooting took place, spotted someone scrambling across the highway and down into a gorge. The driver stopped a short distance away and told patrolling officers what he'd seen.

Trooper Mike Thompson used his binoculars to pinpoint the man's whereabouts. The physical description fit the suspect (six feet one, dark brown hair, wearing brown zip-up coveralls, a denim shirt, and a tan vest) and Thompson was sure he had McQueen in sight.

"I saw him walking out of the edge of the woods along a shallow river bed about thirty feet wide. I yelled to him to lay down, spreadeagled, and he did. Then I told him to get up and walk towards the river. I was trying to get him out into the open. He went about thirty yards up the center of the creek bed, where I told him to lay down again."

By now, the highway patrol's helicopter was hovering overhead and a number of officers from different law enforcement agencies had arrived to help with the capture. It was rough terrain—steep mountain walls and thick, scraggly bushes lined both sides of the creek bed.

Trooper David McMurray, a Vietnam veteran and trained sharpshooter, was the only man with a sniper rifle, so he climbed a rock overlooking the river and aimed his gun at McQueen, telling him not to move or he'd pull the trigger.

Among those who scurried down the bank after McQueen was Trooper Randy Campbell.

"The gorge went straight down and I didn't want to carry my shotgun, so I remember handing it to another trooper before going over the side. There were about ten officers standing at the top of the ridge by then.

"When I reached McQueen, he was on his stomach with his hands behind his head. I pulled my revolver and approached him from his feet. I placed the gun behind his right eye, put my knee in the small of his back, and told him if he moved I'd kill him."

" 'I'm not gonna do anything,' McQueen said.

"Then I put his left arm behind his back and cuffed him. Other officers joined me and someone read him his rights while the rest of us got him to his feet."

McQueen was literally hoisted up the gorge by a rope that had been tied and thrown to the men below.

"About halfway up the bank, we stopped to rest," recalled Campbell, "and McQueen said, 'You've asked me several questions. Now I want to ask you something. Does this involve murder?' "

McQueen was told he wasn't getting any information, but one officer, unable to restrain himself, muttered, "It involves the electric chair, if that tells you anything."

McQueen was silent for a moment, then asked, "Did he have any kids?" An officer answered no.

All the way up the steep bank, McQueen, whose shirt was torn and hands were scratched by the rocks and briars over which he was being dragged, remained quiet and cooperative.

Then his attitude abruptly changed.

"I was behind him, carrying a couple of rifles," said Campbell, "and all of a sudden he started screaming, crying, and yelling that we were hurting him. By this time, we had come up over the top of the ridge and the scene had altered drastically. Earlier, there had been only a few people standing around. Now it was a mob.

"I thought, 'My God, where did all these people come from?' Cars were parked all over the place and spectators were rushing up to see what was going on. The media were there, along with dozens of officers, and the helicopter was still flying overhead. It had turned into a zoo."

Campbell speculates McQueen knew he had an audience and wanted to give them a scene they would remember.

He was taken to Haywood County jail, where he was held without bond pending a hearing. Barker was released, with no charges filed against him.

Six months later, Billy McQueen, Jr., was found guilty of first degree murder and sentenced to life in prison in a trial that lasted only eight days. The case is currently on appeal.

During the courtroom proceedings, he appeared each day dressed to the nines, dark brown hair neatly combed ("He looks more like an attorney than his attorney does," someone remarked), and testified that he remembers only bits and pieces of what had happened the night of April 9.

He said he and Charles Barker had been drinking steadily for about twenty-four hours prior to being stopped at the tunnel. He recalled nothing about the shooting. It was his defense—that McQueen's judgment was severely impaired by alcohol and emotional problems—which contributed to the life sentence imposed rather than the death penalty.

But it was not a verdict with which everyone agreed.

Giles's parents—who attended the trial daily and sat teary-eyed as one witness after another was called to the stand—expressed disappointment that McQueen got off without the death sentence.

"We don't think it's fair this man took our son's life and the jury consented to life sentencing," explained Frank Harmon. "How can you justify this type of person coming into the state and killing another human being who was just doing his job?"

A number of highway patrol members agreed.

"If we get killed as law enforcement officers and the public doesn't choose to back us with the death penalty," said one trooper, "how can they turn around and expect us to protect them?"

"Giles was gunned down execution-style," said another

officer, "and that's justification for capital punishment."

On Friday, April 12, 1985, Giles Harmon was laid to rest in his hometown of Brevard, North Carolina. The service was attended by more than 300 law enforcement officers, friends, and family members. He was twenty-six years old.

His death—as the forty-second North Carolina trooper killed in the line of duty since 1929 and the fifteenth officer fatally assaulted—deeply affected everyone who knew him and even some who did not.

Aside from the personal and professional loss, troopers who seldom worried about their safety on the road began to rethink the possibility that something could, indeed, happen to them.

"I pay more attention to things around me now," said a patrolman who admitted that, prior to Giles's death, he had grown careless on the job. "It's made all the troopers more aware, more cautious. It's taught us not to take anything for granted when we stop someone on patrol."

Five weeks after Giles was killed, that lesson would be painfully reinforced when another North Carolina trooper, 450 miles away, met a similar fate.

II

Halifax County, North Carolina, is rural land, the kind of country where miles of tobacco fields ripple in the breeze, where tin-roofed weatherboard houses are still the norm, and where 25 percent of the total population, mostly black, live below the poverty line. It is also the place where the state's first constitution was adopted. That is its only claim to fame.

Nearby, bordering the Virginia line, is Northampton, a sister county that is just as rural and just as poor as Halifax. Yet it is a region that people come to love in a fierce and protective way. Many refuse to leave it, despite the promise of better opportunities elsewhere.

Among those individuals was Ray Worley, a man as

contradictory in nature as the land on which he chose to live, and on which he died.

Born in Currituck County, on North Carolina's northeastern shore, Worley first joined the highway patrol as a clerk in Elizabeth City, then became a state trooper in 1962. He was immediately assigned to Northampton and Halifax.

He liked the area right from the start, especially the people.

"One day my youngest daughter and I were coming home," said Ray's wife, Jackie, "and saw him parked on the side of the road, talking to a fellow."

"That's why Daddy never gets home on time," remarked eighteen-year-old Wendy.

"Then he'd come flying past us in his patrol car and a few minutes later, we'd pass him again, stopped on the side of the road talking to somebody else."

Despite his friendliness, Ray had a look and a manner that intimidated others at first glance.

Part of it was his physical presence.

Six feet tall, he was big-boned and chronically overweight, seldom tipping the scales at less than 250 pounds. In photographs he never smiled, giving rise to the name "Thundercloud," with which his family tagged him.

"Until you got to know him, he could scare you to death," admitted Jackie. "All of the boyfriends who came to visit our oldest daughter were afraid of him. But he wasn't anything like he looked."

In fact, says Jackie, Ray was sensitive and thoughtful, the kind of person who couldn't say no to anyone in need.

Active in the community, he was a leading force in establishing a local law enforcement association, served as president of the Methodist Men's Group, and was often seen cutting the churchyard grass or fixing an elderly neighbor's roof.

For relaxation, he'd plant a garden or cut wood on his 100-acre farm in Northampton County. Reading was another favorite pastime—mostly inspirational books like Norman Vincent Peale's *The Power of Positive Thinking*, or

Dale Carnegie's guide to public speaking. Though not a college graduate, he was a strong advocate of self-improvement and talked of enrolling in classes once he retired from the patrol, just for the pleasure of learning.

He also liked to cook, whipping up concoctions with no recipe in sight. His weakness was deserts, but he'd try anything once.

"He made a tomato pudding that nobody would touch," said Jackie. "He claimed it was good."

A homebody by nature, Ray was proud of the spacious ranch-style house he helped build (he even picked out the draperies and color schemes) and would fuss and fume about keeping it neat.

"Lots of times, he cleaned up after us instead of the other way around," Jackie said. "And although he liked animals, he couldn't stand dogs in the house. He said he had worked hard to have a nice place."

Home and family meant a great deal to Ray. An only child, his parents were divorced and he too had gone through an earlier, failed marriage (Jackie was his second wife). When her elderly mother and aunt were no longer able to care for themselves, it was Ray who insisted they move in.

"He believed that you look out for your folks," said Jackie. "All the years we were married, he was as good to my family as he was to his own."

At the same time, he had a quick temper and a short fuse.

"My aunt Bernice, who suffers from Alzheimer's disease, grew up on a farm and thinks everyone should get up at the crack of dawn," Jackie said. "One morning after Ray had worked the night shift, she began slamming doors in an effort to get us awake. I knew it wouldn't be long before Ray would lose his cool and tell her off. Sure enough, after she had slammed the door about a dozen times, Ray hauled out of bed, went stomping down the hallway in his underwear, and told Bernice, "Why don't you slam the door five or six *more* times? Just leave it open and you can walk back and forth as much as you like. But, dammit, I've got to get some sleep!"

"My aunt is almost deaf, but she heard that, and she never did it again."

Still, he had a good sense of humor, even when the joke was on him.

"One night he stopped this guy," said Sergeant John Wood, who worked with Ray for more than twenty years, "and the fella got out and ran. Ray went trotting after him and before long an audience had gathered."

"Run, Charlie, run!" they yelled. "That fat boy can't catch you!"

"Ray got a big kick out of that."

What amused him most, however, was aggravating his friends, especially other troopers.

"If you had a week where you didn't feel like doing much or there wasn't much activity, he'd ride your case," said Ervin Marshmon, a pal and co-worker. "He liked to pick things out of you. He'd call you over to his patrol car and— with a real serious expression—he'd say, 'Look, you got anything you want to tell me?' Until I learned that was Ray's trademark, I wondered what he had on me. Then I found out he'd do it to everybody. He said he was always surprised at the information people spilled until they realized he was pulling their leg."

In turn, the officers gave Ray a hard time about his careless habits, like running out of gas or losing his car keys.

He locked his keys up so often that every time he'd walk into a restaurant, the other troopers on break would automatically ask if he needed a coat hanger.

No doubt he was preoccupied, for close friends say he was burdened with financial and family problems.

Yet Smith, one of half a dozen officers Worley trained, called him "sharp and professional."

"He knew everybody in the area and had a memory like you wouldn't believe. He could recall people he had stopped years before and recount every detail about the case. He was rarely challenged in court because he was always well prepared and could relate the facts in a way that people understood."

Like other active troopers, he also worked his share of wrecks, car chases, and fights.

"One night Virginia state troopers chased a guy into North Carolina," said Smith, "and Ray spotted him. He radioed for me to proceed that way so we could set up running roadblocks. Every few minutes, Ray would call and say, 'He's not slowing down, but we've got to catch him because he's running people off the road.'

"The guy took a curve near Jackson about ninety miles per hour on the wrong side of the road, went into a ditch, came out the other side, and careened down Jackson's main street. Ray was behind him the whole time, and I was behind Ray. They looked like two race car drivers trying to jockey for position. Finally, the boy's car swerved, hit Ray, bounced off, and left the road. It came to a stop at the top of the trees, threw the driver out, and landed on top of him. He was killed instantly.

"I walked over to Ray, who was standing there looking at the scene, and said, 'Man, I thought you were going to get it a couple of times.'

"Ray shook his head.

" 'I hate that boy got killed,' he said, 'but he needed to be stopped.' "

In 1971, during another chase, Ray was almost killed himself.

The driver was speeding on a graveled country road with the trooper close behind. Suddenly Ray rounded a curve, slammed on his brakes, skidded off the shoulder, and hit a tree.

He was badly hurt, his left leg broken in twenty-one places, his peripheral vision permanently impaired in one eye. The patrol car was so demolished it had to be towed away on a dolly. Doctors told him the only thing that had saved his life was a seat belt.

At Duke University Hospital in Durham, where he was

transferred for treatment, a pair of foreign interns—neither of whom appeared to speak the other's language—placed him in a body cast and forgot to leave an opening that would allow him to go to the bathroom.

"Well I'll be damned," Ray said, examining his mummified torso, "I think my doctor better have a word with you two."

Bad luck seemed to trail him like a midday shadow.

A few months after he returned to the road, he was standing on an icy bridge with two other troopers when a car came sliding into view. All three officers dived over the railing, but it was Ray who looked back, slipped, fell, and dislocated his shoulder.

"When I opened the back door and saw him propped up by his buddies, no shirt on, and someone's jacket slung over him," recalled Jackie, "I said, 'What have you done *now?*' "

Ray was well aware of the risks involved in his job and never failed to caution the men he worked with about being careful. After Giles Harmon was killed in western North Carolina, he told Jackie, "You can't tell what's going to happen when you step out of that patrol car."

"Well, I don't think you should be on the midnight shift alone," she said, referring to the patrol's policy of having some officers man long stretches of the interstate alone.

Ray agreed, then dropped the subject. He worried about something happening to other troopers, but not necessarily to himself. After twenty-three years as a trooper, he had fallen prey to complacency, a common but potentially deadly hazard among long-term law enforcement officers.

"More than 95 percent of the people you stop on patrol are not going to give you any trouble," explained Trooper Ervin Marshmon. "But the rest—that other 5 percent or so—can hurt you bad. Ray had worked here for years without a major incident and knew everyone in the community. These were people who'd greet him with a smile when he'd stop them. They knew when they were in the wrong and would pay their ticket and be done with it. So he got into a routine of trusting people, of assuming each stop was just another nice one. That's how we all become complacent."

Others believe that Ray's apparently lackadaisical attitude toward his own personal safety may have masked a deepening depression, accentuated by the suicide of his fourteen-year-old son, Ray, Jr., in the summer of 1984.

Though devastated by the loss, Ray kept his grief to himself, returning to work as soon as possible.

"He didn't let it interfere with his job," said Sergeant John Wood, "but to me, he didn't seem as cautious as he had been before."

The following April, Ray decided to accept a promotion, though it meant moving to another county. Rather than uproot his family he would commute, then transfer back to Northampton. Jackie would stay behind, caring for her aunt and two daughters.

Everyone agreed that maybe a change—however temporary—might prove therapeutic.

But no one was prepared for what happened next.

Monday, May 13, 1985. Ray had worked the midnight shift on Interstate 95 and returned home about 7:00 A.M. He went to bed, slept till noon, then got up and told Jackie he was going to a Methodist Men's Group meeting to help prepare food for an upcoming fund-raising event.

About nine o'clock, he came home, tired, but in reasonably good spirits. He was scheduled to work from 11:00 P.M. to 7:00 A.M.

"I wish I could just curl up and go to sleep," he told Jackie as he was preparing to leave. "I don't know why, but I really don't want to go to work tonight."

Nonetheless, he proceeded to Interstate 95 in Halifax County and began patrolling.

About 5:00 A.M., four men driving two vans got off the interstate and pulled into a service station, looking for gas to siphon. They had stolen the vans, then robbed a Pender

County grocery store. Now they were headed north en route to Washington, D.C.

The station was closed but the owner had a German Shepherd dog on the premises. When the animal came running towards the men, one of them shot it with a .22 handgun, scaring it away. Then they took off in the early morning darkness.

Ray was coming north on Interstate 95 when he saw a white late-model Chevrolet van followed by a burgundy Dodge van, both speeding, no headlights burning on either. Accelerating hard to overtake them, he chased the vehicles for two and a half miles, blue light spinning and siren blaring.

Just before the 163-mile marker, thirteen miles south of Roanoke Rapids, Ray pulled ahead of the burgundy van. The white one slowed and came to a halt on the right shoulder of the road. What Ray couldn't see in the darkness was that the passenger inside the front van had tossed the .22 pistol out the window. It bounced against the pavement and came to rest near the guardrail.

As Ray moved in behind the white van, the burgundy van pulled up behind, sandwiching the cruiser between them.

Ray reached for the radio. It was 5:11 A.M., Tuesday, May 14.

"A-147 to Williamston."

"A-147, go ahead."

"I'm stopping two vans, northbound, just north of 561 right near 163. Both got Maryland plates, one temporary, one permanent. Can't give you the [license] number just now."

"Ten-four."

Ray got out of his patrol car, walked to the front of the van, greeted the two young black men inside, and told the driver to come with him to his patrol car. The man's name was Antonio Worrell; he was twenty-eight years old, from Washington, D.C. His passenger was twenty-seven-year-old Mack Eugene Green. It was Green who had thrown the gun out before Worley pulled them over.

As Ray was talking to Worley, the driver in the second van walked up to see what was going on. When he did, Ray told him he needed to see his driver's license too.

"My license is in my luggage and I'll have to go get it," said Timothy Lanier Allen. Riding with him was his older brother, thirty-four-year-old Alex Allen.

While Timothy Allen went to retrieve his license, Ray took Worrell to his patrol car and settled him in the rear seat. Then he climbed in front. Though it was early morning and the start of a working day for most, for Ray the hour was late. He had put in a long night and was tired, perhaps too tired to realize that by not monitoring Allen more closely he had just placed himself in a very dangerous position.

In the shadowy darkness, a figure approached and, as was his custom, Ray reached over to open the front passenger door.

When he did, Timothy Allen pointed a .38-caliber gun inside the car and fired three shots. One struck Ray on the right side of his head behind his ear, one punctured his hand, and the other hit him in the left middle finger. Immediately all three men—Allen, Worrell, and Green—ran and jumped into the back van with Alex Allen and took off. The abandoned van was left with its motor running.

As the men were driving away, one of them glanced back and thought he saw the trooper lift the police radio to his ear.

But all was quiet inside the patrol car. The first bullet had ruptured a major artery in Ray's neck, leading to a quick death.

At the Williamston radio center, telecommunicator Linwood Cowan, Jr., was trying desperately to get Worley back on the line. Several minutes had passed since Ray's transmission informing the station he had stopped two vans. No one had heard from him since.

After twenty-five or so attempts, with no response, Cowan called the Enfield police department, the closest law enforcement agency to Ray's location, telling them they needed to check on a trooper. In turn, the Enfield P.D. called the N.C. Division of Motor Vehicles on Interstate 95 and asked them to send someone from the weigh station. Don Davenport answered the phone.

"Normally, we monitor the troopers' radio broadcasts and would have known what was going on," he said. "But that night our monitor was broken."

The Enfield dispatcher told him that someone from Williamston had been trying to contact Worley for the past thirty minutes, then asked Davenport if he would drive to the spot where Worley had stopped.

Accompanying Davenport was Cecil Alston, a weigh station employee and former telecommunicator. The two men set off for mile marker 163, ten miles north on Interstate 95. En route, they tried raising Worley on the radio.

They could see the patrol car well before they reached it, its blue light, four-way flashers, and inside dome light glowing. The white van, engine still idling, was parked in front.

"There he is," said Davenport. "It looks like he's doing some paperwork."

Once again they tried reaching him on the radio. But there was no answer.

"Something's wrong," said Davenport.

Alston started out of the car and Davenport told him to be careful. For all they knew, the parked van could still be occupied.

With gun drawn, Davenport walked toward the patrol car on the driver's side, while Alston approached from the right.

Shards of glass lay scattered on the pavement and Davenport could see the jagged edges that remained of the driver's window. Then he saw the blood and Ray's erect but lifeless form.

"Oh God! He's been shot!" he told Alston.

Alston jerked the passenger door open.

Davenport reached through the broken window and felt Ray's neck, looking for a pulse. There was none.

Alston, overcome by what he'd seen, leaned over the car hood and put his head down on his arms. Then he raised up and looked at Davenport. Both men were badly shaken.

"I'll go check the van and you call Williamston," said Davenport.

Assuring himself that no one was lurking inside, Davenport walked around the van, while Alston—who had notified Williamston that Ray was dead at the scene—stood near Davenport's car, listening for radio traffic.

Suddenly Alston spotted a small-caliber revolver lying next to the guardrail. Neither man touched the gun, aware that it was a prime piece of evidence.

With nothing to do now but wait for law enforcement officials to show up, they paced. Alston, dressed in a blue, short-sleeved summer uniform, tried to keep warm. The sun had not yet risen on that stretch of the interstate and the morning air felt damp and chilly.

As Davenport walked back and forth in front of the parked cars, his mind churned with questions.

"What son of a bitch would do something like that?" he fumed. "What happened here? What caused them to do it? And where are they now?"

Law officers and the ambulance crew arrived almost simultaneously. Detectives from the State Bureau of Investigation confiscated the gun, while the rescue squad checked the trooper for vital signs. Photographs of the crime scene were taken and other bits of evidence collected. As the medical team was removing Ray's body from the cruiser, a plastic card fell to the ground. Someone picked it up and showed it to a highway patrolman, Sergeant F. W. Horton. It was a driver's license belonging to Antonio Worrell, Ray's back seat passenger.

Now began the process of notifying family members and friends.

Sergeant John Wood was sleeping soundly when his

phone rang at ten minutes to six. It was Alexander Jones, a telecommunicator from Williamston.

"Sergeant Wood, bad news."

"What's wrong?" said Wood, still half-asleep.

"Ray Worley's been murdered. All we know is that he stopped two vans. Then he quit transmitting. Everyone's being notified right now."

"I'll be on my way shortly," said Wood, shocked into silence.

As he passed Ray's home, he glanced towards the house and wondered, "Who's the unlucky person who will have to tell the family?"

He was more than halfway to Interstate 95 when Williamston radioed him to turn around and go to the Worley residence. It was he who would have to relay the news. And he had no idea what he'd say once he got there.

Ervin Marshmon was off duty that morning. When the call came at 6:20 A.M., he knew it must be an emergency.

Like Wood, Marshmon could not, at first, believe what he was hearing. It had been less than a month since he had returned from Giles Harmon's funeral in western North Carolina.

Marshmon dressed quickly and went outside to start his patrol car. Almost immediately, he saw a black man of medium build walking north on the highway directly in front of his house. Turning on the patrol radio, he caught a portion of a broadcast giving a description of a possible suspect in the shooting—a black male carrying a brown bag, wearing dark pants and a light shirt.

Marshmon stared at the man walking along the highway, then picked up his radio.

"Would you repeat that description?" he said.

When the information was relayed again, Marshmon ran back into the house, grabbed his service revolver, and called his sergeant.

"I just saw a man fitting the description of one of the suspects," he said. "He's walking right in front of my house!"

"Get him!" said the sergeant. "But be careful. He's armed."

Marshmon pulled out of the driveway, tapping the horn to get the man's attention. The suspect turned around, looked at the trooper, but kept walking.

"Stop! I need to talk to you," Marshmon called. But Alex Allen continued on.

Marshmon positioned his cruiser between himself and the man so he would have some protection in case he was fired upon. Then he got out of the car, his .357 Magnum in his hand.

When Marshmon pulled the hammer on the gun, Allen stopped.

"Turn around," instructed the trooper. "Face me and get down on the ground."

Allen did as he was told, but placed the bag he was carrying in front of him, so that he could lie on top of it.

"Why is he doing that?" thought Marshmon. "What's in there? What's he hiding?"

Marshmon approached cautiously, grabbed Allen and placed handcuffs on both his wrists. Then he searched him.

"What are you stoppin' me for, man? I ain't done nothing," Allen snapped.

"We just had a trooper killed and you're a suspect," said Marshmon.

"Man, I was just walking up the road."

"Sure," said Marshmon, patting him down for a weapon. His hand struck a hard metal object tucked inside Allen's belt. Marshmon yanked it forward: a .38 revolver with two spent cartridges and one live round.

"I'm taking you into custody," said Marshmon.

Once inside the patrol car, Allen began cursing the trooper and demanding to know why he'd been arrested.

"What are you messing with me for?" he said. "I was just hitchhiking. What the hell did you stop me for anyway?"

The litany went on and on. Finally, Marshmon—still

reeling from the news of Ray's death—could no longer tolerate Allen's presence.

"I was upset, crying, angry, and hurt," he recalled. "Knowing Ray had just gotten killed and knowing that I could be holding the weapon that did it, then having to listen to this guy, made me feel very uncomfortable about having him in my patrol car. I knew I was about to lose my temper. So I did what I thought was best. I called another trooper and asked him to transport the suspect to jail."

Marshmon followed them to the county jail, returned home to pull himself together, then drove to the crime scene. As he stood at the spot where his friend had been killed, his only thought was, "Did he suffer?"

When the four men in the stolen van had left the scene and watched Ray lift the radio to his ear, they were convinced he was alerting authorities. Afraid they'd be seen on the interstate, they took the first exit they approached, turned right, and headed down a rural two-lane highway towards the small town of Enfield, where Trooper Marshmon lived.

Coming upon a graveled driveway that led to an open field, they turned, drove the van into a secluded pull-off, parked it, and took off running. Deciding his chances were better if he went alone, and knowing he had the weapon that killed Worley, Alex Allen headed down Highway 301. The others ran towards the Seaboard System railroad tracks in an attempt to make connections north.

All four had been spotted by a farmer coming to check on his crops in the field close to where the van had been ditched. Realizing that something wasn't right, the farmer stopped at a nearby store and told the owner he'd seen four black men fleeing from a van parked in the bushes on his property, one carrying a brown bag and wearing dark pants and a light shirt.

Local authorities were notified and the perimeter tightened around the Enfield area, east of Interstate 95.

By 9:15 A.M., four hours after Ray was killed, police helicopters had spotted the fugitives at the railroad tracks and law enforcement officers moved in for the capture. The men surrendered with no resistance.

Indicted by a Halifax County grand jury, they were charged with two counts each of possession of stolen property. Timothy Lanier Allen was charged with first degree murder. The other three men were charged with being accessories after the fact.

Ray Worley was buried in Northampton County in the family cemetery behind his home.

Throughout the trial, held six months after the slaying, Timothy Allen showed little emotion or remorse for his actions.

Jackie Worley, Ray's widow, attended the proceedings every day. There were painful moments—especially when Ray's blood-soaked shirt was passed around for evidence—but she had a purpose in being there.

"I went because there were things I wanted to be sure of, questions that needed answers. I had to know they had the right person, because at the time it happened, no one knew who did what.

"I didn't take my eyes off Allen. At times, I tried to stare a hole right through him. But he would not look at me. His attitude was, 'I'm here, but I really didn't do anything.' Did that make me angry? Yes. Even now I get mad. I'm still coping with it."

After four weeks of listening to evidence and more than a dozen witnesses, the jury convicted Timothy Allen of first degree murder. He received the death sentence (now on appeal). His brother, Alex Allen, received sixteen years' imprisonment; Mack Green, fifteen years; Antonio Worrell, seventeen years.

Most troopers felt the sentencing—particularly capital punishment for Timothy Allen—was fair. Some believe, however, that Worrell, Green, and Alex Allen should be serving more time.

For officers who knew and respected Ray Worley, the shooting left its mark in one way or another.

Sergeant John Wood, who notified the Worley family

that Ray was dead, said that for months he woke up every morning at ten till six—the exact time he was told of Ray's death.

"Everyone in our district kind of walked around in a daze for a while," he said. "It was so hard to believe it could happen here, happen to one of us. The new survival training we've gotten from the patrol since then has helped a lot. But we all realize now—it's easy to get killed on this job."

For Erwin Marshmon, another of Ray's close friends, and the trooper who captured Alex Allen, the murder left a strong sense of misgiving about his fellow man.

"For a long time afterwards, I had trouble trusting people," he said. "At one point, I became paranoid about stopping anyone. When I did, I could 'see' them pulling a gun.

"I don't carry on a lot of conversation with people I stop anymore. I watch their hands, watch everything they do. I don't perceive anything as routine because I knew that no one is your friend when you stop them on the road. Instead, they pose a potential threat."

Despite such well-founded cynicism, most troopers—like most people—still assume that terrible things will happen to others, but not to them.

And when you are young and confident that life has only good things to offer, the odds against tragedy striking home seem even greater.

Then something happens that proves you wrong.

III

Bobby Lee Coggins was one of those self-driven people who always accomplish what they set out to do.

And what he wanted to do most in 1984, at the age of twenty-six, was to join the highway patrol. Actually, he wanted to join the State Bureau of Investigation (SBI), but he saw the patrol as the best place to start, a sort of stepping-stone to his future goal.

Even as a kid he knew what he did and didn't want.

He once walked home from a camping trip at three in the morning because the crowd he was with had been smoking marijuana.

"When he came in the house," recalled his father, "he woke us up and told us what had happened. 'That's their business,' he said, 'But I don't want any part of it.' "

An honor student through high school and college, he was academic by nature, yet athletic too, winning awards for many of his sports achievements. Other interests were fast cars, motorcycles, photography, and weight lifting.

"Dad wanted us to lift weights from the time we were little," said Barry, four years younger than Bobby. "It seems like we started right after we were born because I can't remember not doing it. Bobby didn't mind at all—he'd lift for an hour or more every day until he was sweating like crazy.

"But I hated it. When it was my turn, I'd go in the room, close the door, and watch TV. Then I'd splash a little water on my face to make it appear that I'd been sweating too."

Bobby was on to him from the start.

"Yeah, Barry," he'd say, grinning, "you had a real good workout, didn't you?"

The boys grew up in a contemporary rock-front house on a corner lot in Bryson City, North Carolina. A middle-class neighborhood, it was quiet and safe, a good place to live and rear children.

The Cogginses were a close-knit, traditional family. James Coggins, a sales representative for Kraft Company and chairman of the Swain County Board of Commissioners, had firm ideas about how to raise boys, but he was a loving father who genuinely enjoyed his sons. Whenever Bobby took jobs that kept him out driving at night, James would often accompany him so the two could ride around together and talk.

Frances, a small woman with a soft, gentle manner, was the nurturing force, the kind of mother who placed her home and family far above a career.

Growing up, the boys seldom disagreed, despite some real differences in temperament. Bobby was quiet and deliberate, much like Frances. Barry was loud, impulsive, rambunctious. Bobby had straightforward goals and went after them, while Barry tended to drift from one get-rich-quick scheme to another. Both were bright, but Bobby was seen as "the brain," Barry the gutsier, more street-smart of the two.

Throughout his life, Bobby trusted his younger brother's instincts and relied heavily on his judgment in making decisions—even when it wasn't in Bobby's best interests.

One day Bobby was watching television when eight-year-old Barry came to the door, motioning him to come outside. What had started as an argument with some neighborhood boys was about to escalate into a knock-down-drag-out fight.

"I want you to choke this boy till his tongue hangs out," Barry instructed his big brother, "while I stomp those two over there."

"Okay," said Bobby, walking calmly into the fray.

Fully grown, he stood only five feet eight, but was muscular and well-formed, with deep brown eyes and a shock of thick black hair.

Though he neither smoked nor drank, he was a junk-food addict who had to work hard to stay in shape. He'd run five to ten miles a day, come home and down half a gallon of milk at one sitting, then indulge himself in pizzas and Cokes. Sometimes Barry followed him on his workouts, cruising comfortably in his car while Bobby ran alongside, calling him names.

After graduating from college, where he majored in biology and chemistry, Bobby took a job with the U.S. Forest Service as a park ranger. It was his first taste of law enforcement and he loved it.

So he applied to the highway patrol. And waited. Got up at four every morning to run. And waited. Lifted weights every day. And waited. Toured New York City as a student photographer. And waited to hear from the North Carolina Highway Patrol.

One morning he lay sprawled on the living room floor with his head on a cushion, deep in thought.

"You know," he finally said, "I've got all this education, all these degrees, and I can do just about anything physically. Why can't I get in?"

He was nearly in tears.

A few weeks later, he was notified that he had been accepted into the highway patrol.

James and Frances were supportive—whatever Bobby wanted was fine with them. But Barry was opposed to the idea right from the start. He thought the work dangerous and ill-advised for someone with Bobby's educational background.

"You don't need to do that," he told Bobby. "Be a chemist or a biologist."

But Bobby, who could dig in his heels when the occasion warranted, had made up his mind. Not even Barry could dissuade him.

Once enrolled in patrol school, Bobby found it "no big deal," mostly because of his prior academic achievements and his excellent physical conditioning.

From the beginning, he was not the "gung ho" type. Neither the flashy patrol car nor the uniform especially impressed him. Nor was his every waking hour focused on the highway patrol. He seldom talked about his work, preferring not to involve anyone outside the patrol in day-to-day incidents on the job.

When he received his first assignment, he looked it up on the map, and was relieved to learn it was in western North Carolina. Then he went to check it out.

"Oh God," he told Barry, "wait till you see this place."

Buried in the mountains more than sixty miles northeast of Bobby's home, Hot Springs, in Madison County, still has no stoplights, fast-food joints, shopping malls, or theatres. Little more than a village, its largest industry—

whitewater rafting—is seasonal, dependent on the mood of the French Broad River that flows through town.

Once a tourist mecca, it flourished during the 1800s by attracting invalids who came seeking cures at the warm natural springs boiling up from the mountains.

By the turn of the century, when doctors were no longer convinced such "cures" were valid, Hot Springs had lost its appeal and because of its isolation had rapidly declined.

The few businesses still remaining have a sad, deserted look, as though time had peeked in, shook its head, and left. A small bank stands on Main Street along with a hardware store, a park ranger station, a few general shops, and an old-fashioned café with a handwritten sign stating plainly, "NO CREDIT. PLEASE DON'T ASK NO ONE."

Surrounding Hot Springs is country that is pure "back-of-beyond," with ridges so steep and valleys so remote "that even God gets lost without a map," said one native.

Understandably, Bobby Coggins's presence in town—as the first trooper stationed in Hot Springs in more than a decade—was a major event.

What initiated the assignment was a citizen's complaint that troopers in Madison County, whose job it was to patrol the entire region, were spending too much time in one area, leaving large parts of the county unattended. Captain Charles Long, now retired from the patrol, met with local residents to hear them out and at the end of the meeting agreed to do something about it.

"I discussed the situation with the patrol commander," said Long, "and he agreed we should pick the best cadets we could find and send them to places that didn't have a trooper."

"Bobby was the first officer we chose. We thought he was sharp, neat, well-educated, a good person to represent us in the area. And it turned out we were right. He did an excellent job."

His first two weeks in town, he caught the eye of a teenage girl who had never seen a patrol car, much less met a trooper.

Her name was Linda Jo Justice and her parents ran the Carolina Grocery and Video store on Main Street.

She remembers the first time she saw Bobby and the immediate crush that followed.

"I was working behind the counter one day and he came in dressed in his uniform. I thought he was the best thing that ever happened to Hot Springs."

Two days later he stopped by again, struck up a conversation with Virginia Justice, Linda's mother, but could not remember Linda's name.

Undaunted, she whispered to her mother, "Ask him to come for supper."

"You ask him yourself," she replied.

Bobby accepted the invitation, and before long he and Linda were a twosome.

No doubt he was smitten by her beauty. Considered one of the best-looking girls in Hot Springs—if not the prettiest—Linda Jo had a mass of honey-blond hair, big blue eyes, and the kind of figure that could turn a man's head. Dressed up, she easily passed for twenty-one, instead of sixteen.

"Mom didn't really approve of us dating because of our age difference," said Linda. "But she didn't say much. She knew I wasn't going to let her talk me out of it."

Bobby—who in the past had tended to date older, more sophisticated women—took some ribbing from fellow officers.

"Need a baby-sitter for your girlfriend?"

But Bobby would laugh, not really caring what they thought.

He told her about his desire to go into the SBI and that he thought it was a safer job with more conventional hours than the highway patrol.

By now, he'd gotten over his initial unhappiness with Hot Springs and began to relax and enjoy his new assignment. He found most of the locals pleasant and receptive to the idea of having a patrolman in town.

"A few of the rednecks were scared of him," said Linda.

"They had gotten out of hand over the years because the law never came down here. But they learned to respect him."

He spent his first six weeks on the job with training officer Jerry Tapp.

"He fit right into the community," said Tapp, "because he could talk with anybody. And he was easy to train, open-minded, good about listening to what I told him. The only problem we had was that he was *too* talkative. I finally said to him, 'Give me a break. I'd like to ride around in silence once in a while.' "

The one question Bobby asked that Tapp had never been asked before was, "How long do I fight before I have to shoot someone?"

What Tapp didn't know was that before joining the highway patrol, Bobby had never handled, much less fired, a gun. Guns were not allowed in the Coggins home and Bobby had never expressed a desire to have one. Even after joining the patrol, he felt uncomfortable with a sidearm (though he scored high in marksmanship at cadet school), and would remove it as soon as he got home.

Bobby's superiors saw him as an able, conscientious trooper, but somewhat naive about potential danger from the public.

"I noticed that sometimes he engaged in too much conversation when he stopped people," said a line sergeant. "I also warned him about keeping his hands free. He'd hold his flashlight in one hand and his ticket book in the other. If he needed to get to his weapon, he'd have to drop something. Young troopers are taught those things in school but they have a tendency to forget."

James and Frances came to visit often, as did Barry, and were impressed by how quickly Bobby had endeared himself to the community.

"One day he wanted me to ride with him to the post office before he went on patrol," said James. "When we got there, we saw a group of boys sitting on a big wooden spool, drinking beer. Bobby ran around the patrol car, cupped his hands to his mouth and yelled, 'Hey, boys! You better hide that beer! The law is right up the road!' They just laughed and waved at him."

At night, after getting off duty, he'd drive to the center of town and park on the bridge so he could shoot the breeze with the locals. One was a mentally handicapped man who took a shine to Bobby's hat. A few days later, Bobby brought him a U.S. Forest Service hat and told him that now he could help him "patrol."

Mid-September in the Appalachian mountains marks the beginning of a natural wonder that peaks when all the leaves have turned to shades of yellows, reds, and golds. It is a season of change, a last full burst of living color before the bitter gray bleakness of winter settles in.

Along the stark, high ridges surrounding Hot Springs, Bobby often cruised the very places where tourists stopped to catch a bird's-eye view of the fall foliage.

Saturday, September 14, 1985, was one of those days.

Shortly before 4:00 P.M., Linda Jo decided to leave work early. There was little activity at the grocery store in Hot Springs and she wanted to go shopping with her mother in Newport, Tennessee. But she had to go home first to change. On the way, she expected to see Bobby. The couple had become engaged in May, and Bobby was renting a room at her parents' home in Spring Creek.

She spotted him at an overlook, the cruiser parked behind a truck, its blue light spinning. Standing outside the patrol car, he turned to wave as she passed.

Bobby had checked on duty at 4:00 P.M. and was heading up the winding, narrow Highway N.C. 209, which runs through Pisgah National Forest into Hot Springs, when he noticed a '76 orange and white Chevrolet truck with a South Carolina license plate. Watching it closely, he looked for signs of the weaving, irregular pattern drunk drivers exhibit. Suspicious, he turned on the blue light, signaling the driver to stop.

Jimmy Dean Rios, twenty-four, was driving. Seated beside him was William Bray, twenty-three.

The pair had stolen the truck after escaping with three other inmates from the Franklin County jail in Arkansas. Rios had been arrested for theft of property and forgery. Bray had been charged with reckless driving, fleeing from a police officer, having a concealed weapon, and possessing a controlled substance. Classified by one doctor as borderline mentally retarded, Bray carried a .25-caliber pistol Rios had pitched to him as soon as he saw the patrol car. Bray later testified that an hour or so earlier he had smoked marijuana, swallowed four codeine tablets, and consumed six or eight beers.

Of the two, Rios, a former exotic dancer, construction worker, and father of an illegitimate child named "Rebel," was the more complex. Psychologists had diagnosed him as a "mixed personality," a confused individual easily led by others. Those who disagreed said that while he might present such a facade, he was in fact sly and cunning, "a wolf in sheep's clothing."

Both Rios and Bray had fled to Asheville after escaping from prison, where they spent two weeks posing as free-lance photographers, visiting local nightclubs, and trying—not very successfully—to keep a low profile. On the Saturday morning before coming to Hot Springs, Rios was accused of stealing $186 from a pet store. When the police were called, he admitted the theft, but gave the money back. As a result, the manager did not press charges and the fugitives drove off. A few hours later, they were on N.C. 209, looking for a campground where they could spend the night.

Now the trooper was behind them and they'd have to stop.

Bobby got out of his patrol car and walked towards the truck. After greeting the driver he asked for a license.

Rios slapped at his pockets and looked at the officer.

"I don't have none," he said.

"Well, keep looking to see if you can find it. And I'll need to see some registration on the truck too."

In the course of Bobby's questioning, Rios gave his name as "Eric Clark."

"Let's go back to the patrol car and we'll get this straightened out," Bobby finally told him.

Rios got out of the truck and walked ahead of the trooper.

"There's something I need to do before you get in the car," said Bobby.

Rios stopped and spread-eagled himself against the cruiser, ready to be searched. But Bobby, halfway laughing, said, "No, that's not what I meant. I want to give you a sobriety test."

For the next few minutes, he had Rios stand with his feet together, arms out, head tilted backwards, while Bobby instructed him to follow the tip of a moving pen with his eyes.

"Okay," said Bobby, slipping the pen back into his shirt pocket, "you can get in the car now."

With Rios settled in the front seat beside him, he picked up the radio.

"G-151," he said, giving his call number to the Asheville Communications Center, sixty miles away.

"Need 10-28 (ownership information) on a pickup truck out of South Carolina, '85 tag."

"Go ahead, G-151," said the telecommunicator.

Bobby then asked for license and permit information on Eric Clark.

"It's common spelling C-L-A-R-K," he said, "first name Eric, no middle name, date of birth 6-21-62. If you would, check 10-29 [records]."

While they waited, Rios noticed Bobby's photo equipment in the back of the patrol car, asked if he liked photography, and struck up a conversation about his own experience with a camera. He also wanted to know if the pretty young woman who had driven past earlier was Bobby's girlfriend.

In the meantime, Asheville Communications was striking

out on its attempt to locate information on an Eric Clark. What they had discovered was that the vehicle was stolen, and that its occupants were wanted fugitives who were armed and dangerous.

Bray wandered over to the patrol car and stood at the passenger window next to Rios.

"What's the color of that truck?" the Asheville telecommunicator asked.

"It's a two-tone burnt orange and white," Bobby replied.

"Ten-twenty-nines [records check], state of Arkansas, Ozark, Arkansas. Ten-seventy-twos [prisoners in custody], ten-seventy-twos from Franklin County, Arkansas. Go ahead."

Momentarily puzzled, Bobby requested the communications center stand by. Something was amiss but he wasn't sure what.

Almost immediately, the telecommunicator came back on the line.

"G-151," he said, "are you familiar with the old 10-32, 10-32, signal?"

Unaware that 10-32 (an outdated signal that many of the younger troopers did not recognize) meant "armed and dangerous," Bobby responded, "Negative." As yet, a new signal had not replaced the old, and the oversight left the telecommunicator with only one recourse.

"Armed," he stated plainly.

"Ten-four," said Bobby. "Stand by. Everything's ten-four right now." His voice betrayed no fear.

It was 4:38 P.M., just a little over half an hour since Bobby had checked on duty.

Rios and Bray exchanged glances. Both had heard the word "armed" and both knew that once more they'd been caught.

"Shoot him! Shoot him!" yelled Rios. As though on command, Bray reached into his coat pocket, pulled out the .25-caliber pistol and aimed it past Rios, at the trooper. He fired twice, striking Bobby point blank in the temple.

Instinctively, Bobby's right hand went towards the radio, his left hand towards his gun.

"You can't do this," he said.

Those were his last words.

No one knows what happened next. Rios and Bray later accused each other of grabbing Bobby's .357 Magnum and firing the final, fatal shot.

Rios jumped out of the patrol car, shouting "Let's get out of here!" Turning away from Hot Springs, they sped off in the truck, heading deep into the rugged, colorful mountains, carrying Bobby's .357 with them.

Telecommunicators at Asheville headquarters called repeatedly, trying to raise the trooper. Seven long minutes had passed with no contact.

Suddenly an unfamiliar voice came over the airwaves.

"Hello, can anybody hear me out there?"

"Go ahead, person calling," said Asheville headquarters.

"Uh, this is Lee Phillips. I'm up here on, I don't know what road it is, but there's a cop been shot in the head."

"Okay, Lee Phillips, Lee Phillips, this is the Asheville Highway Patrol. Advise what road you are on."

"Don't know. We were just going towards . . . we cut off Asheville highway and cut up towards a national-like park and it's a real curvy road to the top of the mountain, and I'm sitting here with the cop's radio and he's been shot in the head bad. He's bleeding real bad."

"All cars and stations working Asheville, stand by," said the telecommunicator. "Ten-thirty-three (need help quick), ten-thirty-three!"

"Okay, Lee Phillips," the telecommunicator continued. "Give us the name of the road or where you turned off. And give us the number in the rear left window of the patrol car."

"Rear left window is G-151," said Phillips.

"Okay, what road are you on, Lee?"

"I'm from Newport, Tennessee, and I have no idea. Me and my friend just came up this road 'cause I knowed somebody that lived on it a long time ago. We was just riding in the mountains."

"Okay. Where did you turn off? Were you going towards Marshall?"

"Yes, sir. We were going towards Marshall from Newport and we turned the curve. There's a little brown store and they got a three-way turn. We turned off that curve and went up the mountain."

Phillips had passed the trooper's car at the overlook and thought he saw blood on the officer sitting inside. He found a place to turn around, and came back. Unsure of what to do, he picked up the radio, making an automatic connection with Asheville headquarters.

Trooper Rick Terry was sitting at the Mars Hill Police Department, twenty-five miles from Hot Springs, waiting for Bobby and another officer to come to work. His shift, which had started at eight that morning, was about to end. As usual, the radio scanner was on and Terry, with nothing to do but sit, was listening to the Asheville transmission.

"When the information started coming through about the stolen vehicle, I felt I should go down there. So I got in the car and started out, not really in any big hurry. Then I heard them ask over the radio if Bobby was familiar with the old 10-32 code. They waited about ten seconds and said, 'Armed.' At that point, I turned on my blue light and took off."

Two miles out of Hot Springs, Terry, along with dozens of troopers elsewhere, heard the order for all personnel to don their bulletproof vests.

"I knew then Bobby had been shot," he said.

Arriving at the overlook, Terry realized he was the first law enforcement officer there.

"I hurried to Bobby and felt his pulse. There was none. The patrol car was still running and the blue light was on. His hat was on the dash near the steering wheel and I picked it up and laid it on top of the car. But it didn't hit me right away that he was dead. I used his radio to call in, told the communications center I was at the scene and would keep them informed."

A few moments later, Asheville headquarters released a description of the 1976 truck Rios and Bray were driving.

A crowd of people, mostly local residents, were standing near the ambulance when Trooper David Gladden arrived. Terry was still the only patrolman there. Gladden thought the young officer appeared totally stunned by what had happened.

Gladden walked over to Bobby's patrol car, looked in, and turned away. The body had already been removed (prematurely by Terry, as it turned out, for the crime lab had not yet arrived to gather evidence). All that remained of Bobby's last, violent moments were a blood-soaked seat and a half-completed ticket, written in Bobby's neat, concise print.

Unaware that anything unusual had happened, James and Frances Coggins were returning from South Carolina, where James had made a series of business-related stops. Reaching Asheville, they went by Barry's apartment. But he was gone. He had left several hours earlier, looking for them so he could break the terrible news before someone else did.

The day before, Barry had called Bobby because he was thinking of buying a new car, and that was something the two brothers always did together.

A little after 5:00 P.M. on Saturday, Barry went into the living room and turned on the TV. He was sitting back, relaxed, when a news announcement flashed across the screen. "It said something about a trooper getting shot in the Spring Creek community of Madison County," he said, "and I knew it was Bobby. He was the only trooper working there that day."

Barry rushed from the apartment and drove to the highway patrol station, less than a mile from his home. When he pulled in, he saw a sergeant standing out front next to a cruiser. The car door was open and the volume turned up on the radio.

"Could you tell me what's happening in Madison County?" Barry asked.

"No, son," the officer said politely. "The best thing for you to do is get back in your car and leave."

"But I have a brother over there," explained Barry, "and I think it could be him!"

He could hear snatches of conversation coming from the police radio, with the words "Trooper Coggins, G-151," repeated frequently. At that moment, it seemed to Barry the patrol was stonewalling, withholding information he had a right to know.

Anger stirred within him.

"I wanna know what's going on!" he said.

"Wait a minute," said the sergeant. He closed the door on the patrol car and went inside.

A short time later, Barry was led to the communications center where Lieutenant D. W. Reavis, a compassionate man held in high regard by the troopers, gently broke the news that Bobby had, indeed, been killed.

Overcome with grief, Barry left, unsure of where to go or what to do.

"Bobby had told me something about Madison County, the way its politics operated, and I thought, 'It's just a damn place for hoodlums,' " he said. "And it made me mad. I was mad at the people who did it, and mad at the highway patrol for putting him there."

Concerned about his parents, he started out for Bryson City, then changed his mind. He had more questions, and he wanted some answers. So he turned off the interstate and drove towards Spring Creek, Madison County.

"When I got there, the patrol car was still parked and the blue light was still going. Someone grabbed me and told me to stay back. They had already taken Bobby to the hospital. I kept asking what happened and they kept telling me Bobby 'got hurt.' That confused me because I'd been told he was killed. So I went into Hot Springs and stopped by the ambulance service where they said, yes, Bobby was dead. All I wanted to know was the truth."

As soon as the Cogginses, who had left Asheville when they couldn't find Barry, pulled into the driveway of their home in Bryson City, a woman ran out to the car. Frances can't remember who it was.

The only thing she recalls are the awful words she heard next; "Bobby's been shot and killed!"

In Spring Creek, highway patrol officers had roped off the murder scene and were busy setting up a perimeter and command post.

Sergeant Mike Overcash recalls his dismay upon learning Bobby had been removed from the patrol car before any evidence could be gathered about the shooting.

"Had everything been left alone, the holster could have provided fingerprints and the position of the body may have helped determine which direction the bullets came from. As it was, there were questions left unanswered."

The error was due partly to a mix-up in communication, and partly to human nature.

Trooper Rick Terry, the first officer at the scene and the one who had helped move Bobby from the patrol car, had not forgotten what had happened to Giles Harmon after Harmon had been killed in Haywood County months earlier.

"At the time, all I could think of was that when Giles was shot, they left the body in the road for more than seven hours. To this day, I regret putting Bobby in the ambulance instead of waiting for the crime lab. But I was thinking of my friend. I did what I thought was best for him."

The order to remove the body had come by radio from Sergeant Zeb Phillips, who at the time was ninety miles away and thought Bobby was only wounded, not dead.

It had been just two weeks since Phillips had worked with Bobby. The Spring Creek fire department had sponsored a fall festival at which Bobby and Sergeant Phillips had worked traffic detail together. It was the type of assignment Phillips enjoyed because it meant mingling with citizens, establishing the kind of rapport that strengthened the ties between law enforcement and the people it served. Phillips had been pleased to see how easily Bobby fit into his role as the area's sole trooper.

Now the Spring Creek fire department was serving another, more somber purpose. For the next few days, it would become the highway patrol command post for the intense, exhausting manhunt about to begin.

It was apparent from the tire tracks leading away from the scene that Rios and Bray had headed away from Hot Springs and into the remote, surrounding mountains. The truck had pulled out, backed up, then turned towards sparsely populated Spring Creek, the tiny community where Linda Justice and, until now, Bobby Coggins lived.

The area was one which E. Y. Ponder, the seventy-five-year-old sheriff of Madison County, knew well. Born and reared in nearby Marshall, he'd been "the law" in the region since 1950. According to Ponder, all an officer needed to keep the peace in Madison County was "a light pair of shoes and a pocketful of rocks." He never carried a gun; to catch criminals, he relied on his thorough knowledge of the land and his bloodhound instincts. His four trusty deputies did the rest.

A small, wiry man who speaks and moves rapidly, Ponder had wasted no time in getting to the scene of the shooting. He arrived with his deputy, Frank Ogle, after the sheriff's department picked up information on the scanner that a trooper had been shot in Spring Creek.

Ponder knew Bobby as "a nice, personable young man," and considered troopers "a good bunch of boys." He recognized the shooting and the ensuing manhunt as highway patrol business, but this was, after all, his territory. And there was no way in hell he was going to sit back and do nothing.

In fact, his help would prove invaluable to the troopers.

About an hour after Rios and Bray sped off in the truck, Etta Moore Payne was driving down N.C. 63 towards Spring Creek when she saw two men cross the road, running. One of them dropped an object which struck her wheel, then retrieved it after she had passed. She thought it was a gun, but wasn't sure. Continuing on, she saw several police cars and knew something was wrong. So she called the Madison County sheriff's department to report the incident.

When Sheriff Ponder received word of the sighting, he left the shooting scene and started towards Doggett Mountain, just off N.C. 63, accompanied by Deputy Frank Ogle and two patrolmen. None of the officers knew exactly where the search would lead them.

"We pulled up to this little dirt logging road," said Trooper David Gladden, "and Ponder looked at it and said, 'There's been a car here. But it hasn't come out.' You could see where the tires had spun in the dirt."

A short distance into the woods, the men saw a burnt-orange truck with an Arkansas license plate, parked on the side of the road. Ponder, Ogle, and Gladden approached it (the other trooper had stayed behind in the patrol car to man the radio) and began looking for signs of the fugitives.

"You could see footprints where they had gotten out and walked down the road," said Gladden. "About fifty feet from the truck, they had dropped potato-chip crumbs and an empty bag. We did a cursory search of the truck but didn't find much."

Yet it was an excellent beginning.

Deputy Ogle radioed the truck's license number to the highway patrol and received verification that it was the same vehicle Trooper Coggins had stopped earlier.

Names and descriptions of Rios and Bray were then released and the perimeter around Spring Creek tightened.

During the night, no one spotted signs of Rios or Bray. Nor did anything break the next day. Bloodhounds had picked up a scent around 2:00 P.M. on Sunday and a warm campfire was found, but neither was positively linked to the fugitives.

More officers and tracking dogs were brought in, along with helicopters—including one with an infrared heat-sensing device.

In Bryson City, Bobby's parents secluded themselves,

trying hard to comprehend their loss. Both refused to listen to news reports surrounding the manhunt. Barry, however, stayed glued to the radio, intent on learning if and when the men who had killed his brother would be captured and punished.

Linda Jo, who sobbed uncontrollably when she learned that Bobby was dead, told reporters, "When they killed Bobby, they killed me."

There was concern that Rios and Bray would break into someone's home to steal what they needed. Though the pair had guns and a coat (Bray was wearing a jacket when he shot Bobby) neither had eaten for more than forty-eight hours.

Officers knew that sooner or later, hunger would drive them to do something extreme.

They were right.

The house belonged to Rachel Gillespie, a seventy-five-year-old widow who was frightened at reports of fugitives on the loose and had decided to spend Tuesday evening with a friend. Rios and Bray, hidden in the barn next to the house, watched her leave.

They got in through a window and ransacked the kitchen first. Then they went through the house, room by room, looking for anything that might prove useful to them. They took clothes, blankets, quilts, and an old .25/.20-caliber rifle that had hung on the wall for forty years. At one point during the night, they lay down to rest. Before daylight broke, they took their bounty and left, heading northwest onto a ridge, where they made a pallet and settled down to sleep some more.

Within an hour after Rachel Gillespie reported the break-in, Highway N.C. 209 leading to the house was lined with troopers, SBI agents, wildlife officers, deputies, and other law enforcement personnel.

In the woods above the house, Rios and Bray had awakened and realized that officers were moving in on them. They could see and hear the highway patrol helicopter scanning the ridge. It had been sent into the air as soon as the break-in was confirmed. What they didn't know was that the heavy fall foliage was working in their behalf, for the chopper pilot and his spotter could hardly see through the colorful trees.

Then a dog handler on the ground caught a glimpse of two men running through the woods. One of the fugitives (no one could determine who was doing what) turned and blindly aimed the stolen rifle at the trackers. The forty-year-old gun misfired and was thrown to the ground, where officers soon found it.

But the net was closing in on Rios and Bray, for on the opposite side of a ridge they were approaching was a team of dog handlers and SBI agents ready to ensnare them.

Rios had Bobby's .357 Magnum, but dropped it onto the ground when he saw the officers. Then he eased it into a hole with his foot. Bray still carried the .25-caliber handgun he had used to fire at Bobby. They were arrested, handcuffed, and taken to the Madison County Courthouse for questioning.

Under interrogation by SBI investigators, Bray admitted shooting the trooper.

On September 19, 1985, twenty-seven-year-old Bobby Lee Coggins's coffin was lowered under a warm autumn sky in Bryson City. More than 600 people attended the service, many of whom had participated in the three-day manhunt just ended.

After a five-day trial held the following May, William Bray was found guilty of first degree murder. Though the state sought the death penalty, he received a life sentence, plus an additional ninety-three years for breaking, entering, and larceny, larceny of a firearm, and firing into an occupied vehicle. On the witness stand, he cried and said he had not meant to kill the highway patrolman.

Two months later, Jimmy Dean Rios was tried and found guilty of first degree murder, armed robbery, felonious breaking and entering, and felonious larceny.

As in Bray's case, prosecutors sought the death penalty.

But he received a life sentence for his part in the murder,

plus an additional sixty years for the other convictions. The judge ordered that the sentences be served consecutively, making Rios ineligible for parole for more than thirty years.

His family wept when they heard the verdict. Rios, who was calm, even cocky at times during the proceedings, showed no reaction.

Today, both men are serving time in North Carolina's central prison. Their cases are currently on appeal.

Frances and James Coggins attended both trials every day.

"It was horrible," said Frances. "But we felt like we needed to be there."

"If you've ever had a child that's been killed," she added softly, "you come to believe that the punishment should fit the crime."

Barry felt as though his entire family was "on trial" during the courtroom proceedings. He believes that the criminal justice system leans too heavily in favor of the accused.

"The system is set up to protect us," he explained, "but it seems the criminal has all the rights. I mean, two guys can sit up there on the stand and admit they did it, but through technicalities, they don't get the death penalty."

For the troopers who knew and admired Bobby, the loss is different, but just as great. And the bitterness is just as real.

"Rios and Bray got more than what Bobby got," said one officer, speaking on behalf of his colleagues. "They got *life*."

Frances Coggins remembers Bobby standing in the kitchen a week before he was killed, his arms crossed at the chest as he leaned against the counter.

"I've had everything and have everything I ever wanted," he told her, smiling. He had a new Porsche and his girl, and he'd just found out he'd been accepted into the SBI. He looked as happy and content as she had ever seen him.

"I think of that," she said, "and it makes me feel good. At least it helps."

* * *

After these three North Carolina troopers—Harmon, Worley, and Coggins—were murdered while on routine patrol during 1985, much was said about increasing the number of patrolmen on the road. Equipment was improved and an officer survival course was initiated as part of every trooper's training. There was even talk of putting two troopers in every patrol car, or removing some patrolmen from the main highways and onto more isolated areas for backup support. Neither idea proved feasible because too much funding was required.

What happened instead was that troopers became more self-protective. Many changed the way they perceived their work and began, for the first time, to take its hazards seriously.

"I was scared after the shootings," admitted one trooper. "And I've become more demanding on the road. When I stop somebody, they may feel I'm depriving them of their constitutional rights, and for some, that's reason enough to kill me. I get complaints about my attitude. Some people even say I've turned mean. But I think it's helped keep me alive."

One officer who's been on the highway patrol for twenty-one years predicts even more dangerous years ahead for anyone involved in a law enforcement career.

"Our whole society is changing," he said. "There's generally less respect for the law and less discipline among our young people. Family values have shifted and drug and alcohol problems have worsened. It seems criminals have more rights now too, which means that our officers must be more intelligent, more alert, and better trained to deal with a more sophisticated level of crime."

Lack of proper equipment and technical problems in the communications system played a role in all three shootings, too, but some patrolmen believe that the troopers who were killed in 1985 contributed to their own fates, either through inexperience or lack of forethought.

"Complacency and carelessness are the biggest killers

we have," said one officer. "People get aggravated when we say that, or feel that it's an embarrassment to admit these guys may have done something wrong. But if we don't profit from our mistakes, we're backing up. And if it takes a little embarrassment to save someone else from getting hurt or killed, then so be it. Let's not let these men die in vain."

For Barry Coggins, words won't ease the pain, or explain away his brother's death.

"Sometimes I'll be talking to my folks and I'll catch myself saying, 'Be sure to tell Bobby so-and-so.' It's like I can't seem to accept that it ever really happened. And it makes it hard to go on.

"I worry about my parents. About something happening to them. And I worry about being alone. Without Bobby, our family is not the same. And it never will be."

10
Passages

"At first, it's instilled in you that this is the only job there is. Then after about fifteen years, you realize there's more to life than the highway patrol. You begin to look around and see people making a lot more money than you do, and doing a whole lot less."

—A twenty-one-year patrol veteran

Every seasoned trooper knows that, sooner or later, the thrill goes away. No longer is it quite so exciting to don the uniform, drive the shiny car, wear the badge, carry the gun. Sometimes it takes the death of a fellow officer to dim the glow. Sometimes it takes nothing more than the wear and tear of daily routine. In a few cases, the patrol was only a job to begin with, rather than the calling it is perceived to be by most.

Many officers maintain there are clear-cut "stages" in every trooper's career.

"It takes about five years for the idealism to burn out," said one trooper. "Till then, you're 'gung ho.' You live, breathe, sleep, and eat the highway patrol. Then rebellion sets in—especially if the promotion you were expecting doesn't happen. The next stage is apathy, followed by a mellowing out where you're just doing your time. After that, you retire, and talk about how much you miss the guys, the work, and being on the road."

Officers are eligible to apply for a promotion after four years on the patrol. But moving up the ranks generally takes much longer because of a complex process that involves both internal and external politics.

"No one will admit it," said a trooper, ten years on the patrol, "but to get promoted you have to know somebody inside and outside the patrol who will drop a good word for you. We get directives saying we'll be dismissed if we're caught politicking. But the truth is, someone has to like you and recommend you before you'll get a promotion. It's all in the timing. It's always been like that and it always will be, though the highway patrol will deny it to the bitter end."

Political maneuvering isn't the only obstacle to a trooper's advancement. Getting a promotion also means an automatic transfer—something many troopers do not want.

The reasoning behind such a policy, according to the highway patrol, is that an officer who stays in the same location and supervises people he knows is not as effective as one who is sent to new, unfamiliar territory.

But that's not the way troopers see it.

"The patrol's arbitrary rule that you move whenever you're promoted penalizes us," maintained an officer with fifteen years' experience. "It would destroy me economically to take my family and change locations. The 10 percent increase in my salary wouldn't begin to offset the loss of my wife's income if she couldn't find another job. I'd have to sell my home, uproot my children. It just isn't worth it. So I'm not interested in a promotion."

This same trooper says the patrol is losing a lot of officers with excellent potential as supervisors because of its internal political makeup and its unrealistic transfer system. In fact, he added, some of the organization's best people are never promoted: by choice, because they do not have the "right" politics, or because they refuse to relocate.

"What often happens," the trooper continues, "is that troopers get promoted because they want to move, or they've screwed up and need to be sent out of the county, or because they're the 'fair-haired child,' not because they have the best qualifications or would do the best job. I'd like to see more credit given to an officer's educational background, psychological profile, and overall abilities—instead of having so much emphasis placed on whether or not he's a misfit, popular with his sergeant, or willing and eager to change his address."

"I'm satisfied being a trooper," said an officer who has refused a promotion on three occasions. "I like this county. It's home. I love the people and I get along well with them. They know me, trust me, and I feel a responsibility to help protect them. It's not worth a promotion if I have to leave."

"Being promoted is not what a lot of these boys think it is," said another trooper. "It's a lot of responsibility. My wife makes good money. I make good money [top pay for a master trooper in North Carolina was $31,620 in 1987]. Why would I want to worry about whether this trooper is running around or that one is doing his job? I'm almost forty-four years old. I don't have the headaches I'd have if I took a promotion and had to move. I'm happy here. Being a trooper is what I want to be."

Not every officer is so resigned. A large number of troopers have a natural inclination to move ahead, strive for better pay, more responsibility, and a higher position on the management ladder. In that respect, they are no different from other ambitious professionals.

Whether rookie or veteran, each trooper has a story to tell and an opinion to express about his work, his goals, and the passages he encounters along the way. Some officers say that despite its hazards and problems, being a highway patrolman gives them a deep, ongoing sense of satisfaction. Others speak of disillusionment, frustration, misconceptions about who and what they are, and their everyday troubles with the public.

All remember what it was like in the beginning, when they were young, eager to please, and raring to go:

> There was an unwritten law when I joined the patrol that a rookie kept his mouth shut for the first five years. That's because nobody would listen to him. That's not true anymore. Today, we're getting people with a higher degree of intelligence, more education, folks who don't take a back seat to anyone. We've got a lot of smart individuals on the patrol—people who could make a lot more money doing something else. I think that speaks well of the organization and the caliber of people who join it.

> I was stationed in a small county when I first joined the patrol. I was fresh out of school and "gung ho," writing fifteen to twenty tickets a week, while the normal amount was four or five.
>
> One day the sergeant told me I needed to keep a low profile. It seems the mayor and aldermen had gotten together and made some phone calls wanting me transferred because I was arresting too many people. Then one night I caught the county recreation director for speeding. He'd been drinking some too.
>
> When it got to court, the chief of police was sitting there and knew the guy, so they let him off. I had done what I thought I was supposed to do—whether they did their job or not.
>
> Anyway, it turned into a big mess. Newspaper articles were written about people wanting me to leave the county. So I decided it might be a good time to transfer to a larger town. That's what I did. Through it all, I thought I was doing a wonderful job. It just seems I was arresting the "wrong" people.

When you first put that uniform on, you feel responsible, and you think, "Man, I'm *somebody.*" But that's crap. And you realize it in a short time. Or someone makes you realize it.

The first time I worked in a small community, I thought I was better than they were. It was a backward, poverty-stricken county. I'd stop people for a traffic violation and they'd be wearing coveralls, the men unshaven, with tobacco dripping off their chins. Most of them didn't know what the word "citation" meant. They could barely speak decent English.

But it didn't take me long to realize I was at a disadvantage. This was their region and I was the outsider. I knew nothing about the things that were important to them—hunting, fishing, surviving economically in a county where the unemployment rate was 25 to 30 percent. They dealt with hardships I couldn't even comprehend. I went to visit one family following an accident and found them living in a shack with a dirt floor and no indoor plumbing.

That really opened my eyes. I thought, "You dumb-ass. You've missed the boat. These people aren't less than you are. You're the one who can't cope."

I came from a family where I never wanted for anything. My experience in this county shocked me into recognizing that the people were living the best way they knew how, with no education and little hope of ever making their lives any better.

I still wanted out of that county because I felt that I would never fit in. But at least I had gained something from being there. I learned a new respect for people who were different from me. And I carry that with me now wherever I go.

There's always been a tendency among experienced troopers to help the younger guys, to start them off.

Then the rookie gets his feet on the ground and he wants to sit and tell you about who he's stopped and everything that's happened to him. And as an older trooper, you don't want to hear it. You've heard it all before, you've told it all before. But you don't want *him* to know you don't want to hear it.

We all go through that initial stage, where everything is new and exciting. When I first came on, I can remember telling about experiences I'm sure people were bored to death at hearing. Now I have to listen to the same thing.

Here's a typical workday in a small county: You get off at 7:00 P.M. after staying at the firing range all day. It's been raining and you're soaking wet. You go home, but it's your turn to take night calls because there's no third-shift patrol in your county.

About 8:00 P.M., you get a call to investigate a wreck ten miles below the next town, so you've got sixty miles to drive. Meanwhile, the people involved are sitting there wondering why a trooper hasn't shown up.

You return home, start to dry out, and the phone rings again. A car has slid down an embankment. But this is one you don't mind because it's a mother and two little kids. Everyone has their seat belt on and no one is hurt. It just takes a long time to get everything cleared up.

You get back home about ten. At eleven-fifteen, there's another call about a wreck just outside the city limits. The city police say they can handle it. Relieved, you go back to bed. A little after midnight, you get a call about a wreck twenty-five miles away. A man has run over a mailbox. It doesn't amount to much, but there are reports to fill out, paperwork to do.

You come home about 3:00 A.M. and finally drift off to sleep. Then you start all over again.

It was fun to be a trooper in the early days. You could get away with more than you can now. We had two boys stationed in Hickory who drove unmarked cars and would think up pranks when there wasn't much activity. One night they bought a fake gorilla head and rode together, one driving and one wearing the mask. Every time they'd come across someone traveling from out of state—the driver half-asleep at the wheel—they'd cruise up to his window, turn on the siren, and scare him to death with the mask. I don't know how they kept from getting fired.

I also remember a trick we played on a corporal who was always pulling stunts on us.

It gets hot in Hickory and this was during the days when we didn't have air-conditioned patrol cars. One afternoon we were standing on the steps of the office, trying to cool off, when the corporal came out the door. He stood there a minute, put his hat on, and without saying a word, pulled his gun and shot several holes into the ground. Then he drove off.

We ran to a shed and got some motor oil, poured it into the holes, and called the corporal on his car radio. We told him to come back to the office because there was a serious problem.

When he arrived, we explained that he had punctured an oil line. In fact, there it was, oozing right up out of those holes he shot in the ground.

He felt bad about what he'd done, so he got a shovel and began to dig. Well, of course the oil stopped "flowing," and he went on his way. After he left, we poured in some more, puddling it up real good, and called him back, telling him this time the oil leak was much worse.

He started digging again while we sat back and watched. After a while, we were afraid the poor man would have a heart attack or die of heatstroke, so we broke down and told him the truth. It made him mad, too.

Today, the highway patrol would fire you for stuff like that.

The patrol has had to change through the years. It couldn't remain the same and the rest of the world move on. There's more paperwork now. And more stress. Part of the stress for the older troopers comes from having to catch up educationally. These boys coming out of college have typing and business skills. We didn't. Now the patrol comes along with computers. So we're even further behind.

There's some resentment about the increase in the amount of paperwork. But there's not much we can do about it except try and keep up.

Years ago, you didn't question supervisors. The sergeant was respected as much as the colonel. Whatever he said was gospel. Now we're getting away from the highly supervised structure. The new, young troopers are harder to control, better educated, and more likely to think on their own.

I guess that's good, but it has its disadvantages too. I don't think troopers are as dedicated to the patrol or to serving the public as they were in the old days.

Some of the newer troopers don't take time to talk with the public. They get out, write a ticket, and go on to the next one. We older guys call them "computers with a pencil," because the patrol sends them to school, programs them, gives them a ticket book, and turns them loose.

More experienced troopers realize you have to fit into the community first, that writing tickets to everyone you stop isn't as cut-and-dried as it appears. And that sometimes helping people is just as important as citing them.

When I started seeing patrolmen promoted with less time than I had, I began to think, "There's something going on here." I had worked with many of them and knew their competency level. That's when you really wake up. Then you work a couple of years longer and you still don't get a promotion. At that point, you have a tendency to get complaints because you're taking it out on other people. You're no longer satisfied with being a trooper.

After twenty years on the patrol, I have peaks and valleys. Before I got promoted, I was low. Then I went as high as I could go. I've been promoted four years now and the new has worn off. There are more headaches, more responsibilities for those under me. If I want to go to town, I've got to let the patrol know where I am so they can reach me at all times. I also had to move. That's the worst thing about it. It pits you against your family because many times they're against it. My son was about to start his senior year in high school and he didn't want to leave. So we had to move without him.

I realize, however, you can get burned out by staying in one district. You know every curve, every bump in the road, every person you've arrested time and again.

It seems like you never reach a level of satisfaction that you can sustain for any length of time. I don't know if it's ego or what.

I envy the other troopers who say they're satisfied with being a trooper. But I wonder if they're telling the truth. If you have any kind of ambition at all, you surely resent not being promoted.

I think you could be happy if you were promoted and then, if you got disillusioned, could go back to being a trooper.

But you can't go back.

No one has ever told me I had to write a certain number of tickets. But they always bring out this sheet when you're evaluated and put it down in front of you and the numbers are there. You can see what everybody else does. It's instilled in your mind—"the sheet is coming out."

They want you to take the promotional test to show you have incentive. But you've figured out the system. You know there's only a slim chance you're going to make it. And it [the test] becomes a waste of time—my time and theirs.

A lot of people think we're on a ticket-writing quota, but we're not. If you sell vacuum cleaners, you're measured by the number of cleaners you sell. We're measured by the number of tickets we write, the drunk drivers we arrest, and accidents we investigate, how we're thought of by the community, the courts, and our peers.

There's no other way to grade us. But I don't mind. Because I've never written a citation I didn't feel good about. I'm a "company man," but I do what I think is right.

There are different trooper "types."

Some troopers like to be the apple of the sergeant's eye. If he tells them to stay out all night and write fifty tickets, they'll do it just to make themselves look good. Other troopers like to "tell" on fellow troopers because it takes the heat off them if they themselves are doing something wrong. Yet that same type of officer makes sure he's the first one on the scene when the media covers a story about a trooper saving a life.

Some guys don't like to stop and help stranded motorists, or associate with people less fortunate than they are, because they think it's a waste of time. They are a stumbling block in the community rather than a pillar.

But most troopers are the type that quietly go about their business, work their eight hours, and head home.

They're sincere family men. They are the ones who will help you and other troopers on the road. They treat everyone they stop with respect.

And they are the ones who best represent the highway patrol.

I'm a radical trooper. That's different from a troublemaker. The troublemaker is setting out to cause disruption, to tear things down. A radical asks, "Why?" "Why are we doing this?" in an effort to make things better.

But because he's a little out of the mainstream, not strictly a company man or a yes-man, he suffers for it. He has to be a team player if he wants to get ahead in this organization.

The thing that bothers me most about the highway patrol is the cynicism that prevails. The supervisors don't believe anything we say, just as we don't believe anything the public says.

When I find myself believing somebody, I go, "God, I think he's actually telling the truth! How strange!"

Ever since drugs became so prevalent in our society, our job has become a lot more dangerous. It honestly makes me consider changing careers. I'm getting prematurely gray. My blood pressure is sky-high. At night, I look at the ceiling and can't go to sleep.

Is it worth it? That's what I keep asking myself.

One trooper I know down east got into a fight with a guy who had a knife. The trooper should have shot him. But he didn't.

He fought with him, wrestled with him, and got cut up pretty bad. Later, when I asked him why he didn't shoot the man, he said, "All I could think of was that I've got a family here, my wife's got a job here. I'm happy where I am. I knew if I'd shot him, there'd be an investigation and they'd probably transfer me.

And he was probably right. But I think it's really sad.

I like the image we project. It makes me feel good when little boys come up to me and say they want to be a highway patrolman. How many kids walk up to an adult and say, "I want to be a certified public accountant?"

I also like the feeling I get when I go into public places and people turn around to look. Or when kids say, "Can I touch your badge? Your gun? Can I look in your car?"

It's an ego trip, of course. But it pumps me up like nothing else can.

Troopers hate it when parents tell their kids, "You better be good or that cop over there is gonna put you in jail."

Every time that happens to me, I tell the child, "No, I won't do that to you. But I'll put your parents in jail if they don't take care of you."

We're always in the limelight. I can do something wrong and it's not "John Smith did so-and-so." It's "that patrolman" did something. It puts a lot of pressure on us.

Good, dedicated troopers make the effort. And that's the kind of trooper I want to be.

In my opinion, dealing with the court system is one of the worst frustrations a trooper faces.

It gets so discouraging when you take your time and—in some cases—your life in your hands to arrest someone, build a good case, then go into court and watch them fiddle it away on technicalities. You sometimes get to the point where you want to give up.

An officer on the road has to make split-second decisions about whether or not someone has broken the law. But attorneys and judges have days, weeks to prepare a case.

I do the best I can out here and then go to court and stand a good chance of losing the case.

Once I was sent to a wreck where the vehicle had gone into the creek and several people had been injured. I arrested the guy for drunk driving, came to court, and he was found not guilty—even though he registered well over the legal limit on the breathalyzer. He told the court that before I arrived at the scene, he drank half a pint of whiskey, but that it was *after* the wreck had occurred.

The judge said the "time element" in the case bothered him and that's why he pronounced the man not guilty.

In other words, had I arrived at the scene quicker, I might have been able to make a better judgment on the man's driving condition.

But I can't be everywhere at once. And for that, we may have let a drunk driver on the loose.

Generally, the public thinks of us as "Clint Eastwood, shoot-em-up" types.

But I've found in my twenty-three years on the patrol that our best officers are some of the kindest, most forgiving people you'll ever meet. They have a genuine love for mankind and want to help people.

Middle-class people are our best supporters. They know the difference between right and wrong and give us the least amount of trouble. They seldom violate the law and when they do, they accept it when they're wrong.

We see a lot of the negative aspects of humanity. The people we usually come into contact with are down on their luck, drunk drivers, or those involved in criminal activities. It can affect our point of view, give us tunnel vision.

But we realize there are a lot of good people out there too.

People think a trooper has a glorious job, that we get all this recognition. And some officers do. But for most of us, it's a thankless task.

You can't do this work properly if you worry about the publicity or what you're going to get out of it.

But I wish we were better understood.

I've stopped cars many times to tell someone a member of their family is sick or dead. I've run seventy or eighty miles an hour to transport human blood, or take a life-sustaining organ to a hospital. Yet I'm sure people I passed thought I was on my way to get a cup of coffee.

They have no idea what I really do or what might be lying in the seat beside me.

It pisses me off to be treated different just because I'm a trooper. I go into McDonald's and I'm standing in line to order when the cashier says, "No charge."

I want to pay just like everyone else in line. Hell, I'm probably in a better financial position than half of the people standing behind me!

It's embarrassing when that happens. So what I usually do is throw the money down before anyone has time to say anything.

What I like most about being a trooper—and this may sound corny—is doing good. We're a much-needed organization. I see what causes accidents out there, and I'd hate to think what it would be like if there was no highway patrol.

I like the independence that goes along with being a trooper. I go to work at 6:00 P.M. and have no idea what I'll be doing.

I go where I want to, do what I want to, write a ticket to whoever I want—with no one standing over me. If I feel sad, I can ride eight hours without stopping anyone and no one says anything about it.

I meet all kinds of people. I'm in touch with judges, lawyers, governors, people in high office.

After twenty-one years, I still have motivation and a willingness to work on my own.

Not too many people can say those things about their job.

What I dislike is having to deal with some of these disgusting damn people on the road.

Once I stopped a couple from out of state.

"We were just admiring the area, how beautiful it is," said the woman, as I was writing her husband a ticket for speeding.

"Thank you, ma'am," I said.

Just as I was pulling away, she got out of her car and walked back to the cruiser. I rolled the window down to see what she wanted.

"We were looking for a place to stay . . ." she began, and I was just about to tell her how to get to the nearest hotel when she came out with "But, you son of a bitch, you've *ruined* our vacation and we'll never come back through here again!"

Now here's the difference between being on the patrol a year and being on for twelve years. At one year, I would have said, "Fuck you, lady."

But, after twelve years as a trooper, I just laughed and drove away. That made her angrier than ever.

When you walk up and say, "Good afternoon, ma'am," and try to be pleasant and they respond with,

"What in the hell are you stopping me for?" it makes you react accordingly.

"Hey, come on," I want to tell them. "I haven't talked bad to you. I haven't been rude or disrespectful. I don't get paid enough to put up with this crap."

You realize that people will sometimes come across that way, but it makes you mad and you just want to knock the hell out of them.

What I like about being a trooper is that when somebody asks me to help them, I can.

What I hate are the internal politics and the people who think they are above the law.

I've stopped senators, governors, mayors, you name it. I tell every one of them, "I don't give a damn if you get this dismissed tomorrow. I'm doing my job tonight."

We're all critics. We'll be sitting around and somebody will start talking about why he gave a man a ticket for sixty-five miles per hour on the interstate.

Then another trooper says, "Sixty-five on I-40? While you're writing that ticket, someone else is going past you at eighty!"

And the guy starts thinking, "Maybe I'm cutting it too close."

It can affect his attitude towards the job and the public.

Most of us are people who truly enjoy the job, seldom dread going to work, believe strongly in the organization, have good initiative, and if we had it to do all over again, would rejoin the highway patrol.

I'll never make any real money doing this. But after twelve years, I still like being a trooper. To me, that's what counts.

Troopers sit down with other troopers who aren't doing their job and try to help them. If he doesn't listen or shape up, he's left to sink on his own.

I was pretty well marked when I came to town. I had been "beaten down" by an experience and people questioned whether or not I could do the job. Even some troopers were saying I was no good anymore.

When I'd take a break, they'd tell me what I was doing wrong, and that I was close to being fired. I knew I could do the job, but that I was gonna have to alter my ways.

What saved me were those guys coming to me and telling me, "Your job is on the line."

They stuck by me and, sure enough, I proved that I could change. Because I'm still around.

My long-range goal is to be in Internal Affairs. I can move up in that department. I can work regular hours. I can travel across the state. All of that appeals to me.

And I think I'd be good at it.

My belief is that anyone who denigrates the highway patrol has no business being in it.

11
When Good Guys Go Bad

> "I'm personally in favor of Internal Affairs because I don't want to work with a bunch of low-lifes. Troopers in North Carolina are generally well-regarded by the public, and to maintain that, we must have clean laundry."
>
> —*Officer with seven years on the patrol*

It can happen at any time during a trooper's career. Personal problems begin to interfere with the job. Or the stress becomes too great. Sometimes the individual is one of the few undesirables who, despite the patrol's intensive screening process, manage to slip through the net. Whatever the cause, there are some troopers—and they are definitely a minority—who become an embarrassment to the organization. They began as "good" guys who went "bad."

His name is not important. But his story is. Because it illustrates what can happen when a highway patrolman disregards the code of ethics to which all law enforcement officers are bound.

That night, he was patrolling on a remote section of road

in a national forest when he saw a van with no license plate. Signaling the driver to pull over, he stopped and got out of his patrol car. The driver stepped out too, but so did a passenger, who calmly walked up and shot the trooper four times point blank in the chest. Then the two men jumped back in the van and fled.

None of the bullets penetrated the officer because he was wearing a bulletproof vest. Still, he was bruised and shaken. He called for help on the radio and another trooper responded. Shortly after, he was taken to the hospital, where he was listed in good condition and told how lucky he was to have survived.

Within an hour, roadblocks were in place and a search under way for the van and its occupants. By the next morning, more than a hundred state and local officers were patrolling the roads. A helicopter and private aircraft were brought in to assist. A command post was established and the patrol's $100,000 mobile radio van was set up to handle communications.

It was a major manhunt, one that would last three days and cost the state more than $12,000 in patrol salaries and other expenses.

During a routine investigation into the incident, the State Bureau of Investigation and the highway patrol learned of certain "discrepancies" in the trooper's story. In fact, they found there was no van, nor had there been any assailants.

Plagued by personal problems and explaining that the pressures of the job had gotten to him, the trooper admitted he had made up the whole story. The shooting was a hoax.

After voluntarily resigning from the patrol, he cried wolf again, claiming two men had come to his house and fired a bullet at him through the back door. It was another false lead and a sad ending to the officer's career in the highway patrol.

One trooper had such a fear of stopping cars that he wrote "ghost" tickets, using names from the headstones of a local cemetery. After a name he had submitted turned up on an insurance company's computer as a live person who did *not* get a ticket, the trooper was caught.

Still another officer was suspected of stealing personal property during the automobile accidents he investigated. Nothing could be proved, however, and the accusations never got beyond the stage of disturbing rumors.

Throughout the North Carolina Highway Patrol's fifty-nine-year history, there have been few documented cases of serious misconduct on the job. As a rule, the patrol's careful screening process and insistence on high standards tend to weed out those individuals who, deliberately or otherwise, might betray the organization.

But, as in every other profession, it happens.

One of the more sensational cases of misconduct on the patrol involved a trooper who, in 1986, was arrested and tried on charges of fondling a ten-year-old girl he had placed in his patrol car after stopping her on the road. Patrol policy prohibits officers from putting women and children into their cars unless conditions and circumstances warrant it necessary.

Acquitted by a jury, the trooper was nonetheless fired from the highway patrol, which had conducted its own internal investigation.

Two years earlier, a sixteen-year veteran of the patrol was dismissed after reports surfaced that he had engaged in sex with a woman he stopped for speeding. He was also accused of making suggestive remarks to another female, telling her she was "too pretty not to have a man."

And in 1979, two troopers were charged with rape, kidnapping, and crimes against nature when they allegedly abducted a nineteen-year-old married woman, drove her to a wooded area, and forced her to perform sexual acts. A judge found no probable cause in the case, but the officers were relieved of their duties following an internal investigation by the highway patrol and the SBI.

Sometimes greed rather than sex is the motivating factor in a trooper's downfall.

In 1977, an ex-highway patrolman pleaded guilty to

twenty different crimes, including soliciting to commit murder, obstruction of justice, and grand larceny. According to the charges filed, the former trooper was accused of hiring someone to murder the man who held the mortgage on a motel that he owned. Another charge was later filed against the officer for trying to hire a second individual to kill the would-be assassin. As it turned out, no one was killed, but the ex-trooper received a fifteen-year sentence for his role in the solicitations, being an accessory to thirteen counts of breaking into homes (from which he had received stolen goods), and offering money to one of the hired killers if he would agree not to testify at a preliminary hearing.

Lesser charges have also been brought against highway patrolmen for drunk driving, "fixing" tickets to reduce traffic violations in exchange for favors, failure to report accidents, misuse of state-owned equipment (one off-duty trooper drove his patrol car all the way to New York City to see an automobile race), and use of excessive force.

Crooked cops—like corrupt employees in all walks of life—can be found anywhere. In 1982, for example, a seventeen-year veteran of the Massachusetts State Police was charged with smuggling $1.5 million worth of marijuana from the basement of a local police barracks.

"Out of a thousand people in any segment of society, you're going to get a few who will pull things like that," said a North Carolina Highway Patrol supervisor. "For the most part, troopers are honest and decent."

"It's not the individual, it's the job, the profession," a police official was quoted as saying in a *Boston Magazine* article (July, 1982). "There are real temptations out there. And the reason is simple: they can get away with it. They don't have to rob a bank or drive a getaway truck. All they've gotta do is *not* do their job."

Some say there's a thin line between cop and criminal, for they tend to share the same temptations, the same attitudes, and the same understanding of the criminal justice system—which they both know how to beat.

Because of the stresses inherent in their work, police officers can also easily fall prey to alcoholism. One study estimates that 25 percent of all law enforcement officers have a serious alcohol dependency problem. Even worse, a 1979 report found that 67 percent of the police officers questioned in its sample study admitted to drinking *on duty*.

Before 1973, commanding officers in the North Carolina Highway Patrol were responsible for policing their troops and themselves. The trouble was, captains from one region to another held differing views about what constituted a transgression. As a result, the organization had no real guidelines or uniformity for meting out discipline. Nor did the punishment always fit the crime.

"At that time," said a highway patrol major, "one of the worst things you could do was to separate from your wife. You could be fired or transferred over that. Now we realize that society and the family unit has changed and we've had to adjust our standards."

By the mid-1970s the patrol saw the need for a more formalized system of disciplinary action as well as a more organized approach to conducting administrative inspections.

That's when the Internal Affairs division was established.

All complaints, whether of a serious or minor nature, come through Internal Affairs at highway patrol headquarters in Raleigh. Headed by Major William Ethridge, a down-to-earth officer who has a reputation among the troopers for being fair and reasonable, the department is staffed by two lieutenants, a first sergeant, and a clerk-stenographer.

It is the role of Internal Affairs to classify each complaint, determine if a serious offense is involved, and if necessary, send team members into the field to investigate allegations against a trooper.

Complaints are categorized into five "types," from Type Five, the most minor, to Type One, involving serious misconduct on the job.

"Anything that hasn't resulted in injury or loss of respect

for the highway patrol is classified in the minor category,'' explained Ethridge. ''For example, someone complains about a citation—they don't think the trooper should have written them a ticket or they disagree with the charges, so they file a complaint against the officer. That's considered a Type Four or Five. These can ultimately be handled through the district captain or another superior, but are sent here first for review. After a course of action is decided, the reports are returned to us to make sure everything was done according to policy.''

Each complaint is then placed in the trooper's permanent file.

''Lying, or any kind of dishonesty on the job, is a Type One offense,'' Ethridge said. ''If a person complains that he was tried in court and the officer fabricated evidence against him, for instance, we consider that extremely serious. In law enforcement, we must have absolute truthfulness in our people.''

Other kinds of major misconduct include deliberately and without justification causing injury to another person, using drugs, getting caught in a sexual act while on duty, failing to report for duty, drinking on the job, accepting bribes, or engaging in criminal activities.

In between are offenses that range from a trooper not following proper procedures in making an arrest to failing to keep his hair regulation length.

In serious cases, violations of Type One and Two, a thorough investigation is nearly always carried out.

The first person notified is the accused.

''We give the trooper all the facts,'' said Ethridge, ''and allow him a chance to prepare his defense. Meanwhile, we contact all the peripheral people involved—the person who made the complaint, the clerk of court, anyone who might have knowledge of the incident.''

The trooper is brought in, presented with the evidence, and allowed an opportunity to make a statement.

''He must answer all questions,'' said Ethridge, ''and he must tell the truth.'' Unless the complaint involves a criminal offense, he cannot plead the Fifth Amendment.

"If they are truthful with us, we'll meet them halfway. Most will admit their guilt. When they do, we don't bust their knuckles. We just explain what the policies are and tell them what we'll have to do. We're up-front with them."

The colonel of the highway patrol makes the final decision, based on Ethridge's recommendation, whenever the offense is of a serious nature. Even a trooper with a previously clean record can be dismissed or transferred if the findings warrant severe action.

What happens more typically is that over a period of time, a trooper "builds" a case against himself by a series of charges and complaints that go from bad to worse until he is eventually fired.

The exception is a case involving a trooper who breaks the law.

"In those instances, we go to the local law enforcement agency, the district attorney, all the people necessary to conduct the investigation," said Ethridge, "and tell them we're aware of the charges and have suspended the trooper. Then we pick up his uniform, his patrol car, his identification. He is no longer effectively a highway patrolman.

"After that, we do nothing. He's on his own while the criminal investigation goes through. He may be found not guilty and we may still dismiss him because there could be certain information we have that provides internal grounds for dismissal. We may even use a polygraph test [though they are not admissible in court] to help us decide if he's telling the truth."

Between 1978 and 1983, 1,962 complaints were lodged against troopers, but only about 25 percent were ruled valid. Of those, most were in the minor Type Four and Five category of offenses.

"The public thinks it's liquor and women that get our troopers in trouble, but in reality, those are in the minority. And we seldom ever have instances so serious the trooper is fired. Generally, complaints revolve around citations and work-related duties."

Even when a trooper has a stackful of complaints within his file, Ethridge doesn't assume he has a bad employee on his hands.

"What you're likely to have instead," he said, "is a very active trooper. Show me a man who makes a lot of contacts and arrests, and I'll show you a lot of complaints. I don't look at the thickness of a man's file. I look at the quality of the complaints."

Whenever a trooper gets in trouble or is accused of doing wrong, says Ethridge, Internal Affairs can be the best defense he has.

"If the facts are on his side, we'll work our tails off to prove he's innocent. At that point, we're working for him, not against him."

But that's not always how the troopers feel:

> I'm glad we have the option of policing ourselves, but it still insults the shit out of me when somebody comes in to investigate. It can strike terror in a trooper's heart.

> I think today's troopers are living on a legend. It used to be if someone bucked up on you, you'd whip his ass and have no more trouble with him.
>
> Now we've got complaints, lawsuits, Internal Affairs.
>
> Our younger troopers are riding on the patrol's old image. They have to in order to protect themselves.

> Force is justified anytime it's used against me first. I'm big on protecting myself. I'm not going to get hurt if I can help it. They don't pay me enough for that.

> What I always regretted was this. If I ever get upset enough to take physical action against somebody, it takes me a month to get over it. If anybody irks me the wrong way, I'm gonna slap them in the ditch or take whatever action is necessary.

But I always detested having to manhandle somebody because I didn't know when to stop. When I did it—they always went to the hospital.

I play by the rules of how people behave. They are the ones who make the decisions about how they'll be treated, not me. If people put themselves in the position of getting hurt, I have no sympathy for them.

There are some troopers you can buddy around with and they're the nicest fellas in the world. Then they put on this uniform and they become the biggest horse's ass you can imagine—arrogant, self-centered, no patience with anybody.

It's true that something happens when you put on this uniform. You know people expect you to act a certain way. So you take on a macho air. You have the gun, the cuffs, and the authority. And no matter how old you get, it's the same.

I look forward to going to work because I know I'm "the man."

I was chasing a guy one night and he jumped out and ran. I caught up with him and bopped him on the head with my flashlight. I didn't think I had hurt him bad because he was still fighting. So I hit him again. I saw a pool of blood under him and he was hollering and screaming "police brutality."

There was no way I could take him to the courthouse in his condition, so I took him to the hospital. All the way there, he kept saying he was going to sue me.

I told him to go right ahead.

When we arrived I ordered him out of the car.

"You want me out, you'll have to get me out," he said.

So it was on again.

I got a sergeant and another trooper to help me. We

grabbed him and slung him out of the car. He landed against another car and left a smear of blood across the whole side panel. But he was still kicking and carrying on.

"We're gonna have to hog-tie him," said the other trooper.

The sergeant, who had been talking to him real calmly, was kicked in the ear and was cut.

"You son of a bitch!" said the sergeant. Then he helped us tie him up.

We finally got him on a stretcher and the nurse looked at us and said, "You can't leave this man like this."

"You want him untied?" I said. "Then *you* untie him. But we're not responsible for the damages when you do."

We left him tied until he went to X-ray, where he bucked up on us again. He had to have sixty-five stitches to close the top of his head.

My feeling is, if people get hurt, it's their fault. They brought it on themselves.

It surprises me how resentful people are towards the police. I enforce the law, but the public doesn't like me for it. That used to bother me, but now it doesn't matter. Because I'm the one who's got the authority.

Sometimes troopers aren't "going bad" at all. They are simply misunderstood or unfairly treated themselves:

I once got a complaint from a man I arrested who said I "towered" over him. He was five feet tall. I told the sergeant I'd apologize to the guy if it would make him feel better.

All troopers get complaints. But I don't worry about them because I'm just doing my job.

The last one I got was from a South Carolina lawyer

who wrote a letter complaining that I gave his mother a ticket for going the wrong way on the interstate.

Some people are just like that attorney—born-again complainers you can't please no matter what. It's part of the job.

I hate to admit it, but some troopers bring complaints upon themselves by their demeanor. We're in the people business and we have to remember there are some fine individuals out there who don't wear this gray uniform.

It's like when someone files a complaint against you, you've already been convicted. The trooper did it, whatever it was.

You've got to sit down and document everything that happened surrounding the complaint. Half the time you can't remember it because there's really nothing to it.

The patrol tells us to "comply" with the complaint. But they don't tell us what they think about it.

Some troopers will slack up because of complaints. They get paranoid about it—they stop working so hard so they won't get so many complaints. Then they get tagged as "not active enough."

So it can be a "no-win" situation.

I investigated an accident once where a minister was hit by a man taking his wife to the hospital. The guy was in such a hurry—he thought his wife was having a heart attack—that he left the scene without stopping.

I didn't give him a ticket.

A few days later, I was sitting in a restaurant and the minister came up to me and started complaining.

"What would you have done in a similar situation?" I asked him. "Would you have stopped if that had been your wife in the car?"

He said yes, he most certainly would have.

"Then you're a damn fool," I told him.

So he called the highway patrol and complained about *that.*

But I don't regret what I said. I still consider him a fool.

The bigger we grow, the more mistakes we'll make in picking personnel. Part of the reason is that there's more laxness in moral standards among the public. More is taken for granted and attitudes are more liberal.

I don't think troopers are as dedicated as they used to be either. Years ago, when I was a trooper, if I was scheduled to get off at midnight and got a call about a drunk driver twenty miles away, I'd turn around and spend half the night looking for him.

Today's trooper cuts off by the clock and goes home.

Yet that's not true in every case. Sometimes a special assignment comes along that is so demanding, so attention-grabbing, and such a challenge, that it reinforces the dedication and commitment of every trooper it involves, whether he is a good, bad, or indifferent type of officer.

That's what happened in November, 1986, on a remote mountaintop in Edneyville, North Carolina.

12
The Search for Rambo

"He was willing to stand there toe-to-toe with us. It's a dangerous man who'll take as much firepower as he did and still keep going. Very few people want to confront 400 armed law enforcement officers."

—*Trooper involved in Edneyville manhunt*

It started with a simple act of littering.

Henderson County Sheriff's Deputy Jimmy Case was patrolling U.S. 64 East about 6:30 P.M. on Saturday, November 22, 1986, when he saw a passenger throw a beer bottle out a car window. Case pulled in behind the copper-brown Buick Regal and attempted to stop it. But the driver kept going.

The deputy continued following the car for about a mile. Suddenly the passenger leaned out the window, aimed a high-powered rifle at the cruiser and fired. The bullet missed Deputy Case, but struck the radiator hose, crippling the patrol car's cooling system.

Case speeded up, but about half a mile farther on U.S.

64, his car overheated and quit. The Buick, sporting a Florida license plate and carrying two young men, took off.

The driver was Edwin Pete Black, twenty-two, a Hendersonville resident wanted on charges of robbing a bank in Cape Carteret, North Carolina, the day before. The passenger was twenty-one-year-old Michael John Shornook (also known as "Shornock" and other aliases).

Shornook's brushes with the law began in May, 1985, when he stole a Jeep in Morehead City and led nearly a dozen law enforcement officers on a two-hour chase. It ended when he jumped into a river and was apprehended by state troopers who had to swim after him.

A month later he escaped from jail, stole a boat, and was captured again. Sent back to prison, he served ten months of a three-year sentence.

According to Shornook's family, that's when his dislike of law enforcement officers turned to hatred.

"He came back different," Ann Shornook was quoted as saying in a newspaper article about her son. "Prison changed him. He was always a kid who could see things coming, knew things. And the first night he was home, he warned me that something was going to happen, that he was never going back to jail."

"My brother was a hell-raiser," said Jeff Shornook, "but he was a good guy till he went to prison. In high school, he was a bus driver. He got all these plaques on what a safe driver he was. Then he goes and gets his license taken away on some charge and that made him mad. After that, he hated cops and anything associated with them."

Born in Perth Amboy, New Jersey, Shornook was reared in Carmel, Pennsylvania, before moving to Cape Carteret. He was a good student when he applied himself, a quick, intelligent boy skilled with his hands.

The oldest of four children, he was also, says his mother, "the responsible one, the one I could count on to take care of the others."

When his parents separated he moved in with Sandra Horne, a forty-six-year-old earth mother type who taught him how to thrive in the woods. At seventeen, he was showing a passionate interest in guns and becoming a crack shot.

"He had the potential to do anything," Horne told a reporter, "but he told me, 'Everything is going round and round and I can't catch it.' "

Though portrayed by the media as a "Rambo" survivalist because of his penchant for firearms and camouflage clothes, Shornook was in reality a deeply troubled youth who refused to conform to society.

"Even after he was released from prison," said his mother, "he never felt free. Prison had soured him and he decided from then on to thumb his nose at authority. He felt he'd been shit on too many times by a two-faced judicial system and this was his way of paying them back. So he devoted himself to making fools out of cops. After a while, it became a game to him—a game he could have quit at any time—except that it all became too real. But he meant to finish it one way or another."

By fall, 1986, Shornook was running from the law again.

A pawn shop in Jacksonville, North Carolina, was robbed and he was a suspect. A boat was stolen at Emerald Isle and a logbook, believed to have been kept by Shornook, was found nearby. An armed robbery took place at Wrightsville Beach and police issued a warrant for Shornook's arrest. Then he was caught burglarizing a houseboat in Port Orange, Florida. The next day he broke into a house, killing the owner's dog and forcing a woman to fix him breakfast before he took her money and a motorcycle.

On November 21, Shornook and Pete Black donned ski masks and robbed the First Citizens Bank in Cape Carteret. Twenty-four hours later, they were clear across the state in Henderson County, with Deputy Jimmy Case hot on their trail.

Shornook's prediction to his mother that "something is going to happen" was about to come true.

That night, Saturday, November 22, Shornook and Pete Black were invited to a party on Sugarloaf Mountain, in

Edneyville. The host was William Anthony Miller, celebrating his twenty-fifth birthday with a combination of hard liquor, beer, and barbecue. Sometime during the early part of the evening, Shornook and Black left to pick up something—possibly drugs—and were returning to the party when they passed Deputy Jimmy Case.

Miller's home, a white frame, tin-roofed house that sat on a ridge overlooking a huge front yard, was too small to accommodate the thirty or more people who showed up for the affair. So the group moved outside, where they built a bonfire, had a cookout, and got drunk.

Then someone started a fight.

In the course of the argument, twenty-five-year-old Ricky Charles Pack was beaten and his money was taken from him. Pack left, but returned a few minutes later with a carload of angry friends and relatives, all of them bent on revenge.

That's when things really got out of hand.

No one knows exactly who did what, but one thing led to another and guns were drawn. As the bullets flew, the party broke up. Most of the crowd hid in a thicket of pine trees circling the house. Pack tried to escape by shepherding his girlfriend and relatives into a car, but the vehicle was riddled with gunfire and forced into a ditch. Pack got away unharmed with the help of a friend, but his uncle, Dennis Pack, was shot in the stomach. He died three days later.

William Miller ended his birthday by getting shot in the face. Pete Black, the driver with whom Shornook had been riding earlier, loaded Miller into a white Plymouth and started down the mountain toward a hospital. By the time Black reached the main highway, Miller was dying.

On U.S. 64 East, below Miller's home, sheriff's deputies and state troopers were cruising the roads looking for the two men who, a few hours before, had blasted the radiator on Deputy Case's patrol car. They knew a boisterous party was under way on Gilliam Mountain Road because they'd had complaints about cars blocking driveways and too much late-night noise, but they had not yet established a connection between the attempted assault on Case and what was taking place at the Miller house.

"Our intention," said Henderson County detective Lieutenant Randy Case (no relation to Deputy Case), "was to maintain a roadblock till daylight, then get some air surveillance up so we could spot this brown Buick. We felt sure the men were still in the area. We were going up and down the road trying to locate the shell casing from the rifle used in the shooting when a white Plymouth came through our roadblock at a high rate of speed."

When Pete Black stopped, the state trooper who questioned him found Miller dead in the back seat. There was no sign of Shornook.

Black told the officers about the shoot-out and said there were several injured people still at the Miller house.

"We spent the rest of the night investigating the (Miller) murder," said Lt. Case. "The whole time, we kept turning over in our minds that it could have something to do with the patrol car getting shot at."

The officers found more than 140 shell casings scattered around the Miller property, along with fifty- and hundred-dollar bills, drug paraphernalia, and assorted firearms. The few witnesses who emerged from the woods to talk with the police were so drunk their testimony was nearly worthless. But deputies learned that Shornook, who had participated in the shooting (though he was not responsible for either of the murders) was not among them. In fact, no one knew where he was. (Ricky Pack was later charged with the murder of William Miller. Dennis Pack's assailant was never identified.)

Late Saturday night, lawmen sealed off the area and a command post was set up at the Edneyville volunteer fire department. Another post was established farther up the mountain.

About nine-fifteen Sunday morning, two Gilliam Mountain residents told officers they had seen a late-model Buick parked in the apple orchard behind Miller's house. Upon investigation, the deputies determined it fit the description of the car Pete Black was driving when Shornook fired the rifle out the window. A license check showed the vehicle was a leased car, rented with a stolen credit card.

"At the same time we were getting this background information," said Lieutenant Case, "Carteret County officials contacted the Henderson County sheriff's department and reported an incident similar to ours (a patrol car getting shot at). In the conversation, Shornook's name came up."

On Sunday afternoon, Pete Black appeared at the Henderson County sheriff's office and turned himself in. Under intense questioning, he admitted that he knew Shornook and that the two of them had robbed a bank in Cape Carteret. They had met while both were in prison and shared the same dislike for authority figures. Their plan, said Black, was to live a quiet, peaceful life in the scenic mountains of western North Carolina, and travel elsewhere to commit their crimes —sort of like commuting to work.

Slowly, pieces of the puzzle were falling into place.

"We had a meeting," said Case, "and decided there was a strong possibility Shornook was still on the mountain. One of our investigators had seen a man dressed in a black leather jacket walk into an orchard high up on Sugarloaf and then disappear. We were sure it was him."

A short time later, felony warrants for assault on a law enforcement officer were issued for Michael John Shornook, described as a white male, five feet eight, with medium-brown, shoulder-length hair.

Till now, the double shootings and general ruckus at Miller's birthday party had been Henderson County's business, handled—and handled well—primarily by the local sheriff's department. But as the case began to grow in scope and complexity, county law enforcement officials realized they needed help. A fugitive—heavily armed and potentially dangerous—was loose on a mountaintop dotted with dozens of homes.

To get him down would take a major manhunt.

One of the first agencies called to assist was the state highway patrol.

By Sunday night, troopers all over western North Carolina were being notified to report for duty.

Trooper Leah Weirick had been shopping. Her phone was ringing when she walked into the house.

"How are you?" said her first sergeant.

"Fine, sir, how are you?" Weirick responded, aware that something was up. First sergeants didn't normally call just to pass the time of day.

"We've got a manhunt under way and we want you to go," he said.

Oh God, Weirick thought. She was scheduled to be off the next day. This would no doubt alter her plans.

"Sure," she said, "just tell me where and when."

In Asheville, Trooper David Miller had worked a regular weekend shift and was home resting when his sergeant called and said to meet him at the Edneyville fire department at four o'clock Monday, the next morning.

Trooper Keith Lovin, in Robbinsville, had been gone for the weekend and knew nothing about the series of events taking place in Edneyville. When his sergeant called at 10:00 P.M. and told him to report for duty within the next few hours, he began preparing for the 100-mile trip to Edneyville.

His assignment, along with David Miller and several other patrolmen, was to stake out a gravel road just below Mountain Home Baptist Church—less than half a mile from where the party had taken place Saturday night.

"Our job was to stand outside the patrol car and watch the bank," said Miller. "We all decided we'd load our shotguns with buckshot and if he came out shooting, or one of us saw him, we'd shoot back."

Not much happened all day Monday.

Fresh footprints and other signs had led officials to believe Shornook had returned to the car sometime during Sunday night, took food and ammunition, and slipped back into the woods. Throughout the day, six roadblocks were manned over a twenty-mile area, while twenty-five members of a tactical team combed the area on foot. Besides sheriff's department and highway patrol personnel, there were SWAT teams, fire department volunteers, state wildlife officers, State Bureau of Investigation officials, and between thirty and sixty people from the state's Department of Correction Prison Emergency Response Team. In addition, a sheriff's department search plane and the highway patrol's helicopter were brought in to help scan the mountain.

Armed guards were everywhere—even riding the school buses in case Shornook decided to hijack a busload of children.

It was, as one trooper put it, "like a military operation. We had been briefed on Shornook's prior ambush tactics and knew he wouldn't hesitate to fire on an officer. So the atmosphere was extremely tense. We felt like we were in a war zone."

Adding to the sense of uneasiness was the lack of a central law enforcement communications system which would allow one agency to talk with another without having to relay information. Troopers were at a particular disadvantage because not only were they tied to their car radios, but they had little of the proper equipment necessary for conducting an extended manhunt over rugged mountain terrain. Most of the patrolmen had to wear their slick-soled regulation shoes, totally impractical for tracking through the woods, bright-yellow rain slickers—making them perfect targets—and for firearm protection, carry what they had been issued in patrol school, a .357 Magnum and a shotgun. Neither was particularly effective against Shornook's high-powered, long-range rifle and the other weapons he reportedly had.

Some Sugarloaf residents were better prepared to face Shornook than the officers assigned to protect them. Those living in the area were asked to leave, but few complied.

"We're just keeping our eyes open and our guns loaded," said one long-time homeowner.

About four-thirty Monday afternoon, troopers Joey Reece and Gib Clements had parked their cruisers on a dead-end road and were sitting in the woods, watching for unusual movement. Suddenly a twig snapped.

The two men looked at each other.

"Did you hear that?" said Reece.

Clements nodded.

"You go down the road and I'll go around the ridge," whispered Reece. Moments later, they met up.

"I know I heard something," said Reece. Then he stopped, bent down, and glanced upwards. "Come here, Gib. Does that look like a man to you?"

Fifty to sixty yards ahead, Reece had caught a glimpse of what appeared to be someone wearing a blue cap.

"We better call in *now*," said Clements.

While Clements waited, Reece returned to his patrol car and notified the command post of the sighting.

Within minutes, the highway patrol helicopter was hovering over the area. The pilot reported that he, too, saw someone in the woods with a blue cap. It was the first good lead in the case since Shornook had disappeared into the woods Saturday night.

Immediately, the perimeter was adjusted and Shornook's deadly game plan—the one in which he "thumbed his nose at authority"—began in earnest.

Around 7:00 P.M. that night, a hungry, tired Shornook walked up on Ivory Marshall's front porch and, at gunpoint, asked for the keys to Marshall's car.

"He didn't give us that much trouble," Mrs. Marshall said later. "He wasn't trying to kill us or anything. In fact, he talked pretty friendly."

Before driving away in the couple's orange and white Jeep, he took some food, left a hundred-dollar bill on the table, then jerked the phone from the wall. Marshall reported the break-in from an extension phone in another room.

Less than a mile away, troopers David Miller and David Gladden were manning the same dirt road at which they had been stationed all day.

"It was getting dark and we knew someone would relieve

us soon,'' said Miller. ''We had heard about the sighting but thought it was a good distance from us. I got in my patrol car and was preparing to leave when I caught the report on the radio that an orange and white Jeep had been stolen. That's usually what happens during a manhunt. After the area is cordoned off, the fugitive commits a crime—breaks into a home or steals a car—in order to get away.''

Nearby, Trooper Gary Cook had heard the same report. Assigned to patrol the road leading to the top of Sugarloaf Mountain, he had gotten hungry and stopped for something to eat at a church. A field command post had been set up on the church grounds and food brought in for the officers.

''I was standing in the parking lot chewing on a piece of fried chicken,'' said Cook, ''when something came over the radio about a suspect stealing a Jeep and coming out a dirt road at Mountain Home Church. I looked around and saw a sign that said, 'Mountain Home Church.' I thought, 'Wait a minute! That's where I am! And I'm the only trooper here!' ''

Cook radioed his position to officers at another command post and was instructed by a first sergeant to block the main intersection at the church. Help, he was told, was on the way.

Within minutes, troopers David Miller and David Gladden were pulling in. Miller positioned his patrol car nose-to-nose with Cook's cruiser, forming a ''V'' to block the road.

Almost immediately, they were joined by Trooper Keith Lovin. The men stood outside their vehicles, guns drawn, waiting in the dark.

''The plan,'' said Miller, ''was to ambush Shornook as he came over the hilltop towards the church. About that time, a farmer who'd been standing in the church parking lot walked over to us and told us there was another road above the church that Shornook could turn on to. So we moved up about 500 feet, where the dirt roads connected. We were just getting out of our cars when I looked up and saw a vehicle, its headlights on, coming around the curve."

Shornook, driving the stolen Jeep, had spotted the patrol cars straight ahead and veered to the right. He spun off the dirt road into the church cemetery and wheeled around, heading back in the direction from which he came.

A sudden crack of gunfire split the air. Realizing they were being shot at, the officers jumped in the two patrol cars—Miller and Lovin in front, Cook and Gladden behind—and took off after the departing vehicle. In the glow from their headlights, they could tell it fit the description of the stolen Jeep.

Instinctively, Lovin reached up and turned on the blue light and siren.

"Turn off that goddammed siren so I can hear the radio!" snapped Miller.

"G-437, G-437 is in pursuit with Lovin," Miller radioed the command post. "We're going back the way he came."

Each time Shornook rounded a curve on the road, he'd slow down, lean out the window, and fire from a .30-caliber carbine. He was also carrying a .223 Mini-14, two .45-caliber pistols, and a 9-mm pistol. Every few rounds, he'd alternate weapons.

"We've been shot at! We've been shot at!" Miller yelled into the radio mike. "We've been hit! We're still in pursuit!"

One round hit the front bumper, came up through the hood and struck the windshield wiper. Another grazed the fender, while a third bullet hit the condenser on the car's air-conditioning unit.

Neither Miller, intent on maneuvering the dark, narrow mountain road, nor Levin, who was trying to get an accurate aim at the speeding car ahead, fully realized how much danger they were in.

"Everything happened so fast," said Miller. "We could see the flashes and smell the gunpowder but there was no real sensation of fear. We were too busy concentrating on other things."

Miller knew that Shornook's history included ambush tactics.

"To prevent him from stopping and firing on us as we got to him, I tried to stay on his tail. I thought if I could get close enough to intimidate him, he might stop."

In the patrol car behind Miller, Cook and Gladden had the difficult task of staying near enough to provide support for the two troopers in front, while attempting to fire at the Jeep ahead.

"I didn't want to crash into Miller if he had to stop suddenly," said Cook. "But at the same time, I wanted to stay up with him. There were times I was so close my front bumper was right up against his car."

"My greatest fear," said Gladden, "was that I would run out of ammunition. I couldn't remember if I had put a live shell in the chamber of my shotgun, so I loaded and unloaded it at least four times to make sure."

Armed only with a shotgun and a .357 Magnum pistol, Gladden knew that neither of his weapons was an equal match for Shornook's firepower.

"It was like throwing rocks at an elephant," he said.

In the pitch-black darkness, Cook saw a flash in the window of Miller's cruiser, directly in front of Lovin's head.

A fourth bullet, fired from the Jeep, had burst through the patrol car windshield, landed on the dashboard, and exploded in front of Lovin. Shattered glass flew into Lovin's eyes, while a piece of lead—a fragment from the bullet—settled on his coat collar.

Unaware at first that Lovin had been hit, Miller reached up and flicked the glass from his own chair. Then he glanced at Lovin, who was falling forward.

"I reached out and grabbed him," said Miller. "He was talking and there was no sign of blood, so I knew he wasn't hurt real bad. Part of me wanted to continue with the chase, but since I had slowed down to check on Lovin, we had lost sight of the Jeep. So, tactically, we were not in as good a position as we were before. We knew nothing about the road, either, where it ended, or if it was a dead end."

Lovin, now blinded in one eye, spoke up.

"Let's stop and break it off right here."

Miller, frustrated at losing Shornook, continued on.

"Stop, David. I need to stop!" he said. Miller braked and Lovin rolled out of the passenger's side and onto the ground.

"I didn't think my eyes were hurt too bad," Lovin recalled, "but every time I'd blink, I could feel the glass grinding. It was very, very painful."

Cook, who had pulled in behind Miller, believed Lovin had been killed. His first reaction was anger.

"We've got another man dead," he thought. "What are we doing out here chasing this outlaw? He doesn't know us, and we don't know him, yet he's trying to kill us. It doesn't make any sense."

All three troopers rushed over to Lovin and asked if he was all right. Despite his intense pain, he assured them that he was.

Concerned that Shornook might come back shooting, the officers left Miller's patrol car sitting with the headlights on while they retreated to Cook's cruiser. Their first priority was getting some help—both medical attention for Lovin and backup support for themselves.

By radio, Miller notified the command post of their location. The combination of rugged terrain, heavy darkness, and unfamiliarity with the region led to more than a little confusion in getting other officers to the scene.

"It's the dirt road that leads from the church going back to wherever the Jeep was stopped," Miller said. "We're northwest from the church. We're out of sight of him now. We've lost sight of the vehicle."

"Keep us advised," said the telecommunicator. "We'll get you some help on the way."

"Whoever's got a map," Cook interjected, "look for Mountain Home Church. You'll see two roads that go up by the church. Come up and turn left. He saw us there, spun around, and took off. We've exchanged gunfire with him and don't know if we hit him or not.''

''We didn't,'' added Miller.

Unhurt by the barrage of gunfire, Shornook had driven to the end of the gravel road, crashed through a gate, abandoned the Jeep, then fled into the woods on foot.

By the time the backup officers arrived at the scene where Miller and the other troopers were waiting, Shornook was long gone—at least for the night.

Lovin was taken to a local hospital, where he was treated and released. Though his eyes would remain sensitive for two to three months, miraculously there was no permanent damage.

''I didn't need anyone to tell me how lucky I was,'' he said. ''I knew that if the bullet had struck a little higher up the windshield, I would have been hit in the brain. It was all a matter of chance.''

That night, he went home and had a long discussion with his wife about the merits of being a highway patrolman. Two days later, he was back on the job.

After the shoot-out, David Miller had trouble sleeping.

''I don't remember any specific nightmares,'' he said, ''but I do recall twisting and turning a lot. I'd wake up with my clothes so wet with sweat I'd have to change. After that, I refused to think much about it.''

Gary Cook says the incident didn't begin to affect him until it was over and he was safely at home with his family.

''That's the time you look around and wonder if being involved in this kind of work is really worth it,'' he said.

David Gladden maintains the shooting ruined his diet.

''I've been eating junk food ever since,'' he said. ''And I started smoking again. That was the first time I'd been shot at and have it come so close to hitting me. It was not the kind of sensation I expected. In fact, it was the most exhilarating feeling I've ever had—because he *missed*.''

Monday night, a short time after the shooting, the weather took a turn for the worse. By dark, a cloud cover had moved in and thick fog was rolling into every crevice and ridge on Sugarloaf Mountain.

Trooper Leah Weirick, instructed to report for duty on her day off, was among those officers who had to man a lookout post during the night.

"They put me on the road where Shornook had been sighted," she said. "It was cold and rainy. We couldn't sit in our cruisers because we had heard that Shornook would kill a trooper in order to get a car."

For the next twelve hours, Weirick and two fellow troopers sat back to back, Indian-style, around a tree, waiting, watching and listening.

"We couldn't talk," she said, "because we weren't supposed to make any noise. So in a situation like that, you just think. The first two or three hours, I was convinced I was gonna die. I thought, 'This is crazy. I have a fifty-yard-range shotgun and he has a 500-yard-range, high-powered rifle. He can pick me off from anywhere.'

"About the fifth or sixth hour, you realize it's like deer hunting. You sit perfectly still so you'll be the first one to see or hear anything, you'll be the first one to get him. Then fatigue sets in and you start imagining things. I had already been up for two days so I was tired to begin with."

By the next morning, cramped and sore, Weirick's kidneys were sending out SOS signals. At noon, she told the other troopers she absolutely had to go to the bathroom. As quietly as possible, she got up and went behind a tree.

During their watch, the troopers had neither heard nor spotted anything of significance. Later, they discovered that Shornook had also spent the night in the woods—only a hundred yards from where they sat.

"That was enough to give us the shakes," said Weirick.

Tuesday morning, November 26, the search entered its third day.

A contingent of law enforcement officers from various agencies had set up an ambush at Ivory Marshall's home the night before, figuring Shornook would return there for food and shelter. But he never showed.

So Lieutenant Randy Case, of the Henderson County sheriff's department, formed a tracking team to go after him.

With him were three volunteers: Henderson County Deputy Victor Moss and two state troopers, Randy Campbell and David McMurray.

Case and Moss would track, while Campbell and McMurray served as lookouts.

They set off at daylight, amid cold rain and a heavy, damp fog. Driving up the lonely mountain road, Trooper Randy Campbell, seated next to Moss, had a strange, uneasy feeling.

"I felt like something terrible was gonna happen," said Campbell, "and I started to mention it to Vic, but didn't. Then it passed."

During the night, fifteen to twenty officers from the state prison department had secured the abandoned Jeep and were still at the scene when Campbell and the others arrived. The lawmen gathered in a circle, discussing which way Shornook may have gone.

"The prison team had found tracks Monday night," said Deputy Vic Moss, "so we followed those until we got to a place where someone had bush-hogged the trail, causing the tracks to stop. We turned and took a lower road that went across a spring. There were muddy places on it we thought might hold more footprints."

The mud, however, offered no clues.

Another road lay farther up the mountains, but the men had to cross a meadow to get to it.

No one spoke as they started up the ridge toward the meadow, for Shornook could be anywhere, lying in wait.

They walked four abreast, ten to twelve feet apart, Campbell and Moss in the middle, flanked by Case and McMurray. The two deputies and Trooper McMurray carried a .233 Mini-14 while Trooper Campbell was armed with a borrowed sub-machine gun. Randy Case had a hand-held radio for communication with officers at the command post. All four were dressed in camouflage fatigues and wore bulletproof vests.

Halfway across the field, the fog began to lift. From the woods, a sudden shot rang out and the officers hit the dirt.

"My God," thought Trooper Randy Campbell, "he's gonna shoot us in the head!" He raised up, fired off thirty quick rounds, and fell back down. Seconds later, Shornook—hidden behind an oak tree directly above the meadow—released a barrage of gunfire.

Deputy Vic Moss was struck first. The bullet entered the left side of his nose, plowed through the roof of his mouth, and exited out his right ear. To Moss, it felt like everything inside his head exploded.

"I could hear the yelling and the sound of guns, but it seemed a long way off. I remember thinking that since I was hit in the head, I was probably going to die. Then after a few seconds, I thought, 'Well, I ain't dead yet. It's gonna take a better shot than that to kill me.' "

Campbell was lying next to Moss and had just reloaded his gun when he noticed Moss wasn't firing.

"Shornook was just peppering us. It's a wonder he didn't kill us all. Vic was lying with his head on his arms, moaning, so I crawled over to him and lifted his head. The wound looked bad, but not real bad. He asked me if he was gonna die and I said, 'No, you're gonna be all right, but we've got to get you out of here.' "

Case and McMurray, aware that Moss had been hit, told Campbell they'd cover for him while he pulled Moss from the line of fire.

Then Trooper David McMurray called out, "I've been hit!"

"The first thing that passed through my mind," said McMurray, an ex-marine, "was, 'Why doesn't it hurt any worse than that?' I'd always heard gunshot wounds were painful. This felt like I'd been hit with a hammer. So I thought, 'Okay, either I'm not hurt bad at all, or I'm hurt *real* bad.' But I could still move my leg."

In fact, the bullet had struck McMurray's thigh, hit a

magazine clip inside the pocket of his fatigue pants, and bounced off. The impact split the skin and left several large bruises, but did no major damage.

Case asked McMurray if he was all right, and McMurray, now realizing he'd been shot at, rather than shot, said yes. The two men continued firing while Campbell struggled to get Moss off the mountain to safety.

It seemed like hours to the four officers, but the shooting lasted only a matter of minutes. By then, everyone—including Shornook—was running out of ammunition.

Before disappearing back into the woods, he stepped out from behind a bullet-scarred tree and gave a loud rebel yell, followed by "Fuck you, you sons of bitches!"

What Moss remembers most as he was half-dragged, half-carried down the mountains, was the faint but eerie sound of Shornook's laughter echoing across the ridge.

Moss, a thirty-seven-year-old father of four, knew he was seriously hurt, but had made up his mind he was not going to die.

"I never lost consciousness," he said. "My vision had cleared but there was a loud roar in my ears. All of us got in the patrol car—McMurray in front with Randy Case, me in the back with Campbell. I had to hang on to the seat because it was a rough road and Case was driving fast. He wanted to get us out of there so we could get to medical help."

Case, having radioed ahead that an officer was down, worried that Moss might be worse off than he appeared. Moss was thinking the same thing. Despite his wound, he was still able to talk, though his words were somewhat garbled.

"Randy," he called from the back seat, "tell me the truth. Am I going to be all right?"

"All of us reassured him as best we could," Case recalled. "But it was, after all, a head wound. So what we could say?"

On the way to the command post, where help was waiting, Case passed Buncombe County Sheriff's Deputy

Randy Moss, Vic's brother. He was standing by his patrol car, waiting to hear something, anything, about Moss's condition.

"I wanted to stop so bad," said Case, "but I drove right past him. I felt too great an urgency to get Vic off that mountain."

Later, after Moss was transported to the hospital, Case returned and explained to Randy Moss what had happened.

Shot with an MI carbine .30 caliber rifle, Moss suffered severe nerve damage in his facial muscles, a shattered jawbone, and substantial loss of hearing in his right ear. If the bullet had struck one-half inch higher or lower, doctors told him, or the angle had been slightly different, he most likely would not have survived. After undergoing reconstructive surgery, he spent ten days in the hospital and was out of work nearly four months. Today, he still has trouble distinguishing sounds and will probably never have normal hearing in his right ear.

By 5:00 P.M. Tuesday, officers on Sugarloaf Mountain—now four hundred strong, representing thirty different agencies from across the state—had resorted to broadcasting a message over a public address system, urging Shornook to come out of hiding and give himself up. Each announcement was met with silence.

The weather was proving just as stubborn. Continuous rain and fog cut visibility to near zero, hampering the search even further.

One man from Burke County, attempting to track Shornook with a trained dog, said the fog was so thick all he could see at the end of a fifteen-foot leash was the animal's wagging tail.

In another attempt to flush out Shornook, Sandra Horne, the woman who had taught Shornook how to survive in the woods, offered to come to Sugarloaf Mountain and try to talk him into surrendering. Officers, however, vetoed the idea, saying the situation was too dangerous to involve civilians.

It was a frustrating end to a long and discouraging day.

Three officers had been wounded by Shornook so far, and several others fired upon. Even worse, authorities were no closer to a capture. The only good news was that Shornook was finally contained within a four- to five-mile perimeter.

Completely surrounded by law enforcement officers, more intent than ever on apprehending him, his time was running out.

"If the guy doesn't move," said Henderson County Sheriff's Captain Tom Hatchett on Tuesday evening, "we'll stay in our positions and wait until morning before we do anything. Somebody else will get hurt if we rush this thing."

That night, the woods were full of strange happenings.

A Sugarloaf Mountain resident reported hearing her garage door open and close. When officers responded to her call, they found meat missing from her freezer in the garage.

A second family came home and discovered a door partially open. Then someone found an unfamiliar, slick-soled shoe print near the house.

At 5:12 A.M., there were reports of a gunshot and an unexplained light in the woods. Police officers watched for several minutes as the light moved swiftly through the trees, but an investigation yielded nothing.

Even some of the troopers got spooked.

One of the stories circulating about Shornook involved the amount of firepower he was carrying. In addition to rifles and pistols, it was reported he had hand grenades.

Somewhere on the mountain, an explosion went off and a trooper on patrol said everyone in his car—and those in surrounding cruisers—bailed out.

"We just knew the guy had a grenade and was going to blow us apart," he said.

Another officer heard leaves rustling in the woods and got on the radio to call for help.

Trooper Jay Kerr was "roaming"—patrolling up and down a designated stretch of road—when he caught the report and responded to it.

"I had a female trooper with me and we pulled up and got out. It was pouring down rain. Several other troopers had also arrived. Everybody put their lights out and got behind their cars. Then this female trooper looks over at me and says, 'I can't help it. I'm scared to death!'

" 'Well, I'm scared too,' I told her.

" 'You *are?*' she said.

" 'Yeah.'

"So she stands up in the line of fire, jacks a shell into the shotgun chamber, and yells toward the woods, 'Chicken!'

"She got real brave when she realized we were just as scared as she was."

Daylight broke Wednesday morning with more of the same lousy weather.

Around noon, the clouds began to lift and highway patrol officers at the command post agreed the patrol helicopter should go up.

A Jet Ranger with a five- to six-seat capacity, the chopper—purchased from the Pennsylvania state police for $112,000—was worth its weight in gold, particularly in the mountains, where dense, rugged terrain often made searching on foot a difficult task.

The pilot was Warrant Officer Ken Thompson, a sixteen-year veteran of the highway patrol. Riding with him was Sheriff's Deputy Larry Harris and Trooper David McMurray, still recovering from the leg injury he had received when Shornook had ambushed him on Tuesday.

"I was told to stay off my feet for a few days," said McMurray, "yet I wanted to remain on duty. Going up in the chopper seemed the most useful thing I could do."

With him, he carried a Henderson County sheriff's department radio so he could relay information to officers on the ground.

Below him, tactical teams composed of State Bureau of Investigation agents, county law enforcement officers, city police, and other agencies, including the highway patrol, were scouring the mountain, searching every house, cabin, barn, and outbuilding they could find.

"As soon as we got in the air," said McMurray, "one of the detectives on the ground called and asked if I could see him in a large group of people walking up the mountain. I answered yes, and he explained they were on their way to search two deserted barns. So we dropped down and started flying in circles, close enough to see them, but not so close that we became a distraction."

A few minutes later, the same detective contacted McMurray again and told him there were shots being fired from one of the barns. In fact, he said, they thought they had Shornook contained inside the building and wanted to know if—from the air—the perimeter around the barn appeared secure in case Shornook escaped. McMurray assured him it looked contained.

While scores of officers waited, State Bureau of Investigation agents Steve Myers and David Wooten approached the barn. Treading lightly on the hay-strewn floor, they could see a row of wooden stalls, each one with a door, all firmly closed.

Guns drawn, Myers and Wooten kicked the doors open, one by one.

The first three stalls were empty.

Hunkered down in the fourth one was Shornook. As the door swung backwards, Myers could see Shornook's gun pointed right at Wooten's head.

In one swift motion, Shornook turned to his left and fired, wounding Myers in the arm, then turned to his right and shot Wooten in the stomach. As both men fell, Shornook ran from the barn and toward the woods.

McMurray spotted him and radioed from the helicopter that he could see a lone figure running down a ridge, away from the barn.

"Then I corrected myself," he said, "explaining that from the chopper I couldn't identify him as Shornook, so they needed to make sure all law enforcement officers were in their assigned teams."

This time there was little chance that Shornook would get away.

Not only were the barn and surrounding area filled with law enforcement officers, but a four-man tactical team was heading up the ridge as Shornook was coming down. Having heard the shooting, they were ready for anything.

Fifty yards from the barn, they saw him coming their way. Shornook stopped, raised his weapon, and started to say something. His words were cut short when one of the police officers opened fire. The bullet entered behind his left ear and exited the right side of his skull, killing him instantly.

Found near his body were a .30-caliber carbine and a .45-caliber handgun. He was wearing blue jeans, sweat socks, and a heavy camouflage jacket. To the officers who had seen only mug shots of Shornook, he looked older, more physically mature, and stockier than the boy portrayed in the photos.

It was 1:15 P.M., Wednesday, November 26, nearly four days since the manhunt had begun. Only one day away from Thanksgiving.

SBI agent David Wooten, twenty-seven, who underwent surgery for the stomach wound inflicted by Shornook, fully recovered. Steve Myers, also twenty-seven, was treated and released for a gunshot wound to the arm.

Despite all the hullabaloo about Shornook's skills as a "survivalist" and a "Rambo," the autopsy report showed he hadn't eaten in days.

"It sounds good, even dramatic, to call him a 'Rambo,' " said a city police officer, "but the truth is, he was just a kid who happened to know how to handle himself in the woods—much like an experienced hunter."

"He had eluded people in this fashion before," added another policeman. "And he thought it would work again. So there was a logical explanation for everything he did."

As troopers and other law enforcement personnel gathered around their car radios listening to reports of Shornook's death, a calm began returning to Sugarloaf Mountain. Finally, the fear and worry was over, as well as the sheer weariness of manning posts and traipsing through the cold and the rain, wondering if Shornook was lurking nearby, ready and willing to shoot them.

"I'm just relieved it's behind us," said one trooper, speaking on behalf of his fellow officers.

"Yeah," said another, pumping the shells out of his shotgun, "now it looks like we'll have Thanksgiving after all."

Epilogue

It's 3:00 A.M. and Trooper Joel K. Reece has stopped for a cup of coffee with David Miller, another highway patrolman. Outside the diner, city lights are casting soft gray shadows on the empty streets. Even the highways have lost their normal flow. At this hour, they stretch like endless black ribbons winding forward in the dark. There is little activity anywhere, for most people are either home in bed or—like the troopers—on the job.

Back on duty, the two officers are pulling out of the parking lot when they spot an early-model Chrysler slowing down, then speeding up. Behind the wheel is a bearded man in his early fifties. Aware that he's being watched, he refuses to look toward them.

Both Reece and Miller, alert to his odd behavior, cruise behind him. Suddenly, he guns the engine and takes off.

The pursuit continues through a red light, a darkened residential street, and onto a dead-end road, where the man loses control of his car and lands it in a ditch. As he jumps out and runs, the troopers follow him on foot.

Reece slips between two barns while Miller attempts to intercept the man up ahead.

But he appears at one of the barns instead. Entangled in the underbrush, he is trying to escape through a fence.

"Hold it!" says Reece, stepping out of the shadows. "I'm a state trooper. Let me see your hands!"

The man lunges toward him and Reece, sensing a threat, moves in. For several moments, they struggle. When Miller arrives, the troopers together subdue the man, handcuff him, and lead him back to one of the patrol cars.

On the way to jail, the man announces he has something important to say.

"Well, I guess you're big shots now. You've caught a real criminal. You might as well call the FBI because they want me too."

Later, in the booking room at the county jail, Reece discovers the prisoner is telling the truth. In fact, he has a record of armed robberies, shooting with intent to kill, and other serious crimes. The troopers are convinced he was planning a burglary that very night, for he was carrying a ski mask, a folded pillowcase, and a pistol.

The gun, Reece learned, had fallen out of the man's pocket during the scuffle at the barn. To Reece, what kept him from getting shot was a simple stroke of luck. In his rush to prevent the man from getting away, he had forgotten to grab his flashlight from the front seat of the patrol car.

"Had he seen me coming," Reece said later, "I have no doubt he would have fired."

Back on Interstate 40, near the end of his shift, he clocks a blue-gray van with an out-of-state license traveling at a high rate of speed. Its tinted windows have obscured his view of the occupants, but he has already turned on the blue light and the van is pulling over.

Reece puts on his hat, reaches for his flashlight, and climbs out of the cruiser.

In the darkness, his hand deliberately brushes the side of the van. Slowly, too slowly for Reece, the driver is rolling down the window.

Reece pauses a moment, then steps forward. In another hour, his shift will be over and he'll be safely on his way home.

At least that is the best he can hope for on this—and every—routine patrol.